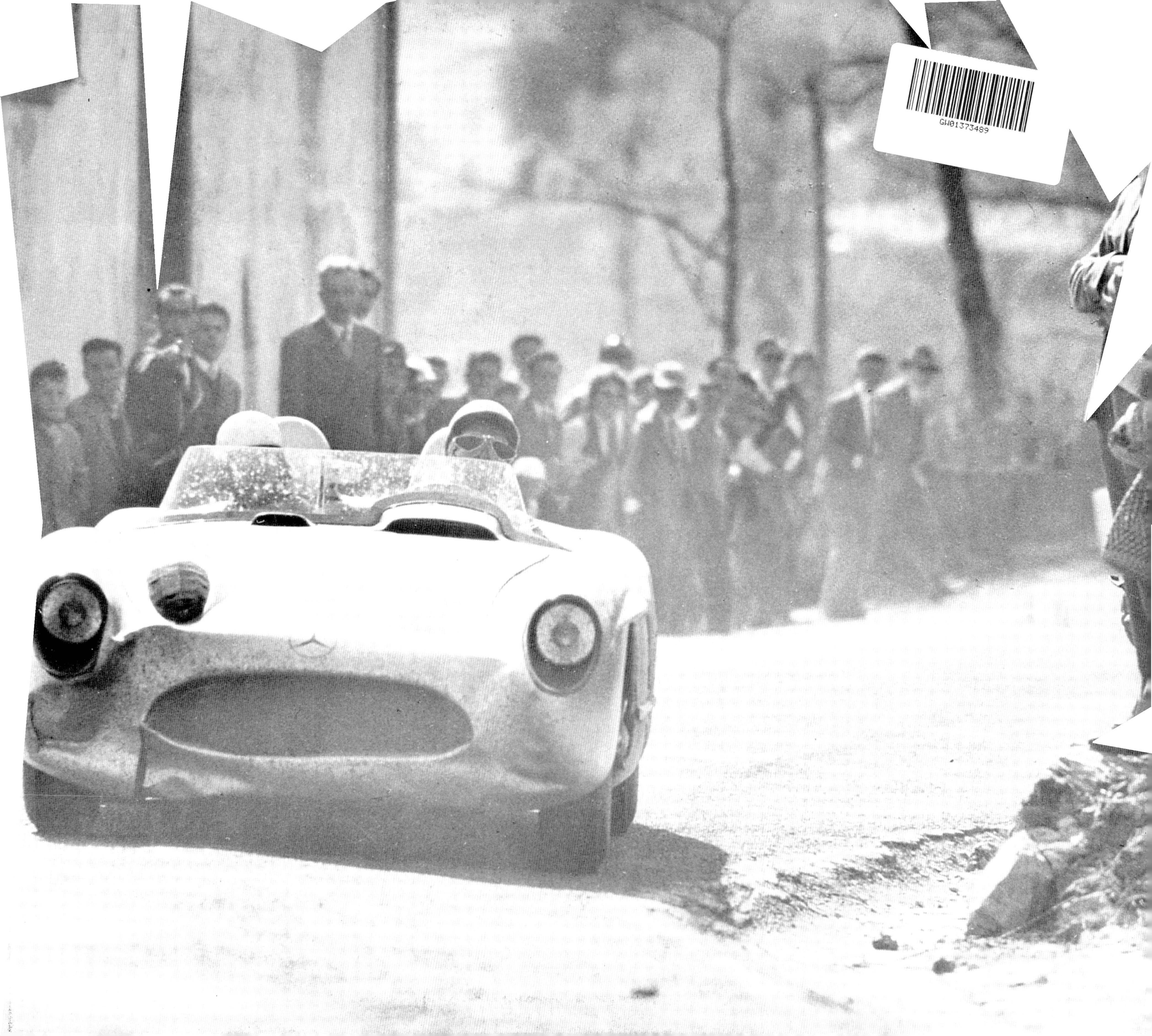

Inside front cover: Jenks and Stirling in the cockpit of their 300 SLR just before the start of the Mille Miglia. *Facing inside front cover:* Mille Miglia magic - insatiable crowds, battered machinery, noble crews, public highways and intoxicating atmosphere. *Top left* - Mille Miglia crowds lined the streets in spite of the cars reaching 150/160/170mph. *Top right* - Glorious victory for Stirling and Jenks after their truly heroic feat to win the 1955 Mille Miglia at record speed. *Bottom left* - The three 300 SLRs of (from left) Fangio, Moss and Kling power away at the start of the Eifelrennen. *Bottom right* - The moment of triumph as Stirling crosses the line a few yards ahead of Fangio to win his first Grand Prix. (DaimlerChrysler Archive)

Stirling Moss Scrapbook 1955

Stirling Moss & Philip Porter

Design by Andrew Garman

Porter Press International

© Sir Stirling Moss & Philip Porter

All rights reserved. No part of this publication may be reproduced,
stored in a retrieval system or transmitted, in any form or by
any means, electronic, mechanical, photocopying, recording or
otherwise, without prior permission in writing from
the publisher

First published in June 2005

ISBN 0-9550068-0-5
ISBN 0-9550068-1-3 (Leather-bound edition)

Published by
Porter Press International
an imprint of Porter & Porter Ltd.

PO Box 2, Tenbury Wells,
WR15 8XX, UK.
Tel: +44 (0)1584 781588
Fax: +44 (0)1584 781630
info@xkclub.com
www.stirlingmossbooks.com

Designed by Grafx Resource
Printed and bound through World Print Limited
in China

COPYRIGHT
We have made every effort to trace and acknowledge copyright holders and we apologise in advance for any unintentional omission. We would be pleased to insert the appropriate acknowledgement in any subsequent edition. We wish to thank the Editors and publishers of the named publications, which we have managed to trace, for their kind permission to reproduce the cuttings and/or photographs. Without their co-operation, this publication would not have been possible.

PHOTO CREDITS
The following have been extremely helpful in providing photographs: Stirling Moss Archive, The GP Library, The Zagari/Spitzley Collection, Doug Nye, Paul Vestey, Matt & Di Spitzley, Geoffrey Goddard, David Weguelin, El Grafico, BRSCC, Ted Walker/Ferret Fotographics, Erik Johnson, Mercedes-Benz, The Simon Thomas Collection, Iacona & Bertschi Archive, and Philip Porter Archive.

INTRODUCTION

This book has been tremendous fun to compile and I hope you will find it fun to read, whether you consume it from cover to cover at one sitting or merely dip in from time to time.

Having written quite a few, rather more conventional, books I thought that 'compiling' one would be rather easier. Not a bit of it. Why am I still so naïve after all these years? Could it be my simple enthusiasm, or maybe I am just a bit simple?

Certainly I have an immense enthusiasm for this subject. For so many, whether they be lifelong, diehard motor sport enthusiasts, or more casual observers, Stirling Moss was, and is, a hero. For me, he was my absolute boyhood hero, and I am far from unique. Indeed, there are, I am sure, quite literally millions around the world who could say the same.

You can perhaps imagine what a thrill and privilege it has been to get to know Stirling and Susie so well in the last few years. How did the idea for this series come about?

I first met Stirling and briefly interviewed him at an event many years ago. I treasured that recording. Subsequently, we corresponded occasionally and during my 10 years of flying hot air balloons and airships, I wrote to him to offer him a flight. He was enthusiastic but I fully realised that with his packed diary and the reliance of ballooning on conducive weather that it was a rather optimistic notion.

Then, in the mid-nineties when I was writing a book on the Jaguar sports racers, I called at his fascinating London home to conduct a more lengthy interview for that tome. He was charming and very helpful and, to my surprise, though it was some years on from our ballooning correspondence, my letter still sat in his in-tray.

Fast-forwarding again, when my wife and I formed the Jaguar XK Club in 1987, the pre-eminent rally driver, Ian Appleyard, kindly accepted an invitation to be our first Patron. Terribly sadly, he died about a year later. We then approached the Rt Hon Alan Clark, M.P., who had owned his XK 120 from new and also owned a Jaguar C-type. He was incredibly supportive and delightfully and outrageously forthright in his views. Equally sadly, within a year or so, he passed away. Both are greatly missed.

I then plucked up courage and asked Mr. Moss, as he then was. He kindly accepted on the understanding that it was a strictly non-participatory role, and he hoped he would survive a little longer than his two predecessors!

We would bump into each other at various events from time and time and correspond occasionally. I then plucked up courage again, in 2002, and asked if there was any way he could be persuaded to attend the Club's Annual Dinner at the House of Commons. He charmingly responded that I drove a hard bargain and, to my complete amazement, accepted.

After dinner I interviewed him and our members just loved his repartee. Refreshingly non-PC and full of hilarious anecdotes, prompted occasionally by "my floppy disc and hard drive" as he calls Susie, his fabulous wife, he had everybody in fits.

Incredibly grateful, I could not quite believe it when he agreed to come again the following year, and the following year, and the following year, which brings us up to date. As a result of all this, I gradually got to know Stirling rather better and occasionally called in to hand over a case of his favourite wine. On one or two occasions, he showed me his wonderful old scrapbooks. Suddenly, I came up with a notion. It would be splendid to share his personal scrapbooks, albums and diaries with a wider audience. They are pure history; they are pure Stirling Moss.

Here we are then. This is the first of what we hope will be one book for each year of his remarkable career. They are a celebration of an incredibly popular hero, a truly extraordinary sportsman and, arguably, the finest all-round racing driver of all time. They are a reminder of the times, of the atmosphere, of the period, of the social scene, of the fun and the unique achievements.

Why 1955? For a start, we are publishing in the fiftieth anniversary year. Secondly, and more importantly, it was a truly remarkable year for the comparatively young Moss. He was signed up by the best Formula One team at the time to partner the current World Champion, Juan Manuel Fangio. He won his first Grand Prix, the British GP no less. He won the Tourist Trophy, Britain's premier sports car race for the third time. He was second to the great Fangio in the World Championship and had shadowed the established master in most of the Grand Prix. He and Peter Collins brilliantly won the exceptionally gruelling Targa Florio. If Mercedes had not decided to withdraw their cars at Le Mans when Stirling had built up a two-lap lead, he would very likely have achieved the 'Grand Slam' of the great sports car races in one season.

Quite exceptionally, he conquered all when he and Denis Jenkinson won the Mille Miglia, the outrageous 1,000 mile race on the roads of Italy. For someone who was not a native of Italy to win this race was quite extraordinary. To set a record that would not be beaten and average, through villages, towns and cities and over treacherous mountain passes, a fraction under 100mph for those 1,000 miles utterly defies belief. It was surely one of the great sporting achievements of all time.

Philip Porter
Knighton-on-Teme, Worcestershire.

Please note that all quotations, unless otherwise attributed, are Stirling's.
There is a glossary of terms employed in this book on page 160.
Acknowledgements will also be found on page 160.

The Story So Far - the prelude to 1955.

Stirling Moss was born, on September 17 1929, into a motoring background. His father, Alfred, had raced at Brooklands and at Indianapolis in the USA, and his mother, Aileen, had been successful in trials (otherwise known as 'mud-plugging') and rallies. As a child, he was taken to competitive motoring events around the country and so motor sport was very much in the blood.

Before he was even in his teens, his father had bought him a little Austin Seven to drive around White House Farm, the family home at Tring in Berkshire. Little Stirling planned a circuit round the fields and spent hours honing his skills. A motorbike followed during the war and, aged 15, a three-wheeler Morgan was purchased by father, who was a dentist by profession and had a number of practises in London and the Home Counties. This thrilled Stirling but it only whetted his appetite for a 'proper' four-wheeler. An MG TB Tickford Coupé followed and then Alfred bought a BMW 328 which he allowed Stirling to use for a few competitions. Meanwhile, the youthful Moss had also been competing successfully in horse-jumping events, a sport in which his younger sister Pat would gain considerable fame before turning to international rallying.

Stirling had saved a little money from his horse-riding successes and, for his 18th birthday, these funds were topped up so that he buy a small racing car. The 500cc single-seater formula was created just after the War by several Bristol enthusiasts as a cheap form of motor racing. The cars employed motor cycle engines and gave a number of well-known drivers a means of starting on the road to success. There is no better proof of this than Stirling himself. One of the first concerns to build 500s commercially was a small Surbiton garage run by Charles Cooper, and his son John. Stirling ordered an early example.

Unfortunately, the famous Shelsley Walsh hillclimb was over-subscribed so his début took place in May 1948 at Prescott hillclimb where he initially lowered the class record but finally finished fourth. The next event was at a venue, Stanmer Hill, that was new to all the competitors. Stirling won. A few weeks later he entered his first races and won all three in one day. He was on his way. The Press and seasoned professionals were already taking note. He ended that first season with 11 wins from 15 starts.

For 1949, he replaced the Cooper Mark II with a Mark III and now had the option of fitting a 1,000cc twin and running in that class. He had another good season with a notable success at the 500cc event supporting the first British Grand Prix. In July he made his international début at Lake Garda in Italy. His little 1,000cc-powered Cooper was laughed at until he won his class by four minutes and chased home two larger-engined V12 Ferraris driven by established stars. He won at Zandvoort and set Fastest Time of Day (ftd) at Shelsley in August. Though the successes were still coming, he was also learning the frustration of retirement through mechanical maladies. However, the maestro of pre-war motor racing, Tazio Nuvolari told Basil Cardew of the *Daily Express*, "Watch Stirling Moss; he is going to be one of the great drivers of the world".

At the dawn of 1950 the 20-year-old Moss was invited to join the under-funded but gallant British HWM team run by John Heath and George Abecassis. Powered by 4-cylinder Alta engines producing 140bhp, they could not really compete with the top continental opposition but gave Stirling a good introduction to longer-distance road racing in mainland Europe. On several occasions 'David' threatened to humble 'Goliath'. At the Naples GP, for example, he won his heat, beating the Formula Two Ferraris, and was leading the final when he suffered a nasty crash. This was his first serious accident. In spite of a broken knee, he was back in successful action in the 500 a couple of weeks later. Throughout the year he was driving a Cooper Mark IV in 500cc form, fitted until August with the pushrod JAP engine and thereafter a more powerful 'double-knocker' Norton.

Stirling's big break came in September 1950. Journalist/driver Tommy Wisdom offered him his Jaguar XK 120 for the newly-revived classic Tourist Trophy to be run on the daunting road circuit at Dundrod in Ulster. The XK 120 had been sensationally launched in late 1948 but, with Britain pursuing an 'export or die' policy after the war, virtually all the XKs went overseas. However, Jaguar had prepared six rather special examples of the earlier aluminium-bodied cars, and 'sold' them to selected drivers or entrants. Wisdom had one and now invited young Stirling, whom none of the British works teams would touch because they feared he was going too fast and would kill himself in one of their cars, the 120 for the TT.

In spite of appalling conditions, Stirling rose to the occasion, beat the established XK drivers, Johnson and Whitehead, and everyone else to record a brilliant win. That evening, as he celebrated his 21st birthday, Jaguar founder and Managing Director William Lyons asked Stirling to lead the works team in 1951. This was to be a serious step up.

For 1951 HWM produced a Formula Two car and retained Stirling's services for another year. Additionally, he continued to race 500s. However, he had now changed his allegiance from Cooper to a new venture in which he played a role. This was named the Kieft and it was very advanced for its time. Though plagued by a few retirements, the Moss and Kieft combination was pretty all-conquering through 1951. The HWM continued to be unreliable and/or out-classed in most of the continental races but gave Stirling some domestic successes and more valuable experience. In one event, at Monza, he dramatically learned the art of 'slipstreaming' and, as a result of hanging on to the tail of Villoresi's much faster Ferrari, finished a brilliant third, beaten only by Ascari and Villoresi who had unwittingly given him the 'tow'.

His Jaguar season started with a win in an XK 120 in the Production Car Race at Silverstone. Next event was the classic 24-hour race at Le Mans for which Jaguar had designed and built the C-type. Though based closely on XK 120 components with essentially the same engine, this was a lightened, more aerodynamically-efficient pure sports racing car. Moss was teamed with the experienced and reliable Jack Fairman.

Stirling was given the role of pacemaker by team manager, 'Lofty' England, and set out to 'break' the opposition. For the first few laps, he diced for the lead with Gonzales in a big Talbot which resulted in the Argentinian cooking his brakes. Stirling repeatedly broke the lap record as he built up a healthy lead while the competition crumbled trying to maintain such a pace. The Jaguars were 1-2-3 and sitting pretty when the Moss/Fairman and Johnson/Biondetti C-types were forced to retire. A copper oil-delivery pipe broke on both cars, starving the bearings of oil, causing them to break up. Luckily, the third C-type, the Walker/Whitehead car, was able to reduce its pace, as the serious competition had succumbed to Stirling's pace, and Jaguar took a famous win which established the company's name and reputation worldwide.

Jaguar were really only interested in winning Le Mans, due to its unique publicity value, and so did not race again until the TT in September. Quite simply, Stirling clocked up his second successive victory in this great British classic.

A week before this triumph, Stirling had experienced Enzo Ferrari at his most unpredictable! Ferrari had invited him to Bari to drive his new 4-cylinder 2½ litre single-seater. When Stirling arrived, he was told it was to be driven by Taruffi instead. Stirling would never forget his treatment by Ferrari and would never entertain driving for him again.

Stirling was always fiercely patriotic and very keen to race and win in British cars. In these early years this principle lessened his chances of success but helped foster his hero status with the British public. These were the days of the B.R.M. project which was so disastrous that it became a music-hall joke. Nevertheless, everyone remained optimistic that it could take on the foreign opposition and Raymond Mays, who 'master-minded' the B.R.M. project, offered Stirling a contract for 1952, as did Ferrari. He accepted neither.

Stirling was a professional racing driver and indeed he claimed in one of his books to be the only full-time racing driver in Britain (all the others ran garages or had other business interests). As such, during the winter when he was not racing, he was not earning and so this led him into the rally world. Consequently, he joined the Sunbeam-Talbot team for the 1952 Monte Carlo Rally in January. Remarkably, he and his novice-crew missed an outright victory be a mere four seconds.

The B.R.M. had driven Stirling to distraction during testing, as it had many a fine driver, and so Stirling desperately looked around for a British alternative. Due to lack of support for the current Formula One, the 1952 World Championship was to be run for 2-litre unsupercharged Formula Two cars. Stirling was persuaded to race the Bristol-engined G-type ERA. It was a mistake. The car was dreadfully unreliable and simply not fast enough when it was running.

Thankfully, Stirling was still enjoying some success with the effective little Kieft-Norton 500 and continuing to race the Jaguar C-types, both works entries and privately-entered ones. This was the period when Jaguar, in conjunction with Dunlop, were developing the disc brake and Stirling achieved the first-ever win for a disc-braked car in an international event when he won the sports car race at Reims in June in Wisdom's C-type.

A few weeks before, Le Mans had been a complete disaster for Jaguar. Concerned about reports of the Mercedes 300 SL's maximum speed, they hastily revised the bodywork and there was a problem in the race with the re-routed plumbing system. As this work was done by Roy Kettle and they boiled themselves out of the race, they came to be known as the 'Kettle Specials'. The irony is that, had they used the previous year's cars, they would easily have won the race.

Mercedes-Benz dramatically returned to top-line motor racing in 1954 and brought Fangio his second World Championship.

Stirling's original Kieft had been written off when aiming to avoid a multiple pile-up and the other examples he raced never quite matched up to the prototype. During 1952 he abandoned Kieft and returned to the Cooper fold which yielded a string of wins.

Stirling nobly continued his quest to find a British car to take on the world and for 1953 was persuaded to drive a car created for him called the Cooper-Alta Special. It was a great disappointment and was abandoned mid-season in favour of a more conventional Cooper single-seater with the same Alta engine. This was a trifle more successful but Stirling finally came to the reluctant conclusion that if he was going to salvage his career and experience the success his talent deserved, he had no alternative but to 'go foreign'. It seems hard to believe now when Britain has been leading the world for more than 30 years in racing car technology but the nascent single-seater racing car industry was in a sorry state in the earlier fifties.

The exception to all this, luckily, was Jaguar whose C-type had been further developed and now enjoyed more power but, above all, had the revolutionary disc brakes. Stirling set a killing pace at Le Mans in '53 and one of the strongest fields of cars and drivers ever seen there gradually wilted under the strain. Frustratingly Stirling, who was sharing with that fine driver Peter Walker, was delayed by two long pit-stops and was stationary for over 10 minutes. He rejoined in 21st place but eventually they finished second to team-mates Rolt and Hamilton.

In the Reims 12-hour race, Moss and Whitehead won by four laps in a C-type and Stirling finished second in the Lisbon GP. His third TT was not as successful as his first two as he was delayed by transmission problems.

The big news for 1954 was that Mercedes-Benz were returning to Grand Prix racing for the first time since creating a tremendous reputation for success pre-War. They signed up 1951 World Champion, Juan Manuel Fangio, to lead the team and Stirling's manager Ken Gregory approached the Mercedes team manager, Alfred Neubauer, about a place for Stirling. Neubauer recognised the young Englishman's talents in sports car but pointed out that he had not really proved himself yet in Grand Prix racing.

Alfred Neubauer, the Mercedes Team Manager, Alfred Moss and Stirling toast the signing of Stirling's Mercedes contract for 1955.

He suggested Stirling should purchase a suitable car, race it in 1954 and then speak to him again at the end of the season.

The Maserati 250F was a suitable car and one was duly purchased from the factory. Finally, Stirling had a car with which to show his true mettle. The combination made their debut in the Bordeaux GP and were the first Maserati home in fourth place. At the May Silverstone event, the de Dion tube broke but at the inaugural Aintree meeting Moss beat Reg Parnell to win by 48 seconds. Another retirement followed in Italy but at the Belgian GP Stirling finished in a very fine third place behind Fangio and Trintignant. Now, that was more like it.

At Le Mans, Jaguar débuted the stunning new D-type. This was the year all three works car were mysteriously delayed by blocked filters due to fine sand in the fuel. All lost precious time but Rolt and Hamilton missed pulling off a remarkable victory by just 105 seconds. Stirling was less lucky. Paired with Walker in the car registered OKV 1, Stirling had been forced to retire when he found himself approaching the Mulsanne Corner at 160mph … with no brakes.

Sadly, his two other appearances in D-types that year were equally disappointing for him. At Reims he had back axle problems and a lack of oil pressure in the TT at Dundrod.

At the British GP, Stirling was going especially well in the 250F and passed Fangio's ill-handling Mercedes Streamliner to hold a safe second place; safe, that is, until axle trouble forced him out. At Caen he finished second and for the German GP at the infamous Nürburgring he was offered a works Maserati after breaking the lap record by eight seconds in practice. Engine trouble put him out on lap two.

By the time of the Italian GP at Monza, Stirling was established in the works team and was effectively their Number One driver. He earned the distinction that day. After slipstreaming Fangio and Ascari, he had the audacity to overtake them for the lead, the World Champions collectively of 1951, 1952 and 1953. He opened up a lead and the race was his, until an oil pipe broke with 12 laps to go. He pushed the dead car for half a mile to finish 10th. Neubauer, who patted him on the back as he passed the Mercedes pit, admired this grit as much as his brilliant driving.

The season ended with some minor wins in the 250F and suddenly

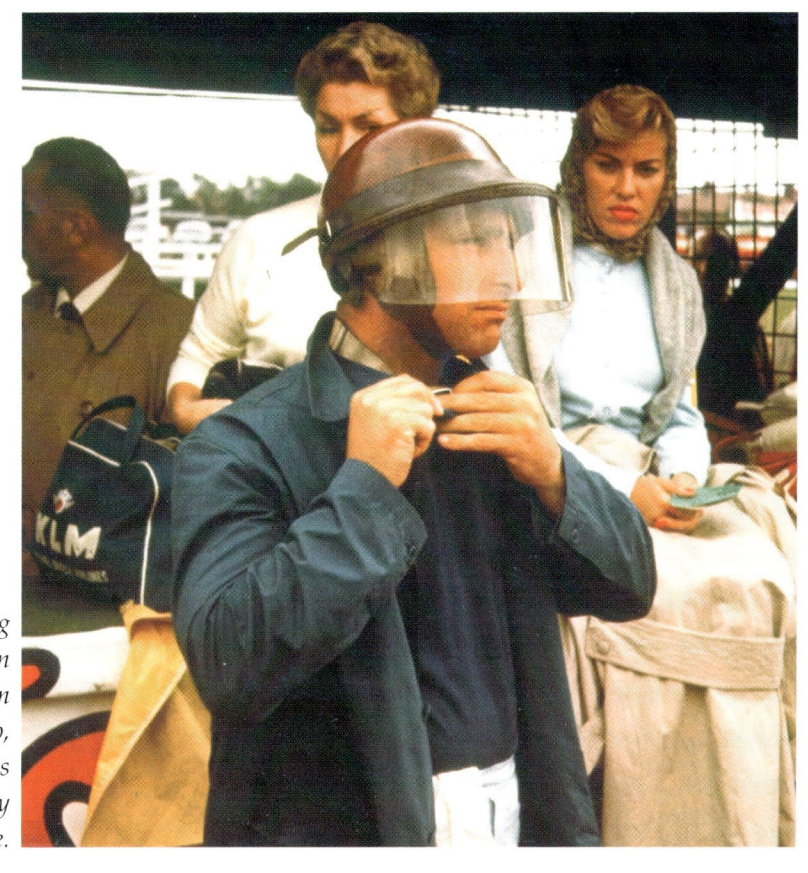

During 1955 Stirling would learn an enormous amount from Juan Manuel Fangio, the man he has always considered to be the very best of all time.

young Stirling Moss was getting the results he deserved after several years of utter frustration.

Things had turned full circle in a year and now both Mercedes and Maserati were fighting over him. He had had discussions with the Italians but nothing had been signed when an invitation arrived from Neubauer to visit him.

"Mercedes asked if would I go over to Germany," recalls Stirling, "to try the Grand Prix car and I think it was Hockenheim. It was a quite cold day. I went there with my father and they brought this thing out, it must have been a W196, a single-seater, and I started to do a certain amount of laps, just to get to know the car."

One thing immediately struck Stirling and impressed him about Mercedes organisation and attention to detail.

"At that time Mercedes had inboard front brakes. You would get dust from the brakes and, with the air coming back over the engine, a slightly oily mist would blow over you. So, we used to get the black face with the white 'panda eyes' showing where you had been wearing goggles.

"I came in and I was fumbling for a piece of rag or something and a German came up to me, I remember it so well. He bowed forward, gave a sort of click of the heels, and in his hands was a bowl of water, not ordinary water, it was hot water. He'd also got a cake of soap and over his arm a towel. I remember it was a bit different to any other team, to say the least!

"I thought, 'Well, that is pretty efficient' and then we discussed the car.

The 196 wasn't a car that you got into and fell in love with, as you do with a [Maserati] 250F. It's nowhere near as user-friendly. It was a great car because of its reliability, sufficient power, quite a good gearbox…

"Driving the car, it was comfortable, but not easy like the 250F. It had a swing axle which is quite difficult in the wet. Anyway, I got out, I was quite impressed, because when you put your foot down it really did have quite a bit of go. I think I am right in saying, they had a Formula One car up to about 300hp which, at the time, was really very good, very good. It was not a light car but the good news was that you had the feeling that nothing would go wrong, a wheel wouldn't come off or anything like that."

There was really no question as to the right decision. In Britain there was criticism in certain quarters but Stirling answered by saying publicly, "I am prepared at any time to drive for a British firm which produces a British Grand Prix car".

The R.A.C. awarded him his fourth Gold Star as the top British driver of the year and Guild of Motoring Writers chose him as their 'Driver of the Year'. Both were a good omen for 1955. Could Stirling Moss finally scale the heights and regularly take on the established stars and challenge them in Formula One, the very pinnacle of international motor racing? It was going to be an exciting year!

The year 1955 was to be the turning point in Stirling's career.

1955

World News:

In February Bulganin replaced Malenkov as Soviet premier. Churchill resigned as Prime Minister in April to be succeeded by Eden. A month later the Federal Republic of West Germany became a sovereign state and later in the year was admitted as a member of Nato, though Nato troops were to remain stationed in West Germany. Also in May seven Eastern Bloc countries signed the Warsaw Pact, a mutual defence treaty. Austrian independence was restored. In July the Geneva Summit took place between the USA, Britain, the USSR and France. Nothing was agreed. Two months later President Eisenhower suffered a heart attack and Argentine dictator Juan Perón was overthrown. In November Russia detonated a massive nuclear bomb in Siberia. In Alabama a young pastor, Dr. Martin Luther King Jr, formed a movement which caused the end of racial segregation in the USA on public transport.

Trivia:

First McDonalds opens
Albert Einstein dies
Ruth Ellis - the last woman to hang in Britain is executed having murdered occasional racing driver David Blakely
Disneyland opens in Anaheim, California
James Dean is killed in a car accident
Fibre optics are developed in Britain by Narinder Kapeny

Television:

TV Shows:
Truth or Consequences
Lawrence Welk Show
The Honeymooners
Lassie
Gunsmoke
Name that Tune
$64,000 Question
Secombe Here
Max Bygraves
The Benny Hill Show

First Televised in 1955:
Picture Book
Look
Life with the Lyons
Dixon of Dock Green
This is Your Life
The Brains Trust
The Woodentops
Crackerjack

10 Oct. Colour television test transmissions began on 405 lines from *Alexandra Palace*

Sport:

'Sugar' Ray Robinson is World Middleweight Boxing Champion
Louise Brough & Tony Trabert win Wimbledon
Donald Campbell breaks the world water speed record at 202mph
F.A. Cup: Newcastle 3 v Manchester City 1
World Series: Brooklyn beat New York Yankees, 4-3
At 100/9 Quare Times wins Grand National ridden by Pat Taaffe
Cambridge wins the Boat Race

Movies:

Marty
The Seven Year Itch
The Rose Tattoo
Smiles of a Summer Night
The Night of the Hunter
Titanic
Oklahoma

The Oscars:
Best Film: *Marty*
Actor: Ernest Borgnine, *Marty*
Actress: Anna Magnani, *The Rose Tattoo*

Significant Films:

Rebel Without a Cause - this cult movie based around rebellious and restless youth is best remembered for spring-boarding charismatic James Dean to stardom. Tragically, aged just 24, he was killed driving his Porsche a few months after its release. Co-stars, Natalie Wood and Sal Mineo also died tragically (respectively, mysterious drowning in 1981 and stabbing in 1976).
The Seven Year Itch - directed by Billy Wilder, this farce starred Marilyn Monroe as a blonde bombshell. The 'seven year itch' refers to the urge to be unfaithful after seven years of matrimony, with a desire to satisfy one's sexual urges ('itches'). The film's promotional tease photographs packaged her as the sexually-endowed girl next door - an ideal fantasy figure.
Kiss Me Deadly - has been described as "the definitive, apocalyptic, nihilistic, science-fiction *film noir* of all time - at the close of the classic noir period". Written by pulp fiction author Mickey Spillane, it features his hero Mike Hammer and opens with him driving his Jaguar XK 120.

Music:

Hits of 1955:
Rock Around the Clock
The Yellow Rose of Texas
Davy Crockett
Love is a Many Splendored Thing

UK No. 1s:

Dickie Valentine	Finger of Suspicion	January 1
Rosemary Clooney	Mambo Italiano	January 14
Ruby Murray	Softly, Softly	February 18
Tennessee Ernie Ford	Give Me Your Word	March 11
Perez Prez Prado & His Orchestra	Cherry Pink And Apple Blossom White	April 29
Tony Bennett	Stranger in Paradise	May 13
Eddie Calvert	Cherry Pink And Apple Blossom White	May 27
Jimmy Young	Unchained Melody	June 24
Alma Cogan	Dreamboat	July 15
Slim Whitman	Rose Marie	July 29
Jimmy Young	The Man From Laramie	October 14
Johnston Brothers	Hernando's Hideaway	November 11
Bill Haley & His Comets	Rock Around the Clock	November 25
Dickie Valentine	Christmas Alphabet	December 12

Money:

Exchange Rates per One British Pound

	U.S. $	German Marks	Japanese Yen	French Francs	Italian Lira	Canadian $	Australian $
1955	2.80	11.76	1008	9.80	1750	2.76	2.50
2003	1.63	2.83	189	9.50	2803	2.29	2.52

National Average Wage

	Week	Per Annum
UK		
1955	£8	£416
2004	£427	£22,183
USA		
1955	$63	$3,301
2003	$655	$34,065

Van Heusen shirts for all sporting occasions

JAGUAR
The finest car of its class in the world
...a record of success unparallele[d] in motoring history

Books:

The Man in the Gray Flannel Suit, Sloan Wilson
Lolita, Vladimir Nabokov
Witness for the Prosecution, Agatha Christie
The Quiet American, Graham Greene
The Trial, Franz Kafka
The Tree of Man, Patrick White
Cat on a Hot Tin Roof, Tennessee Williams
Moonraker, Ian Fleming
The 1st edition of the *Guinness Book of Records* is published

January

1955 Calendar

16   Gran Premio de la Republica Argentina (Argentinian GP) - 4th (sharing with Kling & Hermann) in W196

30   Gran Premio de la Ciudad de Buenos Aires - 1st in heat, 2nd overall on aggregate in 3-litre engined W196

For Stirling Moss, the momentous year of 1955 started on the first day of the New Year with a photo shoot for a publication called 'Everybody's'. With black & white film the norm, colour was still such a rarity that Stirling (SM) remarked in his diary that this shoot was to be done in colour. He then spent the afternoon at the Boat Show with current girlfriend Sally Weston (SW). As he was off to Germany next day, he packed before he and Sally went to the La Rue nightclub. There they had a discussion and decided to finish their relationship!

He was up early next morning and off to London Airport with SW in spite of their 'discussion'. There he met his manager and chum Ken Gregory, legal adviser Felix Nabarro and "Mum & Dad". He caught a flight to Frankfurt which arrived 1½ hours late and went straight to his hotel in Stuttgart.

After a sleepless night, he was at 'Mercs' by 8.50. "Discussed contract and then went to town for a film show. VG." After photos, he went out on the town and bought a Bolex cine camera. A visit to the Mercedes Museum followed where he had a ride on an 1892 Daimler. "The plugs were 2 old hot rods," he wrote.

On January 4th he signed his contract. After some more shopping, he went to the airport to "find I had no visa!" Presumably this was required for his impending visit to Argentina. He flew to Zurich, took part in a half-hour Press reception, flew to Lisbon and there the Press and radio stations made their presence known. That evening they took off for South America.

RACING DRIVER STIRLING MOSS LEFT LONDON AIRPORT BY PAN AMERICAN CLIPPER FOR FRANKFURT. HE WAS ON HIS WAY TO JOIN THE MERCEDES TEAM, WITH WHOM HE WILL LEAVE FOR BUENOS AIRE FOR THE ARGENTINE GRAND PRIX. AT LONDON AIRPORT JUST PRIOR TO EMPLANING FOR FRANKFURT, THE RACING DRIVER STIRLING MOSS CHATS WITH A FRIEND, MISS SALLY WESTON..SHE IS A NIECE OF MILLIONAIRE BISCUIT MAKER GARFIELD WESTON. RUMOUR HAS ROMANTICALLY LINKED THEIR NAMES, BUT THE COUPLE HAVE DENIED THAT THEY ARE ENGAGED.

Bucks Herald 21.1.55

NOT SO FAST AS BROTHER STIRLING, BUT WHO CARES?

All set to get about over the snowy roads around Tring is Pat Moss, well-known show jumper and sister of the famous racing motorist, Stirling Moss. 20-year-old Pat and her mother have used the sleigh more than once during the recent snowy weather to go on shopping expeditions in Tring, where the Moss family live at White Cloud Farm. Doing the hauling work is 24-year-old Dandy Boy, who in his younger days met with considerable success in the show ring. When our picture was taken on Tuesday, Miss Moss said she found the sleigh the most convenient way of getting about in the conditions then prevailing.

Stirling Moss ...

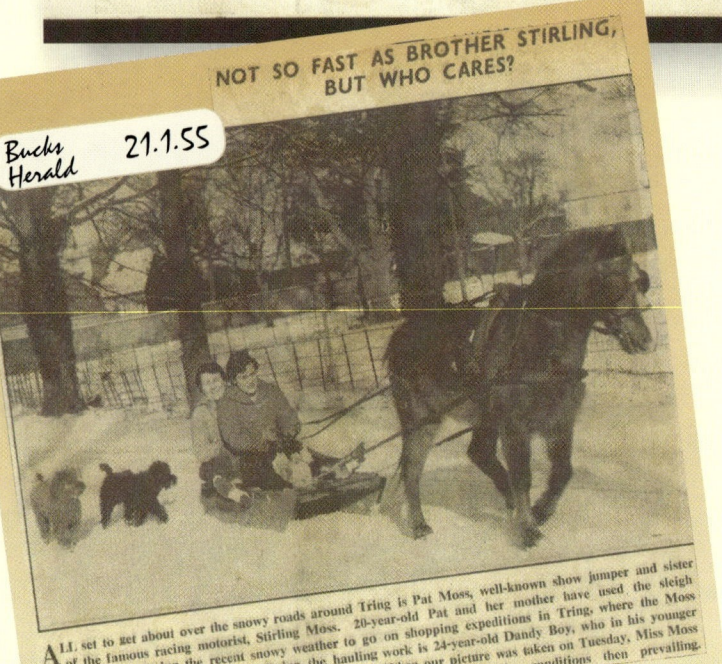

SALLY WESTON

"She was very attractive and had a nice personality but she was a nut. Her real name wasn't Sally Weston. Her real name was Jennifer Claire Tollitt and at school they used to call her 'toilet' - I didn't know all this at the time. She didn't like it and so she said to a friend, whose name was Weston, 'Can I call myself Sally Weston and take your name?' The friend said she didn't mind, so thereafter she became Sally Weston and started to live her life as Sally Weston. She would say to people that she was connected with Weston Biscuits, which wasn't true. She was a very attractive, very vivacious person, whom I don't think for a minute was necessarily that stuck with me. I think she quite fancied Fangio. She spoke Spanish and I often felt that maybe he had a piece - I don't know! She was an attractive person, but we did have fights."

Mercedes-Benz Contract ...

Stirling's contract with M-B stated he would take part in all Grandes Epreuves (Grand Prix events counting towards the World Championship) and four sports car events. These were the Mille Miglia, Le Mans, the 1,000 Kilometres at the Nürburgring and the 'Panamericana'. He was allowed to drive other cars when not required by Mercedes. There was some suggestion the car might be painted British Racing Green but this was not to be. However, a small Union Jack was to painted on the car, plus the crest of the boys' comic, 'The Eagle'. Apparently, Neubauer offered to include a pig amongst the car's decorations in acknowledgement of 'Poppa' Moss's farming interests!

The fee was rumoured to be £25,000 but was in reality a regular retainer and a percentage of the starting money and other earnings. He was also to be provided with a Mercedes-Benz 220A, which cost £2,123 to purchase in the UK. To put this into context, the average wage in 1955 was just £8 week.

On the eve of his departure for America, where he makes his first appearance for the German Mercedes-Benz concern in the Grand Prix of Argentina, famous racing driver Stirling Moss explains the mysteries of his own car to a couple of racing drivers of the future. Moss will drive the new eight-cylinder petrol injection Mercedes, developed from the 1954 Mercedes Grand Prix machine, which has yet to make its debut in competitive events.

Sunday Chronicle 5.1.55

Stirling with Mrs McDonald Hobley at the Limelight Ball for the Blind on New Year's Eve. McDonald Hobley was a well-known announcer and broadcaster, and a friend of Stirling's.

An excellent night's sleep was ensured not only by the payment of $1,000 but also due to "two 'pheno' pills - slept 10/11 hours, slept though Dakar stop, filmed Rio and Sugar Loaf, wrote 16 cards as little else to do. Really hot. Discovered Lancia have a charter DC6 five hours in front of us with five cars and 16 people. The Recife hostesses (3) are very jolly and quite cute. There was chaos at the airport. We were met by Fangio & Co." That evening, "Many drinks were ordered and N [Neubauer] told the waiter to charge room 405 (Artur's) but AK heard and shouted 'No'." Referring back to the flight, SM noted, "Today the hostesses gave us bibs like babies, also toys to play with!"

Next day, Stirling was paid another $1,000 and noted, "Neubauer is still as funny as ever. Saw Harry Schell." That night he went to bed at 4am!

On Friday January 7th, "Entertained at German Embassy by Ambassador. Then lunch at Merc showrooms. Sightseeing and water skiing in Chris-Craft. Still very hot. Windstorm. Bed at 3.00am."

After spending Saturday at Paul Vincent's home with team mate Hans Hermann, he went to a club on the Sunday and swam all day. He also recorded, "We are being allowed 21 pesos to the $ = $420 per day."

Next day he was paid 10 times that sum and went off to see the circuit, commenting that "Hans and I have a [Mercedes] 300 to share". After lunch he bought two shirts to race in and then went back to the circuit. "On route poor Hans hit a small van and bashed the right (my) side of the car. He told Binder who has arranged to have it done overnight so Neubauer won't see it. Did 15 laps. Fangio 1.44.3! Kling 1.45, Hans 1.45.8 & SM 1.46 (5 times). I really don't think it will be possible to drive 90 or 100 laps in this heat. I was dead beat after 10! The brakes are really hairy and Uhlenhaut is trying to get me a servo fixed. We are reaching 220 kms [137mph] but are geared for 234 [145mph], so we should be quicker with the correct ratio. Had food at Rivoli - VG."

January 11th "Bought a pair of shoes (29/-) [£1.45] and Union Jack for Mercs to copy for my car. Terrible diarrhoea. To circuit. My car already has servo fitted and seating modified! No time to do axle ratio. I found a new way with the car while driving slowly & recorded ftd [fastest time of day] in 1.44.3, Fangio & Behra 1.44.8. The brakes are much lighter now but the

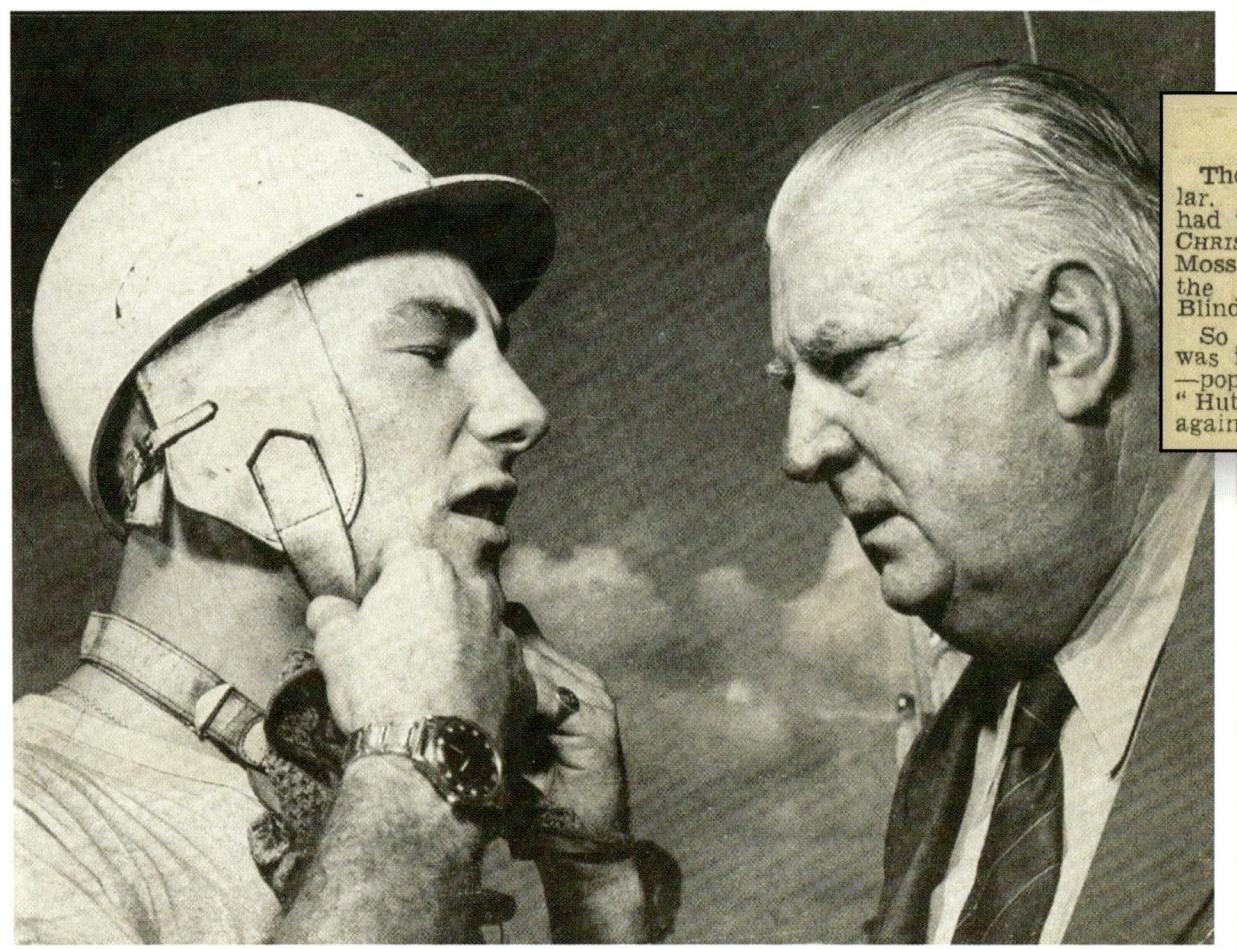

Speed men

Those trumpeters were popular. The Pigalle in Piccadilly had them. The Savoy (where CHRIS CHATAWAY beat STIRLING Moss in a miniature car race at the very Limelight Ball for the Blind) had them.

So did Quaglino's — where I was in time to hear "HUTCH" —popular, cabaret - minded "Hutch"—capture the house again.

Stirling with the irascible but paternal Alfred Neubauer, the famous Mercedes Team Manager, who was also known as 'Don Alfredo'.

Alfred Neubauer

Alfred Neubauer was an Austrian who had a modest career as a racing driver before realising that his talents lay in another sphere of motor racing. 'Don Alfredo', as he was often known, invented the role of team manager. Stirling wrote the foreword to his book, 'Speed was my Life'.

"As a team manager he has no equal in the history of big-time motor racing. In fact, it was Neubauer who virtually created the role of team manager and made it an indispensable feature of international motor racing.

"I enjoyed driving in the Mercedes team enormously. This was largely due to my affection for Alfred Neubauer as a man and to my admiration for him as a team-leader. He possessed to a high degree qualities which I particularly respect, combining intelligence with efficiency and scrupulous attention to detail.

"It seems almost superfluous to mention his genius for organising.

"This too I appreciated as a Mercedes team driver. Alfred Neubauer's experience of men and motor racing was so vast that he could read a driver's thoughts - on or off the job.

"Everyone who has seen him in action knows what an unpredictable temper he had, but he 'exploded' only when people were slow to understand, forgetful or careless; he did not suffer fools gladly. There was only one thing I really disliked about him - he made me (and others) get up too damned early!

"As an Englishman I loved his humour and his rare sense of fun. I cannot imagine anyone being unable to enjoy himself in his company, for one of 'Don Alfredo's' accomplishments is that he is a linguist and can be funny in three or four languages! He became a team manager because of his love of cars; I am convinced he could have made a success of almost any career - in business, or even the stage, had he so wished."

It is interesting that during his year as a Mercedes driver Moss paints a totally different picture of Mercedes' supposedly fearsome 22-stone [308lbs/140kgs] team manager than is usually presented. Rather than an austere and formidable figure, Stirling found him to be a very amusing man. His diary is littered with anecdotes that illustrate Neubauer's capacity for humour and self-deprecation. On the plane to South America, Moss noted that "He [Neubauer] was filmed reading and then brought the mag up to show an ape on the cover. Neubauer was unable to enter the toilet without turning sideways & some pushing."

Artur Keser, Head Of Mercedes PR

Artur Keser was a brilliant journalist-turned-PR man. He wrote under a pseudonym made up of his initials - A.J.K. - and was often addressed as 'Kaj' by his intimates. Keser was recruited to help with Press relations during the abortive trip to Argentina to race the pre-war Mercedes single seaters in South America in 1951. Subsequently, he was persuaded to give up journalism and join Daimler-Benz full-time as 'Presseleiter' (Head of the Press Dept.).

Keser was a keen motor racing enthusiast and had a fund of stories about 'Don Alfredo' (Alfred Neubauer). For example, when the W196 Streamliners failed to win at Silverstone in '54, he was spotted putting a case of 'victory celebration' Champagne into the boot of his own car!

During the war, Keser was 'Town Major' of a town in the South of France and the locals persuaded to him to have printed and distribute posters saying, "Help stamp out ****", the name of a pestilential bug which the French had given to their occupiers!

Stirling's belt burst

SIR:

I saw Stirling Moss crash at speed on the Castle Combe track in Wiltshire two years ago and afterwards picked up this souvenir—his safety belt. It has clearly been ripped from its moorings on either side and thus become useless. That is why I wonder whether the safety belt, which Moss recommends in his Spring Guide to Motoring (ILLUSTRATED supplement, April 2), is as safe as he suggests. I should also like to know how Moss expected to undo this belt in an emergency; it has three buckles and no quick release.

T. L. COELL
Frampton-on-Severn, Glos.

. *Stirling Moss replies:* This is an ordinary webbing belt which burst when I was flung out of the car at sixty miles an hour. A racing-car safety belt comes over the shoulders, like an airman's, and has a quick release. I do not wear a safety belt in racing. One reason for this is that the fire risk from the highly volatile fuel is so much greater.

Stirling and Sally seen at the Boat Show before he departed for South America.

Punta del Este...

Punta del Este, known as 'the St. Tropez of Uruguay' and 'the Pearl of the Atlantic', was popular with Argentine and Uruguayan upper middle class families who, escaping the stifling January heat in Buenos Aires, rented cottages along the shore or stayed in elegant hotels.

Another year of Shell successes

More and more racing, rally and trials competitors, motor mechanics and engineers, in fact all those responsible for preparing high performance engines, consistently use Shell X-100 for every kind of event. They realise that this oil—exactly the same as you can get at your garage—reduces wear to a minimum, and prolongs engine life to a remarkable degree.

Free!

SHELL SUCCESSES 1954

A 64-PAGE BOOK CONTAINING an exciting record of motoring and motor cycling events—all won on Shell Motor Oil. It's a handsome book illustrated with superb photographs, and containing articles specially written for Shell by Stirling Moss, Mike Hawthorn, Ken Wharton, Sheila Van Damm, Francis Beart, Bill Boddice and others. Write for your copy to your nearest Divisional Office of Shell-Mex and B.P. Ltd. (see telephone directory for address).

SHELL X-100 MOTOR OIL

for longer engine life
it fights acid action

SAE

Rudolf Uhlenhaut...

Rudolf 'Rudi' Uhlenhaut was the softly-spoken head of the research department at Mercedes-Benz. Born in London in 1906, his mother was English and his father was a German bank manager. He joined M-B in 1931 and was responsible for the 300 and 190 SL sports cars, and W196 GP car and 300 SLR sports racer. Famously, he was such a fine test driver than he was only marginally slower than several of the team's professional racers. He was also widely described as the finest automotive engineer in the world.

pedal travels too far. I have some slots for extra air which help some. Returned and had our medicals. Every day we see 2/3 cars wrecked due to the wheels falling off!"

The heat was exceptional for Europeans and was making life difficult in various ways. For this reason, plus the noise and the fact that he was receiving phonecalls intended for Artur Keser, SM changed hotel rooms. The drivers lunched at the local Mercedes factory and Stirling noted that "Fangio is mobbed everywhere". It was raining hard that day and he did 20 laps in the training car. His best was 1.45.6, whereas Fangio did 1.44.5 and Kling 1.44.3 in the short car. "I now discover that there are only two short cars, one for Fangio and one for Kling! Cocktail party at the Ambassador's, met John Camden of the [Daily] Express for food at the California. Bed at 1am."

Stirling was up early next morning and off to the garage to check the new pedal positions. He then tried the car round the block! At 3pm Stirling went to the circuit and did 10/15 laps. "Used new tyres, awful, 1.49. I could only do 1.46 on the others. Hans did 1.47.4, Fangio 1.44.1. Wow. Kling broke the practice car. Dinner at the English Club. Bed 1.30am.

"Up at 7.30 and off to see Perón at 8.15. This wasn't possible as his brother died yesterday; so we saw the Mayor instead. I hear Perón saw 14,000 persons last year in audience! Later got my passport back but had to pay $100 fine as well of fee of $100. In the evening I met Teddy and went out with some friends of his, very boring. Bed at 3.30. Gonzales lapped in 1.43.2 & Ascari in 1.43.1. (How?)"

Final practice took place next day. "Best I could do was 1.44.6. Gonzales 1.43.1, Fangio 1.43.3, Behra 1.43.8, Hermann & Kling 1.45. Just heard impossible to get into Punta del Este, too full due to the film festival. 8th fastest, only 1.8 secs separated first 10 cars! Bed at 12.30.

"Up at 10.30 to find the day hotter than ever. Yesterday it was just on 90°. We had a drivers' meeting and Neubauer explained all the signals to me. It's been decided to let us all have a go. I still have slight diarrhoea. I had a good start and was 4th. 1st Fangio, 2nd Ascari, 3rd Gonzales. We stayed like that for 5 or 6 laps and then later Ascari left the road, Gonzales stopped due to fatigue, & Fangio 1st SM 2nd, Schell 3rd. Then my fuel pump packed up, I collapsed and that's that."

With his mechanical problem, SM had stopped out on the circuit and climbed out of

Moss did not have sunstroke

STIRLING MOSS, the British racing driver, who was fourth in the Argentine Grand Prix, did not suffer from sunstroke as was at first reported.

He ran out of petrol and went off the track. The ambulance crew, who did not understand English, bundled him into an ambulance and placed ice on his head before an interpreter could intervene, according to the Mercedes-Benz Press officer.

Moss re-entered the race and was among the eight finishers.

The race was won in intense heat by Fangio, who drove his Mercedes-Benz at an average speed of more than 80 m.p.h. over the twisting track. The heat forced several drivers to give up.

Manchester Eve News 17.1.55

Drivers

Moss on: Harry Schell ...

"Very likeable. I don't want to say buffoon but he was the one we would play pranks on. Nice guy and a man who, at the end of the year, always went a bit quicker so he'd be sure of getting a drive for the following year. He was always gambling. For instance, he'd play various cards games with de Portago. He was the original Innes Ireland, if you like!"

'Pheno Pills'

Moss is possibly referring to the drug Phenobarbital, which is used for the control of epilepsy and as a sedative to relieve stress and anxiety. It was also commonly used for the short-term treatment of insomnia in the 1950s.

Stirling lacked confidence in his brakes in practice for the Argentine Grand Prix which may in part explain why he was on the third row of the grid.

MANAGER 'CLEARS' STIRLING

Medical card goes to Mr. Shinwell

By BASIL CARDEW

MR. EMANUEL SHINWELL, Socialist Minister of Defence in 1950-1, will get a letter this morning containing proof that racing driver Stirling Moss was put in Grade 3 by a National Service medical board.

It is a Photostat copy of the grade card issued to Moss on August 19, 1947—one month before his 18th birthday.

The sender is his 23-year-old manager, Mr. Ken Gregory, who has written a similar letter—but without the Photostat—to all other M.P.s.

Mr. Gregory said last night : "I am singling out the Photostat for

"Stirling discussed the matter with me before he left to race in Sunday's Buenos Aires Grand Prix and my letters have his full approval."

The letter to M.P.s comments : "Presumably as a result of the low medical grading, Mr. Moss has not been called for military service, but he has at no time taken any

steps to secure deferment or exemption, nor has he at any time deliberately stayed abroad for this purpose.

"You will, therefore, appreciate that the references to him, both in the House of Commons and elsewhere, have caused him distress and embarrassment."

Stirling Moss, driving a German Mercedes, has so far put up the fastest practice times in Buenos Aires.

Daily Express 15.1.55

Wheeling out the W196 for Stirling's début race with Mercedes-Benz, the Argentine Grand Prix. Withstanding the heat was going to be his biggest challenge.

January

Stirling Moss Scrapbook

15

the cockpit. He lay down on the ground for a moment and was promptly put on a stretcher and carted off by some over-zealous medics. As they spoke no English and Stirling did not have a word of Spanish, he was in the local hospital before he knew it. Finally, he managed to extricate himself and returned to the circuit where Neubauer immediately put him in Hermann's W196.

Returning to his diary notes, "Later I drove 35 mins in Hans' car, also driven by Karl. Fangio is fantastic - he drove all the 3 hours alone!! Ferrari were 2nd & 3rd and then Hans, Karl, SM 4th. Ferraris used 4 drivers per car. It was so hot my gum melted in my pocket (104°)." Next day, he noted, "Track temperature was 55°C (134°F) yesterday".

Stirling did not do a lot for the next few days apart from arranging a flight to Uruguay ("our passports are being fixed by the German Embassy!") and taking part in one practice session on the revised, more twisty circuit to be used for the second Argentine race in a fortnight's time. He noted: "My car now has special _air_ ducting and is _much_ cooler. The under-bonnet temperature is 80°C (170°F)." As this race was not being run to GP rules, larger power units could be used and M-B fitted 3-litre engines in place of the 2½-litre power units allowed in GP racing.

On January 21st he did meet President Perón. "He was very charming," wrote Stirling who also recorded that, "Pres. Perón's room had two tractors (toys) on the table, a Pan-Am Strat [Stratocruiser], an American jet, a stuffed toad and b. great vulture doings as well." SM was not feeling at all well but in spite of this he and some chums left in pouring rain for Miramar. "We had a job to find accommodation. In the end we found a room for four men and a double for the girls. Room = 5/- [25p]. Bed at 3.30."

Next day the party went to Mar del Plata and SM, who always watched the pennies, was impressed to find "a room for 70 pesos (incl. of all!)". Next day was spent on the beach in wonderful sunshine. He sunbathed and walked three kilometres.

The following morning he enjoyed more of the same. "It was very hot with a good wind so we really burnt up. After lunch swam in the big breakers (2m). At 11pm we went to 'Duel in the Sun' with Jenny Jones & Peck VG. Bed at 2am."

Five and a half hours later he was woken by "a phone call re. an offer to drive for Boris at Sebring. Left Mar del Plata, covering 230kms in

Race Report

Gran Premio de la Republica Argentina

The appearance of the full M-B GP team in South America caused great excitement. It is said there was some panic among Mercedes technical staff regarding carburation and axle ratios, due to their unfamiliarity with the circuit and the extreme conditions. Rumour had it that the red Italian machines would out-class the silver German ones. The local heroes were Fangio and Gonzales, and, after practice, four different makes graced the front row of the grid - Lancia (Ascari), Mercedes (Fangio), Ferrari (Gonzales) and Maserati (Behra).

"The Argentine autodrome was a short, twisty one of just under 2 ½ miles," recalled Stirling, "but it accommodated a quarter of a million people. In the blistering heat, which was well over 130° [F] on the circuit, the start was really terrific, with half a dozen of us snarling away in a fight for the lead. To the delight of the crowd, Fangio and Gonzales whipped away from the start with Ascari, Farina and myself close-up, but by the first turn Ascari had roared by Gonzales and I had managed to pass Farina. After three laps, Ascari had gone by Fangio, and Gonzales and I were still chasing them with only a fraction of a second between the lot of us."

Crashes then eliminated Behra and Villoresi, Berger and Menditeguy (who collided head-on!), Bayol and Stirling's team mate Karl Kling. After 20 laps, the leader Ascari skidded on oil and went off, hitting a fence. Gonzales pitted on the point of collapse and Trintignant took over his car. Indeed there was much driver swopping in the Ferraris. Farina, also about to pass out, handed over to Magliol.

At 30 laps Stirling, now lying second, had his vapour lock problem and charade with the over-zealous medics. On the 34th lap Fangio pitted, drank a couple of bottles of lemonade, gave himself a quick towel-bath and three minutes later was on his way again in third place. Another local, and the only other driver to complete the entire race solo, Roberto Mierès briefly led. Soon, however, Fangio was established again in the lead and led home two Ferraris, each of which had had three drivers (Trintignant had taken stints in both, as had Farina!). Meanwhile, Kling had taken over Hermann's W196, "sweated it out for a few laps, then handed it back again," as Autosport Editor Gregor Grant delightfully put it. Stirling took it over and the trio finished fourth.

Never before had there been such driver swopping and the result caused a real headache for those in charge of the World Championship points scoring. In those days it was eight points for a win, six for second, four for third, three for fourth and two for fifth, with an extra point for the fastest lap. Farina and Trintignant were finally awarded 3⅓ points each, Magliol 1⅓ and Kling, Hermann and Moss 1 point each!

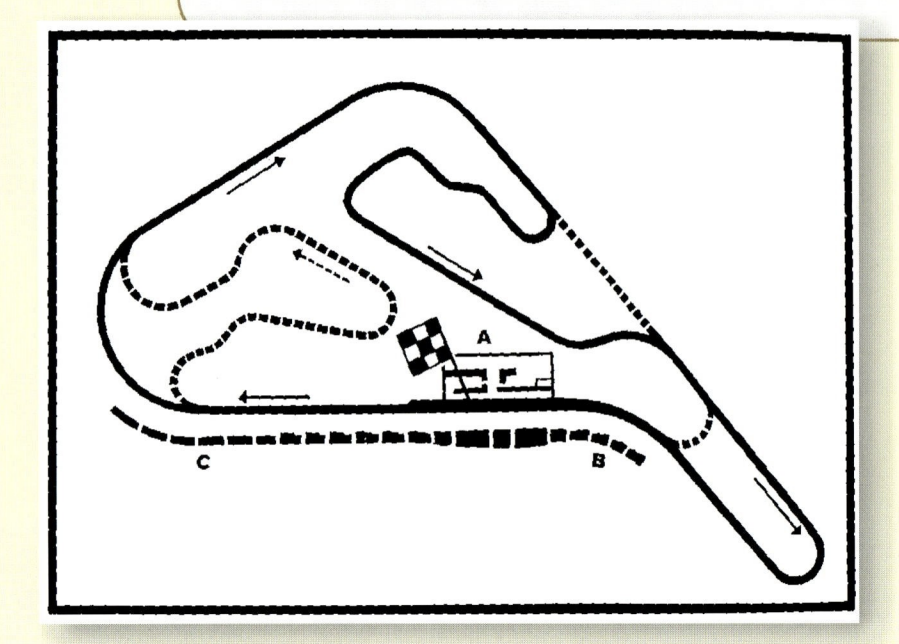

The Buenos Aires track was known as the circuit of '17th of October'. The outer course of 2.48 miles (4.2 kms) was used for the Argentine GP.

Stirling Moss ...

FANGIO'S FEAT

"It was incredibly hot and especially inside the cars. They tried to create some air intakes but even the air was incredibly hot. I was very tired and the thought of getting back in a car was not too great a one!

"Fangio's feat was indeed extraordinary. He had built up his exceptional stamina competing in the long-distance South American road races earlier in his career. He also had some little pills to help him withstand the heat and fatigue."

SE INICIA LA GRAN CARRE

It appears that 1954 World Champion Juan Manuel Fangio has already departed. Gonzales (12) can be seen in the foreground in his Ferrari, followed by Alberto Ascari (32) in the Lancia with its distinctive pannier tanks. Jean Behra, in the works Maserati, is on the far side of this shot and Stirling's team mates, Kling and Hermann, can be spotted in the middle of the pack. Stirling himself, in his distinctive white helmet, is on the far left of the picture.

The Popular Image

The perceived exhilaration and danger of racing as a profession coupled with the drivers' often high profile capacity for fun and womanising, hold the key to their fame at this time. Given that the horizons most people could aspire to in 1950s Britain were limited, drivers such as Moss, who travelled the world, pursued ostentatiously glamorous lifestyles and were believed to earn big money, quickly became the superstars, indeed the 'Beckhams', of their day.

However, it is important to note that, despite the seemingly advantageous terms of his employment, his finances were not all that they might sound. One headline from 1955 records his frustration with the British tax laws, which meant that despite earning over £14,000, tax had left him with only £1,200.

Stirling Moss keeps a promise

Sunday Chronicle Motoring Correspondent

STIRLING MOSS, 25-year-old racing driver now in Buenos Aires as a member of the official Mercedes Benz team, will drive a British car in the Sebring 12—the American Le Mans — in March.

The British ace has cabled Mr. Donald Healey, maker of the fast Austin Healey 100, offering to drive one of his cars in the race.

This follows Stirling Moss's article in the *Sunday Chronicle* last week in which he declared: "I will drive for Britain."

His manager, Mr. Ken Gregory, said yesterday: "Mr. Healey in a cable to Stirling has raised the question as to whether the company would be able to pay the fee a driver of his calibre normally commands.

"Moss cabled back saying:

"'SO KEEN DRIVE BRITISH, PREPARED TO DO SO WHATEVER THE FEE.'"

Good recovery

Moss won the Sebring race last year, driving with the American W. Lloyd, an Italian Osca entered by the Briggs-Cunningham stable at an average of 73.65 m.p.h. for the 12 hours.

Following Moss's exhausting drive in the Argentinian Grand Prix last week he was ordered by doctors to rest.

Messages reaching London say he has made a good recovery and will practise with the Mercedes team during the coming week in readiness for the Buenos Aires Grand Prix next Sunday.

Sunday Chronicle 23.1.55

2 hours! Shopped, bought Pat a bridle and bit. Dinner and danced.

"I hear Mercs think Hans and I are not serious," he said in his diary next day. "I wish they would come out and speak and not do it behind our backs. I reckon it's Korf & Kling. 3pm to circuit. All did 2.21, then Fangio idled round in 2.17.7! Wow. The 3 litre is fantastic and has some 320hp but so much torque it isn't true. I hear our 2½s had from 280-288hp. Had dinner with Uhlenhaut and Keser."

On January 27th he had a look at a friend's Porsche 550 and then went to the circuit and used a 2½ because his 3-litre had a split oil tank. He managed a 2.20.8 while Fangio did 2.21.0 in the same car and Kling 2.22.2, with Hermann on 2.22.6. That night he sampled the Caso's Club. As an aside he commented, "Mercs also made a special breathing tube with harness to try out".

A day later Neubauer paid him $2,250 (for his 4th place finish in the GP) and $6,000 (presumably his retainer). Stirling also asked if it would be possible to buy a Mercedes 300 for a friend but the answer was, "No!" He wrote, "Official price $140,000 but always $300,000!" Following practice when both SM and Hermann clocked 2.19.9, "My car is very critical on tyres; we are wearing these out very quickly". That evening there was a party with Mercedes.

Final practice for qualification for the race was rather traumatic. "It was raining hard and the front brakes on my 3-litre kept locking. Also the tyres were clapped. Later I used a spare 2½ and was equal 2nd ftd in 2.33.6. Fangio 2.33.2 in a 3-litre. The track was awful and heaps water badly. Had cable from Briggs re. a D-type at Sebring."

On the day of the race, "To circuit. 80% humidity and 46.6°C on the track. In the first heat, I took the lead for some 15 laps from Fangio and Farina; my front brakes were locking badly and I got very tired. Later Fangio lead and then Farina. Finish was Farina, Fangio, SM, Kling, etc. I had to drive 4 laps with canvas showing in patches on my left front tyre due to brake-locking."

The Continental tyres, which Mercedes were using to combat the heat and expected greater wear with the more powerful cars, were too hard. Changing to softer compounds for the second heat made a big difference.

"In the second heat, Fangio lead and I followed at 1 metre all the race till 26 laps and then overtook him and equalled Farina's lap

Though he was battling with the heat, Stirling had worked his way up to second place at quarter distance.

The intensely patriotic Stirling seen with the Union Jack flag which Mercedes painted on the car for him. As the season progressed, the M-B team would be increasingly cosmopolitan in its choice of drivers.

Give Me Some Air

In an attempt to combat the heat, at one stage during practice Stirling had a pipe from an air vent strapped to his chest, hoping for a direct stream of air to his face. "But even that was no good!"

Note the cooling vents.

Fatal! Stirling lay down for a moment to recover … and is whisked off to hospital.

CHRIS-CRAFT …

The Chris-Craft boat is an American icon, an internationally recognised symbol of performance and pleasure. The Chris-Craft Cobra was launched in 1955.

The Mercedes party in South America.

record of 2.19.5. Fangio was slower than me on the mid-speed curves and a bit faster on the fast one, until later when I was about the same. My water was 105° and I only used 7500 [rpm]. Fangio was using 2nd more than I. I think this was my best race. Returned to BA and Merc dinner. Antonia gave me $500, three suits and a beautiful set of Argentine bow lassos, knives, etc. Bed at 3.00.

"Up at 7.45 after no sleep, possibly due to the pill the doctor gave me yesterday between races. Afternoon took off for Montevideo but had to circle due to clag, in and out again of Sao Paolo but had to return to Monte at 10.30! Phoned SAS and fixed with a sleeper on the 04.05 plane! KLM allowed me to use the sleeper on the DC6 until SAS arrived."

So the month of January was quite an adventure. In only his second event for Mercedes-Benz, he beat his team leader and World Champion, Juan Manuel Fangio. At last, Stirling had cars and a team worthy of his latent talent.

When Moss pulled off the track with his fuel problem in the Argentine Grand Prix, the locals quickly gathered around to assist. Marshalling standards were a little different in those days!

Stirling Moss ...

MEETING PERÓN

"I met Perón at one of the events, I remember it quite vividly. I was mopping my brow after the race, you know, because it was pretty hot. I had all the black round me and Perón whipped out a hankie, the most fantastic hankie, incredible fine Sea Island cotton and said. 'Do take this'. I had this black face and I wiped it because he gave it me and here was this thing now, absolutely ruined and I thought, 'God, I can't give it back to him' so I kept it. Unfortunately, I don't know how, but somehow the damned thing got lost, so I haven't got it now. But it was unbelievable, the mess that I made of this poor man's hankie. He was very gracious at the time, I think he congratulated me. Fangio, of course, was much, much closer to him." There is a suggestion that, as the handkerchief was such a fancy one, that it might have belonged to 'Evita' who had died just a couple of years before.

TAIL VIEW

WITH no justification, beyond that it was told at Bedford and I enjoyed the narration, I print the yarn told against himself last week by British Racing Motors Ltd. publicity director, Rivers Fletcher.

It concerns the time he was taking photographs of Stirling Moss trying out the latest B.R.M. Moss had suggested Fletcher stand on the track with his cine-camera and "I will beetle up to you at about 120 m.p.h. plus, slide round and you can obtain a good close-up."

Fletcher agreed and took up his position. Moss duly "beetled" up, but much closer to Fletcher than the amateur photographer appreciated. Telling the story, he concludes: "And Stirling always says the next thing he saw was my backside disappearing through a hedge."

N. Hants Even Tel 20.1.55

'Duel In The Sun'

The appropriately-named film 'Duel in the Sun' was branded 'Lust in the Dust' when released in 1946. An epic western starring Jennifer Jones, Gregory Peck and Lillian Gish, it was about a sexually-charged half-breed woman. The movie was produced by David. O. Selznick whose great classic was 'Gone with the Wind'.

'Pig Brother' watching...

☆ IF he doesn't watch out, STIRLING MOSS will have "pig brother" watching him every time he takes the wheel of his Mercedes.

The 25-year-old white-headed boy of motor racing spends a great deal of time helping to run his father's pig farm in Hertfordshire.

Alfred Neubauer, Mercedes team manager, is also a pig enthusiast. I heard yesterday that he has offered to paint a pink porker on the side of Stirling's silver car.

If Stirling accepts the offer, the vehicle will soon be looking like a Christmas tree. It already carries a Union Jack and a lucky horseshoe.

Yesterday his father, Mr. Alfred Moss, said he would be discussing the matter with Stirling when he returns after racing for Mercedes in South America.

STIRLING MOSS

Newcastle Journal 20.1.55

Juan Perón

Juan Perón, whose father was a farmer, was born in a province of Buenos Aires in 1895. After military school he rose to the rank of colonel and played a significant role in the military coup of 1943. He held various government posts before becoming President of Argentina in 1946. His politics were a blend of fascism and socialism, and his ideology would become known as Perónism.

His first wife died of cancer in 1942 and in 1945 he married Eva, who become known as Evita. Tremendously popular with women and the working classes, she died, also of cancer, at just 33 years of age in 1953. With her death Perón's popularity waned and his economic difficulties increased. In June 1955 Perón crushed an attempted coup but succumbed to another in September that year. He went into exile. In 1973 he returned to be re-elected President by an overwhelming majority but died a year later.

Local hero, Juan Manuel Fangio, takes well-earned refreshment after his extraordinary feat in the intense heat of Buenos Aires.

For the second Argentine race, the W196s were fitted with larger 3-litre engines.

Stirling Moss ...

BUENOS AIRES GP

"For the second [Argentine] race the car was even better to drive, a lot more torque obviously. I remember we had a lot of problems with cracking brakes there. I mentioned that this was a problem because when they cracked, the brakes grabbed. As a result, they squirted a little oil into the brakes."

Larger Engines

For the Formula Libre Buenos Aires GP, three long-wheelbase W196s were fitted with the 3-litre engines being developed for the 300 SLR sports racer. With cast alloy blocks, they produced around 320bhp but there was some difficulty fitting the engines due to their greater size and they could not be canted over to such a degree as the 2½-litre power units. In wet practice, Stirling was actually faster in a 2½-litre.

Moss On: Dr. Guiseppe Farina ...

"Farina was really tough, dirty. On one occasion, earlier in my career, he really carved me up something awful at Spa while lapping me. I was in an HWM, and in passing me he went too wide and then I got passed him on the exit and he had to re-pass. Fangio came passed laughing his head off. I mean I was a lap behind and he pushed me out of the way. As he'd overdone it, I just kept going which I thought was really fun. I think that Fangio sat there thinking, 'Well boy, you deserve that!' He was a tough driver and not very gracious. He did crash a lot."

Safety First Guarantee

This Certifies that I, the undermentioned female, about to enjoy sexual intercourse with—

_____

am above the lawful age of consent, am in my right mind and not under the influence of any drug or narcotic. Neither does he have to use any force, threats or promises to influence me.

I am in no fear of him whatsoever; do not expect or want to marry him, don't know whether he is married or not, and don't care. I am not asleep or drunk and am entering into this relation with him because I love it and want it as much as he does, and if I receive the satisfaction I expect, I am very willing to play an early return engagement.

Furthermore, I agree never to appear as a witness against him or to prosecute under the Mann White Slave Act.

Signed before jumping into bed, the _____ day of _____ 19___

By _____

Address _____

(SEAL)

How I lost—by Stirling Moss

'Si, si' just not enough!

By STIRLING MOSS,
as told to the Sunday Chronicle Motoring Correspondent

BUENOS AIRES, Saturday.

LIFE is ironic! A year ago I slithered and skidded my way over the last 200 miles of the Maritime Alps and down to the Riviera in the Monte Carlo Rally.

I expected to do the same again this year—and I gather it was the cruellest run anybody can recall—until the Mercedes offer came along.

And, instead of ice and snow, I was in a sun-drenched inferno, for that is what the Argentinian Grand Prix was.

Never have I driven in conditions like it—the temperature was 105 deg. and humidity 88—and yet, contrary to reports, it was not sunstroke that wrecked my chances, although indirectly it was the heat. This is what happened.

After lying about seventh I had worked my way through the field until, on the 25th lap, I was second to Fangio, who was driving superbly, as usual.

It was on that lap that my car spluttered and stopped. The trouble was a vapour-lock in the petrol system, which starved my engine of fuel, and I pulled in to the side of the track.

Sunday Chronicle 30.1.55

After the unremitting and intense heat experienced in the Argentine GP, the Mercedes engineers made a number of changes for the second race, the Buenos Aires GP. Stirling's car now seems to be positively riddled with louvres, vents and heat deflectors. The large 'boards' seen below the cockpit were presumably intended to act as heat shields on the opposite side from that shown here to deflect the heat from the exposed exhaust pipes.

In the first heat, Stirling followed his team leader but in the second heat Stirling passed Fangio and took the flag ahead of the great Argentinian, though finishing second on aggregate. Stirling considered this to be his finest race so far and it must have given his confidence a great boost. Opposite: Fangio was Stirling's great mentor during the 1955 season.

Light On His Feet!

Stirling, unlike certain others drivers, preferred a very light brake pedal. Ken Gregory described him as being "light and springy on his feet", even likening him to a ballet dancer. Apparently, a servo from a Chevrolet saloon was used initially on the W196 when Stirling was unhappy with the brakes.

El Gráfico

BUENOS AIRES
4 DE FEBRERO DE 1955
Año 36º — Nº 1851

FEBRUARY

Calendar
1955

Practising for the Mille Miglia (MM)

February began for Stirling in Rio after a bumpy flight. "Read most of the day," he noted, "and took my pills." On Wednesday 2nd, he flew to Lisbon and then Geneva just catching the London flight. Next day he spent at the office before having dinner with his father at the Steering Wheel Club. After dinner he called on Sally Weston in Pitts Head Mews. He got home to bed at 3am.

That Friday, after visiting SW and Sandersons about wallpaper for his flat, he met Denis Jenkinson for lunch at Sheppies to discuss the Mille Miglia. After working through the afternoon, he took 'Audrey' to see *Young At Heart*. "G. Food at La Rues. Bed late."

On Saturday he met his legendary racing mechanic Alf Francis for lunch at the 'Wheel'. After visiting the flat to check on how the workmen were doing, he drove to his parents' farm at Tring to relax. "Neubauer phoned but I wasn't in!"

On Monday he was interviewed by John Hall of the Star for an article in the Chronicle. That evening he met SW and "we saw 'Carmen Jones' VG & food at the Colony". Next day he took Audrey to *There's No Business Like Show Business* (VG) and dined at the Mirabel. Wednesday saw him up early and, after visiting Donaldson & Williams, his London tailors, Stirling had a photo session with Lance Macklin and the Healey they would be driving at Sebring. He lunched with Donald Healey. That evening he saw "SW, row over the hire of a Minx. Later to Epicure for food. VG."

SW collected Stirling next morning and drove him to London Airport where he and Jenks flew, via Geneva, to Milan. From there they were driven to Brescia. "We met all the

The Motor — February 9, 1955

A NOD seems as good as a wink to the Mercedes technicians. When Stirling Moss recently mentioned that he found the brakes a little on the heavy side for his liking, they promptly fitted a servo. And after the trouble at Buenos Aires with tremendous heat in the cockpits that very hot day, they immediately fashioned bigger air vents and fitted wind-deflector strips, rather like the familiar splash-guards, to prevent heated air from the engine and the simmering road surface from playing on the cockpits.

* * *

MOSS, returned from the Argentine, is leaving for two practice laps of the Mille Miglia course where he is to drive (April 30) Mercedes with Fangio and Kling.

The Motor 9.2.55

Stirling's flat

STIRLING MOSS, back from racing in the Argentine, soon got to work decorating his new flat.

His racing programme—he is now driving for the German Mercedes firm—gives him little time to be down on the farm at his father's home in Tring so he has set up his own flat in West Kensington.

Stirling Moss's next race is an all-British affair. With Lance Macklin he will drive an Austin-Healey in Florida.

His official German racing car carries a miniature Union Jack on the bonnet.

YORKS Eve. Post 7.2.55

Stirling Moss ...

WHY JENKS?

"I knew him quite well because he raced bikes in the old days when I started. I was in the 500cc cars and they often had cars and bikes at the same meetings. He was a highly intelligent man, very knowledgeable, a very critical person. I mean, if Jenks had said to you after a race, 'You didn't half go that time' it was the highest accolade you could get. I knew how weird he was and how exact and very pernickety, which I felt were the things needed. I knew how courageous he was because he had been a motorcycle sidecar passenger and [with Eric Oliver] had been World Champion three times. So he was an obvious choice."

MOSS TO RACE AUSTIN HEALEY

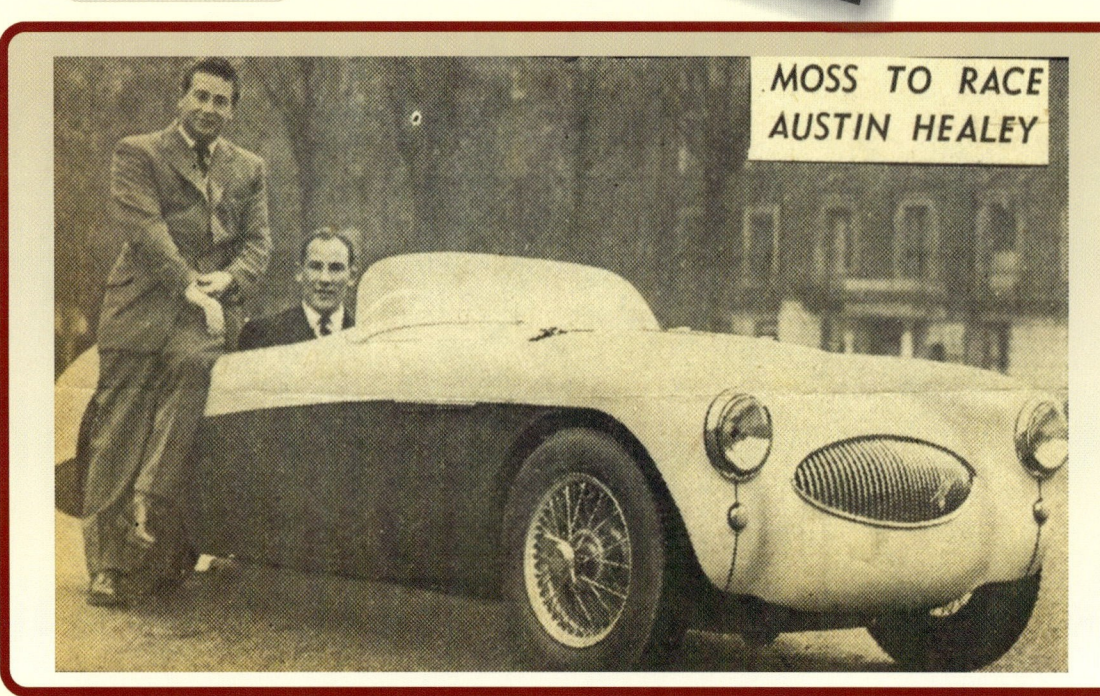

STIRLING MOSS, British Grand Prix driver, will be at the wheel of an Austin Healey 100 S in the Florida International 12-Hour Grand Prix of Endurance at Sebring in America, on March 13.

Announcing this today, the Austin Motor Company said that Moss's co-driver will be Lance Macklin, another experienced Grand Prix driver.

Last year Stirling Moss won the Sebring race, and Lance Macklin won the three-litre class, was the driver of the first British car to finish, and was third in the general classification.

Picture shows Moss and Macklin with an Austin Healey 100 S.

B'ham Eve. Despatch 15.2.55

Stirling Moss ...

COMMUNICATING

In the open 300 SLR it was impossible for Moss and Jenks to hear each other at speed.

SM: *"We tried out the very latest intercoms, made by companies like Decca. We were doing a lap in the SLR, a recce, and we'd been going for 20 minutes and I stopped and said, 'What's up?' He said, 'Well I read the notes to you' and I said, 'I never heard them'. Many, many years later, we met a guy from Cornell University, who said if you are really flat out concentrating you don't feel pain and you can't hear things - it's the 'stay alive' response. The reason I hadn't heard was because I was concentrating too hard to hear what he was saying. Jenks said, that just shows you, these rally drivers, if they are really at 10/10ths, would never hear the pace notes! So that's why we didn't use an intercom, but we certainly tried them out."*

As a consequence, they devised a set of hand signals.

SM: *"The thing about hand signals is that there are very few you need. There were places going round the circuit where you could see the road but there were places, such as the brow of a hill, that you could really take flat out, but you wouldn't know. That's somewhere where you could save time. There were other places where you thought you could see the road but there might be a wiggle in between, somewhere where you could get hurt. The only places we were interested in were where you could gain time or where we should slow down, but which didn't look slow. So that's what all our notes were based on and the hand signals had to be something you could see while driving, without transferring vision from driving."*

Above: Stirling, with the 220A which was on loan to him, and Jenks.

A Flat—And A Flag

STIRLING MOSS, who has returned from his triumphant racing in the Argentine, spent today decorating his new flat.

His racing programme—he is now driving for the German Mercedes firm — gives him little time to be down on the farm at his father's home in Tring, so he has set up his own flat in West Kensington.

Stirling Moss's next race is an all-British affair. With Lance Macklin he will drive an Austin-Healey in the classic Sebring International in Florida.

His official German racing car carries a miniature Union Jack on the bonnet.

Moss In Practice Crash: Unhurt

STIRLING Moss, the British racing driver, was uninjured when his car ploughed into a flock of sheep and was in collision with an oncoming Italian car near Rome last night.

Moss, who is to take part in the classic Italian Mille Miglia road race in a German Mercedes in May, was familiarising himself with the route when the accident occurred.

chaps and then saw the car; it's an SLR! No clothing, we were expecting an SL.

"Up at 6.30am and we left at 7.45. We stopped about 35 kms out for a plug check and then on. Arrived at Pescara at 1pm. Average 132.6 kph! Lunch and on to Aquila. Av. 133.3, thence to Viterbo. Overall average = 124.6 kph. Time 7 hr 40 min. 955 kms. Denis was sick due to fumes so we made a deflector but NG. Car averaged 100 kms/20.7 litres. Geared for 274 kph @ 7,500 = 172mph. We got 6700 but traffic too heavy. 7500 in 4th = 152 mph."

The duo were out again next day and drove to Siena, Firenza "and then the Futa, etc., to Bologna. This 101 kms section took us 1 hr 4. Av = 100.3. Last year fastest was 1 hr 4 and in '53 it was 1 hr 2! We continued through Modena where a policeman waved us down. I didn't stop. He followed in a 1400 Fiat and cut across the front, but I nipped round and continued to Parma for lunch. Overall average 119.4. Stage 138 kph! On to Brescia. Saw Neubauer, they changed the clutch, checked the brakes, etc. Dinner and bed at 9.30, tired and unwell. Car does 100 kms/27 litres in hills. Tyres only 1/3 worn in 1600 kms."

Stirling now had a stinking cold. He still managed to average 155.5 kph (97 mph) next day until the radiator sprung a leak and they had to stop the night at Pescara. The following morning he was woken by the Merc mechanics at 5am but did not rise until 7.30, leaving an hour later in a hailstorm. Unable to see, they had to stop for a while. "Continued, then snow all the way to Pescara, then OK. Then at approx 3.15 I hit a bloody sheep. The man threw a stick at it and it ran across me. I was doing about 100 kph. The car was rather bent, especially the rear left wheel." Hermann and Kling picked them up in a 220 saloon and they drove back to Brescia next day.

"Neubauer was wonderful and laid no blame. He thought I had hit a Jeep, not sheep!"

"I had some metal in my eye so saw a Doc." It was now mid-month and SM flew back to London, riding in the cockpit as they crossed the Alps and landing in a snow-covered Britain. Apart from lunch with Jack Fairman, he worked a long day in the office before appearing on the BBC Sportsview programme. That evening, he went to the Colony with SW.

He spent the next morning with TV personality McDonald Hobley, taking three hours to make a four minute clip for the film, *The Man of the Year*.

Stirling Moss ...

HAIL & SNOW

A hailstorm and snow must have been pretty exciting in an SLR! "Yes. At least in those days we had one tyre, whether wet or dry, and you just drove accordingly and snow is just hard rain. The SLR in the wet was fairly difficult to handle, because it was a pretty large car and if you start getting that amount of size and weight sliding, it obviously takes a bit of controlling."

This is presumably Brands Hatch where Stirling went for a photographic session in later February. The photography was rather ruined by the unexpected snowfall, but Stirling still indulged in a little fun in the Gullwing 300 SL Merc. That fun included generous handfuls of opposite lock.

Stirling Moss ...

HIGH AVERAGE SPEEDS

You were pressing on! "Yes, I would have, depending where it was. On the Futa, for instance, I would have pressed on because you could really see for miles and I knew if a car was coming. In principle, I would never have been on the wrong side [of the road], unless I was able to check it was clear. Having said that, in a car with the potential of the SLR you could get out of the way pretty fast. We would certainly have got up to quite high speeds when you could see that the road was OK."

Stirling Moss fined 30s.

Racing motorist Stirling Moss was fined 30s. at Bow Street, London, yesterday for causing an obstruction in Adelaide Street, Strand, by parking his car for 45 minutes opposite a cab rank.

Moss, who pleaded not guilty, said: "I maintain that where I was there was no obstruction."

News Chronical 26.2.55

Stirling Moss ...

ITALIAN POLICE

As to the incident with the police: "I was obviously in a hurry. What happened was the policeman waved me down, I didn't take much notice and he got a bit upset. I managed to nip round him and out-ran him in the hope that he wasn't able to radio ahead. I assume we probably looked at the car to see if there were any aerials and all that sort of stuff. You are talking '55 when it wasn't quite so sophisticated. It was obviously something I did that was a bit naughty!"

Above: The chap talking to Stirling is John 'Autocar' Cooper, so known to distinguish him from John Cooper, of Cooper racing cars fame. The former was so-called as he was Sport Editor of *The Autocar*. He was apprenticed to Alvis in 1933 and held various appointments in the industry before entering journalism in 1949. He was involved in creating the prototype Kieft 500 for Stirling. In 1952 they shared a Sunbeam-Talbot 90 with Desmond Scannell on the Monte Carlo Rally and, on their very first rally, finished second by a mere four seconds. The following year they were sixth. In 1953 John Cooper and Ray Martin built the Cooper-Alta Special for Stirling to go Grand Prix racing. Cooper was tragically killed in an accident in March at the age of 38.

Left: Stirling purchased a Bolex 16mm cine camera on his first trip to Germany in January and filmed extensively in South America. He later edited his films and used to show them to family and friends.

That Sunday he was photographed, in colour, with sister Pat for 'Illustrated' and for the MG company. In the afternoon, he edited and showed his Buenos Aires films. "OK" Next evening he dined at the House of Commons with Bill Shepherd M.P. and "after we went to the Cabaret, Eve and Coconut Grove. Bed at 3.45am."

The following morning he had a meeting with Sir William, Sir Reg and Brian Rootes. "Fixed up truck, etc." This would have been for his privately-owned Maserati 250F which Stirling had raced in '54 and would lend to a variety of drivers in '55. After an afternoon of interviews, SM and SW saw *Theodora* and *Three Pilates*. (F) They ate at L'Epicure.

Wednesday 23rd saw Stirling taking a 300 SL to Brands Hatch for photography but there was four inches of snow there. Rest of the day was taken up with press interviews and then he and a friend went to see *The Boy Friend*. "Saw Doreen for food later."

Thursday evening Stirling and SW went to see *The Slave* (F) before food at Sheppies. His days were being filled with a mixture of interviews, photo sessions, meetings and work at the office. That Friday he also had to go to court to pay a fine of 30/- (£1.50) for causing an obstruction with his car in the Strand. Though feeling under the weather, he called at Ken Gregory's flat where he changed into evening dress, collected SW and went to Madame Tussaud's to be filmed by the television cameras with his wax bust for the Arthur Askey Show. They then went on to the BR & SCC Dinner but left early.

The following morning, a Saturday, he went to the Daily Express offices for an interview with Robert Glenton. After lunch with Audrey, he flew that evening to New York, via Shannon. Arriving in the early hours of Sunday (local time), he flew National to Miami and then Pan-Am to Nassau. "To B.C. ["British Colonial - one of the better hotels." Considered extremely expensive at £9 per day for full board.] changed, food and met many GB press chaps. Then Duncan [McLean] showed us the lights in honour of the Princess." The final day of February was spent water-skiing, touring the island and playing golf.

Stirling Moss ...

PRACTISING WITH TRAFFIC

Was it hairy practising with ordinary traffic on the road? "Yea, it was really. But practice was really limited to checking one's notes, more than actually practising. It was practising in as much as, if there was a bit where we could see, we'd have a go. You had to be very careful, because you could have easily brought the sport into disrepute and all that sort of stuff. We did certainly have considerable care when we were practising."

Cars

300 SL Coupé

2-seater closed sports car with distinctive 'Gullwing' doors, launched at the New York Auto Show in February 1954, production commenced later 1954 until 1957, 1,400 built, tubular steel space-frame chassis, in-line 6-cylinder, 2,966cc, two valves per cylinder operated by rocker arms off chain-driven overhead cam, Bosch fuel injection, 240bhp (SAE) at 6,100rpm, 5-speed manual gearbox, independent front suspension with double wishbones with concentric coil springs and telescopic shock absorbers, rear suspension by independently coil sprung half axles, drum brakes, maximum speed 135 mph (217 km/h), 0 - 60 mph in 8.8 seconds.

A Roadster (convertible) version was introduced in 1957 with a revised chassis, conventional doors and different rear suspension.

Stirling would spend a good deal of time in April practising for the Mille Miglia and would use a 300 SL for much of it.

From right to left, Valerie Agnew, Stirling, Rivers Fletcher and his wife Penny. This was the time of year for dinners and awards ceremonies. When Malcolm Campbell wanted to race his one-and-a-half-seater GP Delage in the 1928 Junior Grand Prix at Brooklands, it was still a regulation that one had to take a riding mechanic. His normal mechanic, Leo Villa, was too large to fit in and so he took Rivers who was still a schoolboy. He was later apprenticed to Bentley at Cricklewood and spent 18 years working for B.R.M.

Pat Moss, Stirling's younger sister, made a considerable name for herself in the show-jumping world in the fifties. In the days of Pat Smythe, Ted Williams and Alan Oliver, she became well-known to the British public as the sport was regularly televised. Later she would have an extremely successful career as a rally driver. Having passed her driving test in a Morris Ten, she acquired a Morris Minor which Stirling's racing mechanic Alf Francis tuned for her. She had an MG and a TR2 and later competed for a variety of works teams including Ford, Austin-Healey and Lancia. A wealth of successes included 2nd overall in the San Remo Rally and 5th overall on the 1964 Monte Carlo Rally. She won countless Coupes des Dames and married rally champion Eric Carlsson.

Why we lead the world in export cars
by STIRLING MOSS

Sunday Chronicle 27.2.55

Another's Fame

IT CAN BE very awkward having the same name as a famous person. So awkward, in fact, that a Yorkshireman is to change his by deed poll.

"The last straw was when I was stopped by a policeman for a driving offence," explains he. "When the bobby asked my name I had to reply 'Sterling Moss.' Needless to say, he didn't believe me. I'm twice the age of the Stirling Moss.

"I plan to take my wife's maiden name, hyphen it with mine and call myself Halliday-Moss. That and the different spelling of our Christian names ought to end the confusion."

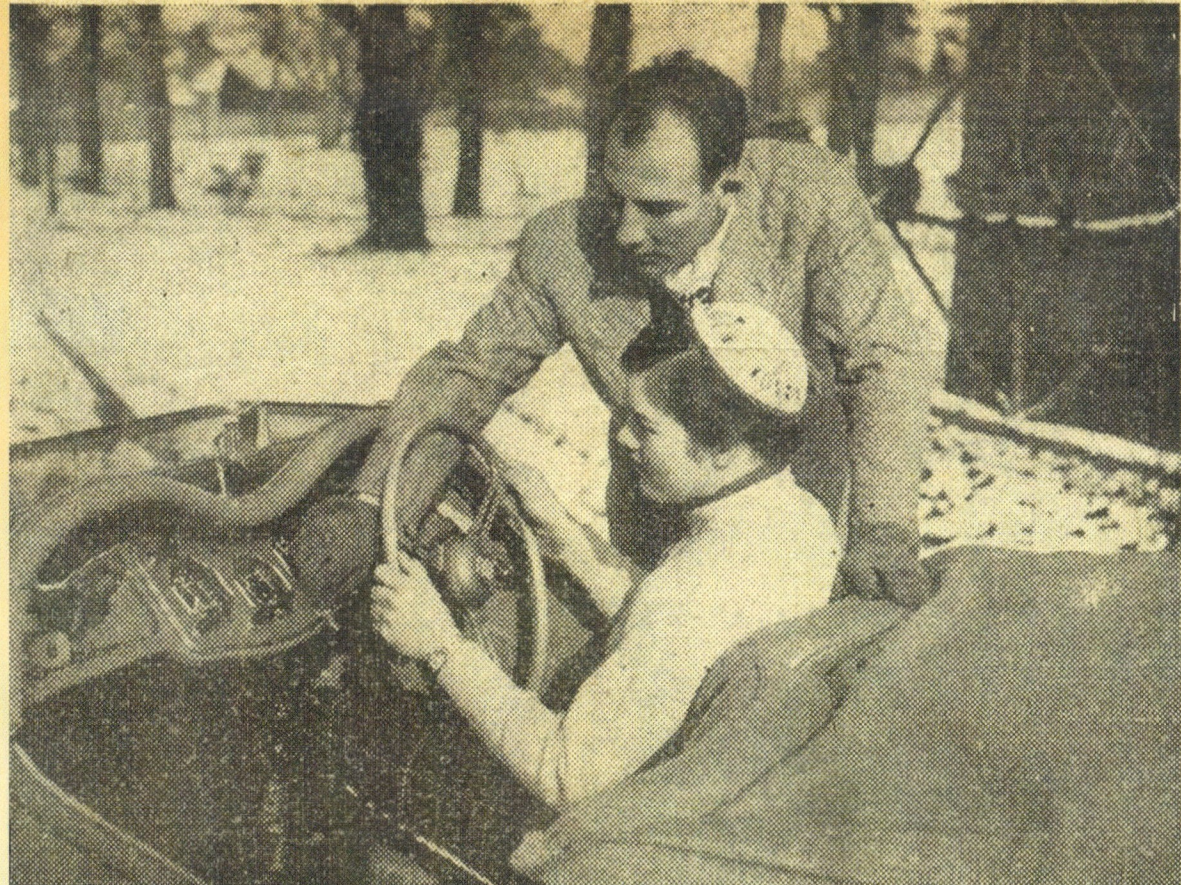

Sunday Despatch 27.2.55

Fast Moving

HOTFOOT from Mme. Tussaud's, where he had unveiled a waxwork of himself, STIRLING MOSS dashed last night to the British Racing and Sports Car Club dinner to receive the Victor Ludorum Cup. And to-night he is flying back across the Atlantic.

For the next three weeks he and his racing manager, KEN GREGORY, will be dividing their time between Sebring, in Florida, and Nassau, Bahamas, on the first joint venture of "Stirling Moss, Ltd."

The twenty-four-year-old British champion driver will be attempting this year in a British Austin Healey to retain the Sebring Cup he won last year. He and Gregory have been asked by the Bermuda authorities to run sports car races in the island.

Evening News 26.2.55

A BROTHER TO ASSIST HER....

Champion racing driver Stirling Moss gives useful tips to his sister, Pat Moss, the 19-year-old horse-jumping personality, who is to "invade" her brother's sport next month when she competes in the R.A.C. British International Rally from March 8 to 13.

N. Daily Mail 23.2.55

MARCH

1955 Calendar

13 Sebring 12 Hours, USA - 6th overall & 1st in Production Car Class (sharing Austin-Healey with Lance Macklin)

March began with Stirling spearfishing in Nassau and he shot a sting ray. This was followed by water-skiing and shopping. "Then we met Donald Healey & went to Red Crise's yacht to watch fireworks. NBG. Imperial to hear Simionette. Bed at 1.30am."

Wednesday March 2nd was similarly stressful. In the evening, "Ken and I went to Sir Victor Sassoon's for a R.A.F.A. 'do'. Left & saw *The Silver Chalise* F. I didn't feel well." Next morning he went spearfishing with Marianne, saw a barracuda, had lunch with David Brown (of Aston Martin fame) and in the evening saw Edward E. Horton in *White Sheep of the Family*. (VG) Thursday was spent relaxing and in the evening he was taken to the 'Silver Slipper'. Bed at 3.30am. A similar day on Saturday concluded with dinner at Lord Carden's and dancing at the 'Drake'. Bed at 3.30am - again!

In spite of the climate, Stirling was suffering from a cold but was fit enough to meet and dine that evening with Nancy Walker at the Cumberland.

Monday 7th: "Up early, packed then skied. Also Ken & Nancy. Lunch with Duncan & Phyll & then to Oakes field. Returned Johnny's Minx and took off at 3.30pm. To Miami and usual problems with customs, etc., thence to Havana. Met George Gray at the Nacional. Food at the 21, then visited the Mambo. Saw a film at the Shanghai. Bed at 2.00am." Next day was spent shopping, including buying five yards of Dacron charcoal grey suit cloth for $70. "Then we saw the fabulous show at the 'Tropicana'."

Next morning SM went to Miami and collected the Healey he was to drive at Sebring. He bought an air-conditioner for $214 and a clock radio for $41, and checked into the Mardi

Short, long or wavy, sir?

MALE hairstyles came under discussion at the annual dinner of the Fellowship of Hair Artists.

According to president Mr. Philip Woolf, "It is no longer considered cissy for a man to have a wave pressed in front of his hair. With Englishmen that is a very great advance."

There are four top styles of haircut at present:

ALBANY is best suited to the man about town. It features a blow wave front, with sides brushed straight back. Nigel Patrick and dress designer Norman Hartnell choose this style.

CITY TRIM, for the business man, has no sideboards, a right side parting and the hair tapered at the sides. Donald Sinden and Bernard Braden are good examples.

BOND STREET, for the young, gay man, is short and springy. Stirling Moss has this haircut, so has Bonar Colleano.

Evening Standard 9.3.55

Stirling Moss ...

"Nancy Walker was a very cute American girl, very pretty in a chocolate box sort of way. She really was very attractive. She was the sort of girl that would have probably been a cheerleader. I went out with her."

Donald Healey (left), Stirling and Lance Macklin at Sebring in the Austin-Healey they would share in the 12-hour classic in Florida. Stirling's patriotism led him to drive the British sports car and their success must have done Austin-Healey sales a power of good in the important US market.

Stirling Moss fined for obstruction

RACING motorist Stirling Moss, who gave an address in William IV Street, Strand, London, was fined 30s. at Bow Street on Friday for causing obstruction at Adelaide Street, Strand. He pleaded not guilty.

P.C. W. Lees said that Moss's car was parked for 45 minutes opposite a cab rank and traffic was reduced to a single alternate line. Moss told him: "I wouldn't have left it here, only I couldn't get into William IV Street."

In Court Moss asked: How many cabs were parked on the rank opposite?

P.C. Lees: There was one period during the time your car was there when it was full right up, with 16 cabs.

Moss said in evidence that he had worked at William IV Street for two or three years and had never yet seen the taxi rank full. When he parked there were only one or two taxis right down at the other end of the rank and circumstances were the same when he returned. "I maintain that where I was there was no obstruction," he said.

Police Inspector H. Kimberley said that Moss was convicted for a similar offence last December.

Bucks Herald 4.3.55

From right; Sir Sydney Oakes, Donald Healey, Lady Greta Oakes and Stirling. Lance Macklin is on the extreme left.

Silver Slipper Club

The **Silver Slipper Club** was very popular and had an open-air dance floor. Undesirable elements who were barred would drink outside and chuck their empty bottles over the wall, often landing on the dancers. To combat this, the owners had hung a net over the dance floor. However, on occasions two bottles would meet in mid-air and smash against each other, showering the hapless dancers in shards of glass. As a result, the locals danced with their hats on!

Stirling Moss ...

SM: "I think that Marianne was a blond."

PP: "Ken says in his book that you didn't go to bed for two days because you were partying."

SM: "Well, if Ken said that in his book it's probably true. She was fairly well to do to have a Cadillac."

Organisation At Sebring

The organisation was a little 'relaxed' at Sebring in those days. At one point, during the night, a marshal, wanting to get to another part of the circuit, drove his Mk VII Jaguar round the circuit in the opposite direction to the racers!

Gras Motel at $7 each a night! "Saw *Garden of Eden*. F Watched TV wrestling."

Thursday and Friday were spent at the track with co-driver Lance Macklin doing a few laps each. On Saturday SM did just one lap due to brake and tyre wear. On Sunday, "I began with a good start at 10am. Was 2nd at the line from 33rd! Carried on until 1pm when we were 7th. Getting 4,400 with the 5.50 x 15 tyres. I lapped in 3.54. Lance drove until 3.30 at 4.01 and then I took over until 5.30. Lance till 7.30 and I finished minus brakes.

"We put on four tyres at 1pm (unnecessary), fuel only at 3.30, four tyres at 5.30 and fuel only at 7.30. We won the Production Car Class and were 6th. 1st Jag, 2nd Ferrari, 3rd Maser, 4th Maser, 5th Ferrari. Packed up and drove 80 miles along the Miami road and found a motel."

That Monday SM and Ken Gregory flew to New York where they met up with Marianne and Nancy and called at the Morocco. Bed at 3.30! Next day was spent shopping and buying "gadgets of all kinds". After more shopping, they "saw Hank Flynn and he showed the films we took at Nassau. VG. Later saw Nancy and Marianne. Saw *The Pyjama Game*. VG. We had a presentation bottle of Champagne at the Stork and Ken got high! Food at a hamburger stall and then a drive around in Marianne's Caddy. Bed at 4am."

Such was the quantity of their purchases that it took two taxis to take Stirling and Ken to the Queen Mary on which they were returning to Blighty. They had a final "noggin" with Marianne and Nancy but the sailing was delayed due to fog. The evening consisted of dinner, dancing and bingo. Bed at 4am.

"Up at 10am and a swim, food, table tennis and a second swim. Saw *Simba* F in the afternoon. Later Ken, Viola, Glenys and I went to Mr. Wilcox (the Purser's) for cocktails. Had food at 8.30 and played horse racing. No dancing due to the swell, so community singing instead."

On Friday he saw another film - *A Prize of Gold* (QG) and met Lord Essendon (who raced pre-war under the name of Hon. Brian Lewis) "en route from sunlamp treatment and had a drink". That evening Stirling boosted his earnings by winning £4 at bingo and also won "a special dance with Viola".

The sea was extremely rough and Stirling got little sleep. That morning he was shown "the 140,000 hp engine room and saw the 164 ft

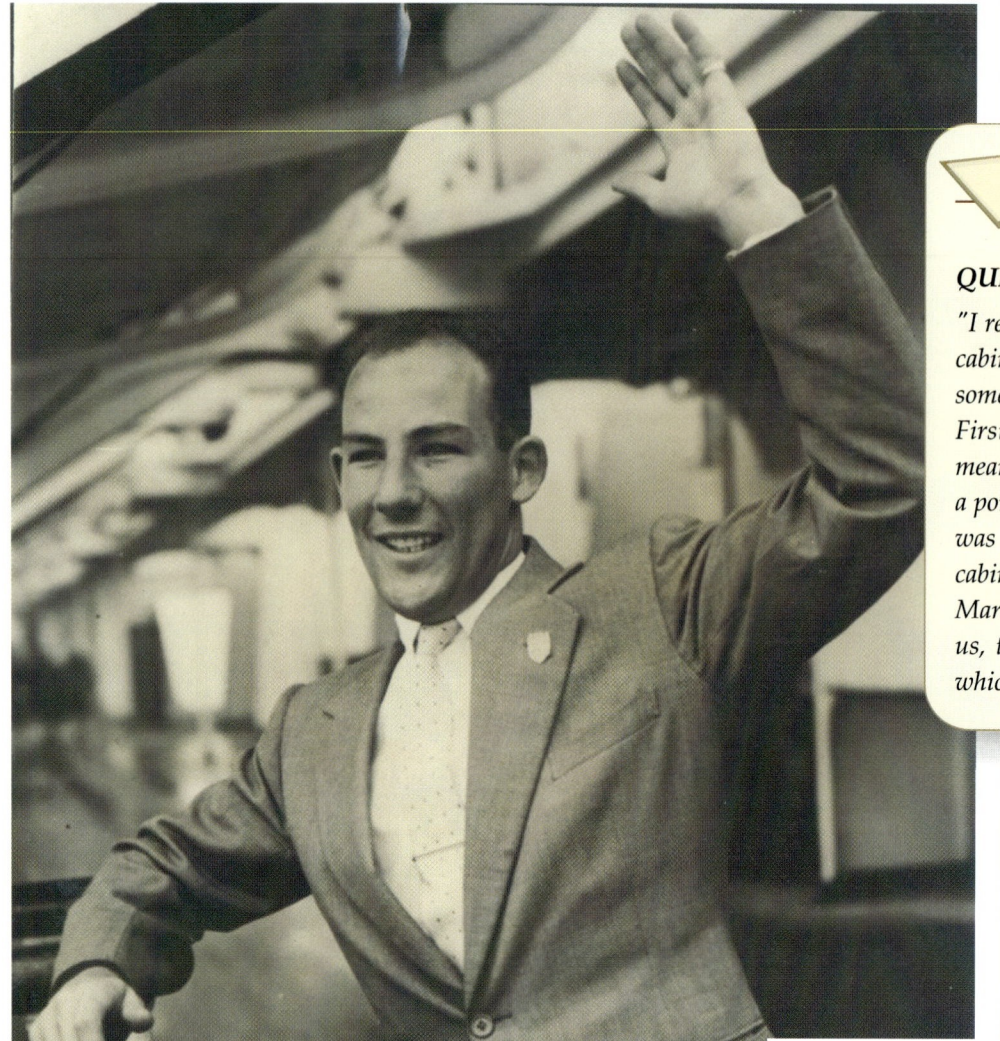

Stirling Moss ...

QUEEN MARY

"I remember the crossing, because we had no great cabin, I can tell you, but we managed to engineer something. I think we went Middle Class, but ate in First Class. But the cabins were pretty ordinary, I mean nothing like we would expect today. If you had a porthole it meant you were on the outside, which was a big deal. I remember when we arrived in our cabin some girl we met gave us a very nice gift which Marianne had managed to get somebody to plant for us, to remind us that they still thought about us, which I thought at the time was fairly romantic."

Stirling's voyage across the Atlantic on the Queen Mary was a chance to relax and indulge in the pleasures of what was then the world's finest liner. The Queen Mary, which had been built in 1937 to succeed the Titanic, was bigger and faster than that ill-fated ship. She made 1,001 Atlantic crossings, held the record for the fastest crossing, was converted into a troop ship during the war and participated in the D-Day invasion. She was sold by Cunard in 1967 for $3.4m.

Stirling Moss ...

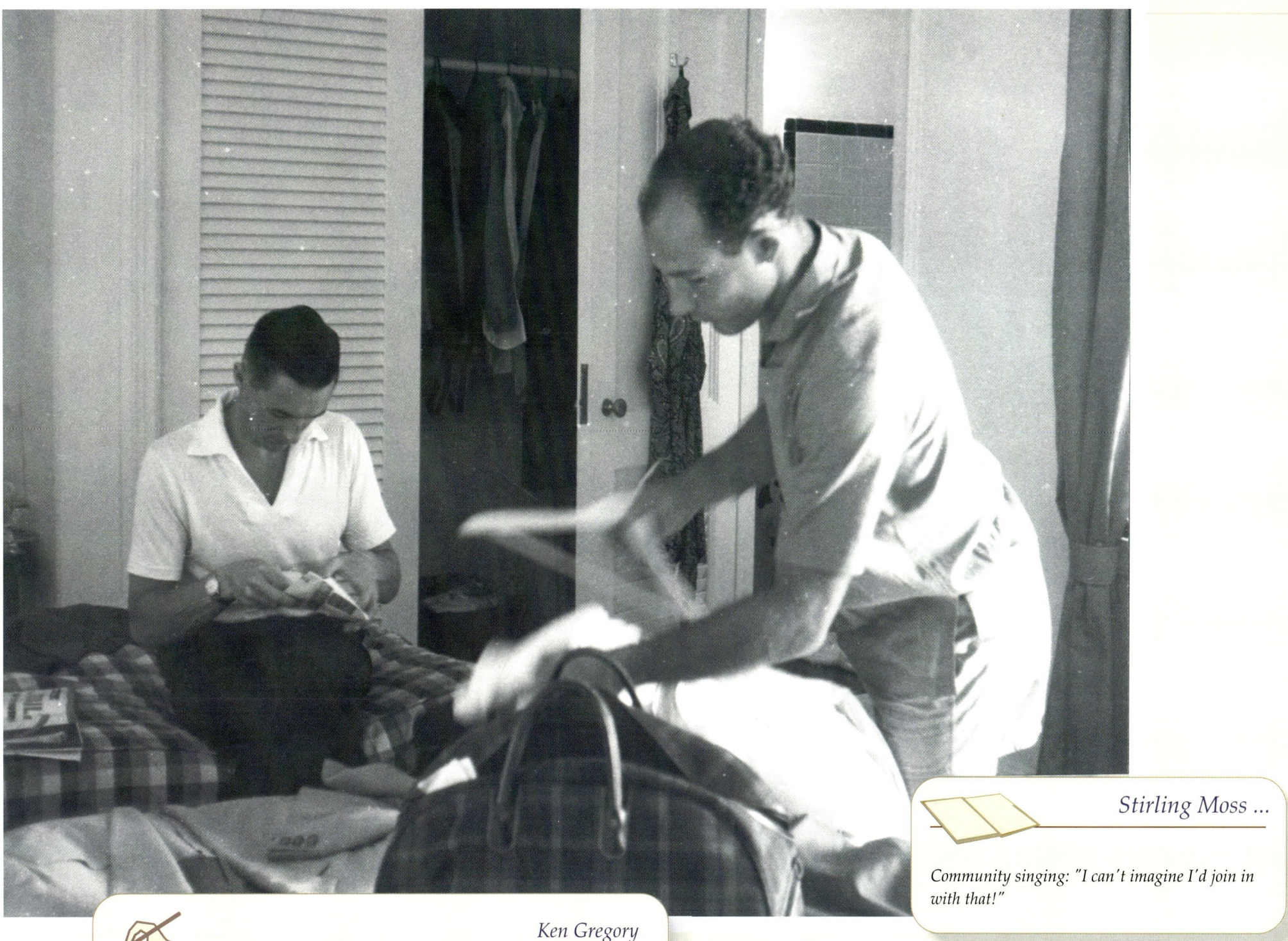

Community singing: "I can't imagine I'd join in with that!"

Ken Gregory

After seven years in the army, Ken Gregory joined the RAC in an administrative capacity. He soon became Assistant Secretary of the 500 Club (for 500cc racers) and organised the annual dinner and dance. There he shared a table with Stirling and Peter Collins, who was also racing 500s with great success. Ken did not take a girlfriend "but Peter and Stirling had made up for this by bringing at least two each," he later wrote. Ken and Stirling became great friends and began attending race meetings together. On occasions, Ken also raced a 500.

In 1952 Gregory become Stirling's official Manager, looking after all his travel arrangements and negotiating contracts and suchlike. In late 1954, the 500 Club, which had become the Half-Litre Club, changed its name to reflect its growing stature and became the British Racing and Sports Car Club. Ken continued to run this Club and look after Stirling's affairs for many years to come.

props." That night he danced until 5.30am. Sunday morning saw him playing Ken's records in John Greenwood's cabin, watching *Brigadoon* (F) and then "Tea and noggin with Lord Essendon and then a special dinner. Fois Gras, Turtle Soup, Sole Bonne Femme, Filet Mignon sauce Bearnaise, Crêpes Suzettes and fruit salad. Bingo, dancing and bed at 5am."

They docked Monday morning and Stirling comments that there were swarms of photographers. Friends met him with his Standard 8 and a Rover. "I paid only £38 tax on my things, including the air-conditioner, spit, radio, etc. Met SW, unpacked till 4am."

After a day working in the flat and the office, Stirling, sister Pat and SW went to Tring. Next day was spent at Silverstone, though it started off blowing a gale and pouring with rain, engaged in tyre testing with (presumably) his 250F Maserati. "Took Pat round in her M.G. She did 2.32 VG (SM 2.23)."

On Thursday 24th, Stirling received what he described as the 1st RAC badge from Chairman Wilfred Andrews. He then went to the Ferodo Trophy presentation at the Dorchester. Friday he went to friend's funeral and then met a journalist from Newsweek at L'Aperitif for lunch. "To Pan-Am and received my doings for the Clipper Club. To RAC and met Leslie J. [Johnson] until 5.30 when to office until 7.50pm. Spoke to Shelagh for 50 mins. Took SW to see *Lucretia Borgia* B. Then to Colony. Excellent cabaret. Fay de Witt. Bed at 3am."

"Up late and cleaned flat. To Goodwood with Sally. Saw Pat win her first race easily. She did 2.03.5 damp in her M.G. T.F. (VG)."

That Sunday he flew to Milan, collected "my super 220A" and drove to Brescia where he met up with Neubauer and Jenks.

"Neubauer says his secretary is 60 and he wants to change her for three 20-year-olds!

"He also says the reason Denis isn't with Eric anymore is because his beard got in the carb and Eric had to stop to free him. It was a case of the beard going or else!" The Eric referred to here would be Eric Oliver with whom Denis Jenkinson had won the motor cycle sidecar World Championship in 1949. Jenks, who as *DSJ*, was the Continental Correspondent of *Motor Sport*, was to prove the ideal companion to ride with SM in the Mille Miglia, and his beard would be less of a problem in the 300 SLR!

Stirling Moss ...

TEACHING PAT

"I remember going round with Pat in her MG. She wasn't going that quickly and so I said to her, 'Listen. Next time I say stop, I want you to stop as quickly as you can - an absolute emergency stop. I was sitting there watching her and, as soon as I saw her foot lift a fraction going into Stowe, I said stop and she stopped. And of course she stopped before the corner. I said 'What did you stop for' and she said 'Well, you told me to'. I was just showing her that no way should you back off this far from a corner which you haven't got to. Then she realised what I was talking about and started to go and got the hang of it."

Car colour

MORE colour about your cars please, much more, and not those conservative greens, maroon and navy blues. Ace racing driver STIRLING MOSS, home yesterday from America, makes this plea to our manufacturers. Lighter, brighter shades—salmon pinks, heliotropes—that is what will sell British cars to Uncle Sam.

The Americans are not so much concerned, he says, with chromium plating or with the majestic size of an automobile, but they don't want to drive around in a vehicle that looks like a hearse.

With his manager, KEN GREGORY, he went to America primarily to compete in the 12 hours' race at Sebring, Florida.

Second object was to investigate the possibilities of racing in the Bahamas. He will take part in a December event.

NICE WORK, SISTER! (Right): Stirling Moss congratulates his sister, Pat, after she won her first race by more than 18 seconds.

AUTOSPORT

Stirling Moss ...

MILLE MIGLIA PRACTICE

SM: *"You have to realise that, even going like hell, it took two days to do a complete lap in practice. You are talking about 500 miles in a day and, even starting very early in the morning, that's still a hell of a lot.*
PP: *"And those wouldn't be closed roads, so that would slow you down?"*
SM: *"Yes. Realistically to put much over 55 miles into an hour in some places, like the towns and cities, was quite difficult and when you were doing 500 miles per day, you can't just pop in an extra lap, like on a circuit. So we only had a certain, very limited amount of full laps, actually.*

"After a race elsewhere, we'd go straight back to Italy and get into the practicing. It was a very involving event, you know.
PP: *"That must have curtailed your social life a bit, all that practicing?"*
SM: *"Well exactly!"*

Stirling and Lance Macklin were good 'mates', having both been members of the H.W.M. team for a couple of seasons.

Even on holiday there must be excitement and a turn of speed somewhere for British racing motorist Stirling Moss. He finds it here, water-ski-ing in the Bahamas

Daily Mail 16.3.55

Cars

Mercedes-Benz 220A
6-cylinder in-line, 2,195cc, 7.6:1 compression, 85bhp at 4,800rpm, ohc, dual-downdraught carbs, 4-speed gearbox, coil & wishbone independent front suspension, swing axles & coil springs at rear, 4-wheel hydraulic servo-assisted brakes, weight: approx. 2,920lbs (1,324kgs); max speed: 95mph (154kph), UK price, including Purchase Tax, £2,123.

On Monday they drove to Pescara and Rome where they stayed in the Parioli which SM noted as "expensive". Tuesday they lunched at Modena, called on Maserati and picked up eight 48mm inlet valves (for 16,000 lire) and carried on to Brescia where they met up with Fangio. Wednesday saw SM and Jenks up at 5.45am and off to Pescara at 6.30. "Rain all the way. Juan used the SLR and Kling the SL. Hans has two days off. Continued on to Viterbo for the night."

Thursday, March 31st: "Up at 9am (late!) and off at 9.45 to have lunch at the Raticosa Pass. On to Brescia, arriving at 6.15. All plans are altered now. We use an SL tomorrow and an SLR on Sunday. Home on Tuesday! Poor Mantovani has had to have a leg amputated following an accident at Turin in practice. My 220 averaged 61 mph from Bolgnia to Brescia and 24.3 mpg."

Stirling Moss Honoured
Stirling Moss is to receive Sports Members' Badge No 1 at the Royal Automobile Club tonight.
His sister Pat is to take part in her first race at Goodwood on Saturday. The British Automobile Racing Club are staging an event for women only.

No. 1 badge for Stirling Moss
Stirling Moss, Britain's No. 1 racing driver, was awarded the first badge of the Royal Automobile Club motor sport section, at R.A.C. headquarters in London last night.

Daily Mail 25.3.55

Stirling, No. 1
Stirling Moss, Britain's No. 1 racing driver, was awarded the first badge of the Royal Automobile Club motor sport section, at RAC headquarters in London last night.

Morning Advertiser 25.3.55

APRIL

1955 Calendar

	Practising for the MM
11	Goodwood Race Meeting - Sports Cars up to 1,500cc - ret'd in Beart Rodger Climax; Chichester Cup - 3rd in Maserati 250F; Richmond F1 Race - ret'd in Maserati 250F
	Practising for the MM
25	Bordeaux GP (non-Championship F1 race) - 4th in Maserati 250F, broke lap record
	Practising for the MM

"Up at 6.00am for a day of woe," begins Stirling's diary entry, rather ironically, for April 1st. "We left in the SL behind Hans's SLR at 7.00am and came to Ravenna and Forli at an average of 78 mph. Then, four kms after Ravenna, a truck (military bombs) pulled directly across me and we hit it and smashed the SL. This was at 9.45am. At 8.30pm we were still in Forli with the police who were most helpful."

Next morning Stirling saw Neubauer. "He says the SLR's brakes have had it so we will all go home." That night SM stayed at the Palace in Milan. The following day he flew back to Heathrow and was met by his mother and father, "as Ken had mucked up his leg at Oulton". That night he saw SW.

Next day he worked and saw *As Long As They're Happy* (QG). After another day of work, he took his father to see *Hippo Dancing* (VG) on Tuesday evening. He collected his Gannex overalls on Thursday and on Friday he went down to Blue Mist, which was where Sally's parents lived. Here he edited his cine films and showed them.

Saturday was spent at Goodwood testing (mainly) the 250F, "after a lovely breakfast. Tried Beart's car but bad clutch slip, later this was OK. Very bad oversteer. 1.47.5. I was happy about this, 'cos it wasn't finished until 6am today. The Maser motor is fantastic. Got 7,800. 1.34.4 but handling awful. Found we had the wrong hubs

MOTOR RACING

MAY 1955 — OFFICIAL ORGAN OF THE BRITISH RACING & SPORTS CAR CLUB — MONTHLY 2/-

Diminutive Beart/Rodger 1100cc sports car driven by Stirling Moss in its first race at Goodwood on Easter Monday. This is one of several promising new British 1100cc sports cars.

NEW ITALIAN RACING CAR

Cars

BEART RODGER CLIMAX

Francis Beart made such a name for himself that he became synonymous with air-cooled racing engines. Such Beart-prepared power units powered many motor cycles and 500cc racers to glory. Stirling, Alan Brown and Stuart Lewis-Evans drove 500s prepared by Beart.

At the beginning of 1955, Beart decided to turn constructor and build a small sports racing car fitted with the new FWA four-cylinder all-aluminium engine which Coventry-Climax had developed for a Government order for lighter, more powerful fire pumps.

To help him design the car, Beart brought in Bernard 'Bernie' Rodger who had previously been chief engineer to several British teams. The multi-tubular chassis frame was of lightweight construction, with independent front suspension and a de Dion arrangement at the rear. Steering box was off a Fiat 500 and the king pins came from an Austin A30. The Beart-designed gearbox was mounted in the centre of the car. Together they designed a multi-plate clutch which Rodger machined out of solid dural. It could handle 100bhp yet weighed only 6lbs (2.7kg). Testing was due to start by the end of February!

As Stirling says in his diary, it was actually finished at 6am on the morning of April 9th and was unpainted! Why did Stirling, now a works F1 driver, bother with such a humble machine? "I suppose just because I liked driving and competitions."

Motor racing isn't one of the arts, but I think it's as near to art as you can get mechanically. There's a kind of poetry of motion to it, a feeling of rhythm, of perfect balance.

— *Stirling Moss*

STIRLING MOSS
Clown is his lucky mascot.

Lucky Seven

LIGHT chatter in the pits before a big race is not appreciated by Stirling Moss, the racing motorist. It is not that he is on edge, but words and figures mean something to him.

For instance, if you wish him good luck he will take it as a bad omen. Stirling Moss, it must be admitted, is very superstitious.

"That accident I had in the Mercedes would happen when I didn't have my lucky clown mascot with me," he told me.

Moss attaches great significance to the number seven. His Standard Eight carries the registration number SFM 777, and before that his Jaguar was also 777. Once at Aintree he won at 77.77 m.p.h.

Grand Prix rules prevent him from having seven as his number on the racing Mercedes. Instead, he has chosen 14—two sevens.

The official British racing colour, green, brought him no luck in his Maserati, so he painted it dove-grey.

The little Beart Rodger Climax, seen in its naked unpainted state at Goodwood, was going well until put out by a minor ailment.

German Press...

QUESTION MOSS'S ABILITY

Apparently, after the incidents with the sheep and the army lorry, one German newspaper questioned why one of their beautiful and magnificent cars was being entrusted to an English idiot. It would be fascinating to see what they said on May 2nd!

on it! Dunlops !X! Saw a film *Hunters of the Deep F.*" Sunday was spent working on his Standard 8, shooting and wood-cutting. Next day was Easter Monday and SM was back at Goodwood with SW. "Raced the 1,100. It went well and I was 1st in class and 3rd overall when the throttle broke. Lap 1.45! The Maser was awful due to the wrong wheels. I was 3rd in the Libre. Retired in the F.1, fuel blockage."

On Tuesday he was photographed for Trico for advertising purposes and in the evening took SW to see *Deep in my Heart*. "G. Food at La Rue." Next evening he saw *Above us the Waves*. (G) Two days later he was at Goodwood again for testing with Alf Francis. "Ran the Mas. and my best was 1.34.4 using everything." They then removed the fuel injection. "1.31.8! Wow!"

That Sunday, Stirling flew to Milan, picked up his 220 and drove to Brescia via Calino, for more Mille Miglia practicing. Next day, he was up at the ungodly hour of 4.55am and was on the road at 6am in an SL - "not a good one". After lunch at L'Aquila, where they changed the plugs, they "continued to Florence and stayed at the expensive Select Hotel. Covered 1200 kms today!"

Next morning he negotiated the famous Futa Pass in 1 hr 13 and motored on to Brescia. Wednesday 20th saw him up at 5am and off by 5.45am in an SLR. "All was OK to Rimini, then it stopped, noises from the bell housing (broken crank!). We waited from 9am until 2.30 when the Merc boys arrived. Set off again in my 220 at 3pm. Took a short cut to Viterbo, arriving at 9pm."

Another early start resulted in them reaching Brescia at 1.45pm. "Left Brescia at 3.45, at Malpensa [Airport] at 5.10. Plane delayed so we changed after much fuss to TWA and left at 7.45. Came to Paris at 10.15, via Zurich. At Miriani at 11.30pm." Next morning he and Jenks flew from Orly to Bordeaux where they were met by Alf. Stirling was to race his private 250F in the non-Championship Bordeaux GP against opposition which included the works Maserati team.

In practice that afternoon, he found the plugs too hard, the gearing too high and the pick-up poor. "Brakes fantastic, [braking] 30 yards later than anyone else." Alf Francis had spent time at the Jaguar works in the winter fitting disc brakes. Practice on Saturday was not much better, especially when someone covered the course in oil. "Had a cocktail party and then

Stunning shot of Stirling four-wheel drifting his 250F at Goodwood on Easter Monday. Unfortunately, it was a frustrating day for him.

Stirling Moss ...

GANNEX

"Gannex, I met a man called Joe Kagan - he was later Lord Kagan - and he had developed and patented a material called Gannex, which was supposed to breathe and yet be waterproof. It was quite a novelty and they made suitcases and all sorts of things. He said, 'For the Mille Miglia you need a pair of my overalls' and so a pair was made. But it didn't really work. I think probably the material was a bit too heavy in itself to wear as a base garment. It certainly worked to a good extent in driving rain when water would normally have gone through on the stitches, but they weren't really successful enough so I didn't use them."

Prime Minister Harold Wilson would make Gannex raincoats famous in the sixties and ennobled the founder who was locked up for fraud soon afterwards!

WEEK ENDING APRIL 2 1955

ILLUSTRATED

4d Every Wednesday

Mercy killing—
Alderman Dingley stands firm

STIRLING MOSS
a wonderful pre-Easter supplement

SPRING GUIDE TO MOTORING

How to buy—
   how to look after—
     and how to drive your car
with tips by Raymond Baxter, Mrs. Jack Hawkins, Vera Lynn, Manny Mercer, Dirk Bogarde, Tony Hancock, Dickie Valentine and Barbara Kelly

Cover couple:
STIRLING MOSS and Sister Pat

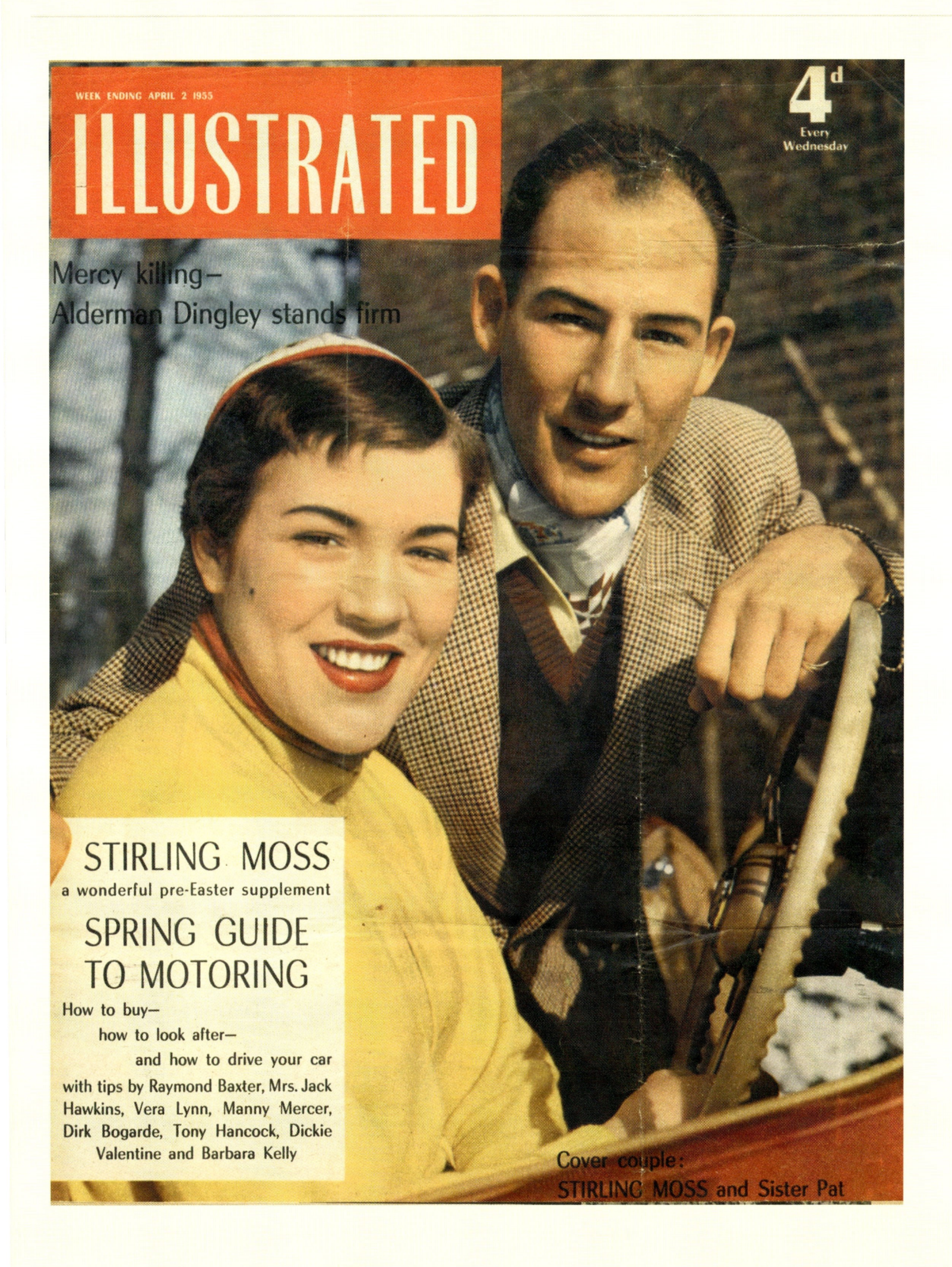

Alf Bets Stirling...

The handling of the 250F had become very difficult and Stirling and his father were convinced that Alf Francis had altered the dimensions of the track or wheelbase, or the suspension in some way whilst modifying the car to take disc brakes. Alf was insistent that that was not the case.

"The car oversteers very badly," said Stirling to Alf, and does not want to travel in a straight line… it goes absolutely haywire."

Easter Monday Goodwood was pretty disastrous for the Moss equipe and hence they met for testing a couple of days later. Francis was convinced that the problem lay with the engine and more precisely with the fuel injection. The power was coming in with such a bang that it was upsetting the balance of the car.

"Look Stirling," Alf quoted himself as saying in his book 'Alf Francis - Racing Mechanic', "I'll give you my week's wages if I am wrong. Let's put the car on carburettors tomorrow and I will prove it to you."

Alf won his bet and they ruefully reflected they could have won at Goodwood with the carb set-up.

Futa Pass ...

A significant route through the Apennines, the highest peak being 903m, the pass was built by Consul Caius Flaminius in 187BC after the defeat of the Ligurian populations of the Tuscan and Emilian Apennines. Livy tells us that it was the route taken by Flaminia Minor and it was probably used by Hannibal in 217 BC. Throughout the centuries, the pass has been used by tourists, pilgrims, crusaders and popes (Moss and Jenks were just the latest in a long line of adventurers). It was of considerable strategic importance during the Second World War, when it formed part of the famous Gothic Line and was heavily fortified. The pass fell to the allies after intense fighting in Sept 1944 and is now the site of several war cemeteries.

food with Bernard Cahier, Denis, Dad and a Yank."

The race took place on Sunday. "A good start but my car's acceleration was very poor. Brakes locked at the front and I dropped to 8th. Then I tried hard and came to 4th, then my tank strap broke. Lost three laps and continued. Worked my way up to 4th, just 40-50 secs behind. I got the lap record 1.20.3! Went to the 'do', very tired."

On Monday SM and Jenks flew to Le Bourget Airport, went into Paris and flew out from Orly, via Zurich, to Stuttgart. They visited the M-B works and the Competition Dept. "Stayed till 7.15 being fitted for my seat, etc., also Denis." They then had dinner with Fangio, Kling, Keser and others. Next day they drove their SLR to Hockenheim where they spent the day testing. "Got 7600 rpm (=170 mph!). Wind buffeting was very tiresome and we did many tests without much success."

After SM had had his portrait photograph taken at the Mercedes factory next morning, they flew via Zurich to Milan, met SW at Lecco and the three went for dinner. Then, "To Maggi's". This would be Count Maggi with whom Stirling was based for the event. Next morning he met SW at Brescia, had a drink with Pete (probably Collins) and collected journalist Charles Fothergill from Malpensa Airport.

He was up early on Friday 29th and attended a Drivers' Meeting at Brescia. "Later to Maggi's with all the Merc people for lunch VG. To Brescia shopping, then tried the SLR with new windscreen; it seems much better. To Maggi's and tea. Later called on Sally at Isco then we went to Maggi's 'do'. Bed at 11.30pm.

"Up early and to Brescia. Food there with Mr. and Mrs Macklin, Heath, etc." This would be Lance Macklin's parents and John Heath of HWM fame. "Later stooged around. Met John Manusis. Had food and bed at 8.45pm."

An early night made enormous sense, for next day Stirling was going to drive flat out for 1,000 miles and achieve one of the greatest feats in motor racing history.

Count Maggi ...

Conte Aymo Maggi was an Italian nobleman from the Brescia area. His ancestry could be traced back to early Venetian merchants who held a Vatican licence to mint their own coinage. As a boy, the young Maggi learnt to drive sitting upon the knees of the family chauffeur. Like many Italians, he was obsessed with cars and speed. Both he and his best friend, Count Franco Mazzotti, took up motor racing.

In 1921, the first Italian Grand Prix was run on a 90-mile course in the Brescia area. To the disgust of Maggi and many other Italians, it was won not only by a Frenchman, but by a Frenchman driving a French car. This was an affront to Italian automotive pride. Something needed to be done to retrieve the situation.

However, to the very considerable anger of the Brescians, the following year the Grand Prix was purloined by Milan to be run on the new Monza Autodrome.

How could this double disaster be addressed? Maggi, Mazzotti and friends, Giovanni Canestrini and Renzo Castagneto, discussed the challenge. They needed to create an important new race that would inspire their compatriots. They thought of a race from Brescia to Rome, but reflected that Rome would take all the glory. Then they had it. A race from Brescia to Rome and back to Brescia again. When one of them asked the distance and another replied about 1,600 kilometres, Mazzotto, who achieved fame as a record-breaking pilot and was used to thinking in miles, pointed out that that was 1,000 miles. That sealed it. They had had their brainwave.

However, it is one thing having an idea and quite another putting it into practise. How could they persuade every town, village and district? Maggi delivered a letter to Mussolini's right-hand man, whom Maggi had luckily saved from assassination. The police and authorities were instructed to help. The quartet's publicity stated that it would be "the most important manifestation of Italian motor sport ever".

Maggi was then 23. The race, though it fired the imagination and was an enormous success, always courted controversy. It was banned, after an accident, in 1938 but resumed in 1940, after Maggi had driven to Berlin to get permission from the German High Command.

After the war, as if the race was not sufficient of a challenge, it was spiced up with the risk of land mines and the added difficulty of missing bridges. Count Maggi's race continued until finally banned in 1957 and he died four years later. Saddened as he was, the Mille Miglia had certainly achieved its aim of acting as a catalyst to inspire budding Italian racing car constructors and drivers.

By tradition, the British drivers were the guests of Count Maggi at his magnificent castle at Calino, 10 miles from Brescia.

Seat Fitting ...

At Jaguar, when Stirling had once asked for a different seat in the C-type, he was told he would sit in what he was given. At Mercedes-Benz attitudes were a little different and he notes in his diary having a 'seat fitting'. "A seat fitting then was nothing like as sophisticated as it is now and seats were not made as they are today. In fact, if you look at an SLR you can see they weren't that great. The sort of thing they would take notice of was the angle you wanted to be at, the amount of stuffing in the cushion and things like that. Ten hours on the road is quite a long time so they made the seat as good a fit and as comfortable as they possibly could." Stirling liked the back of his seat reclined at 17° with firm support around the hips.

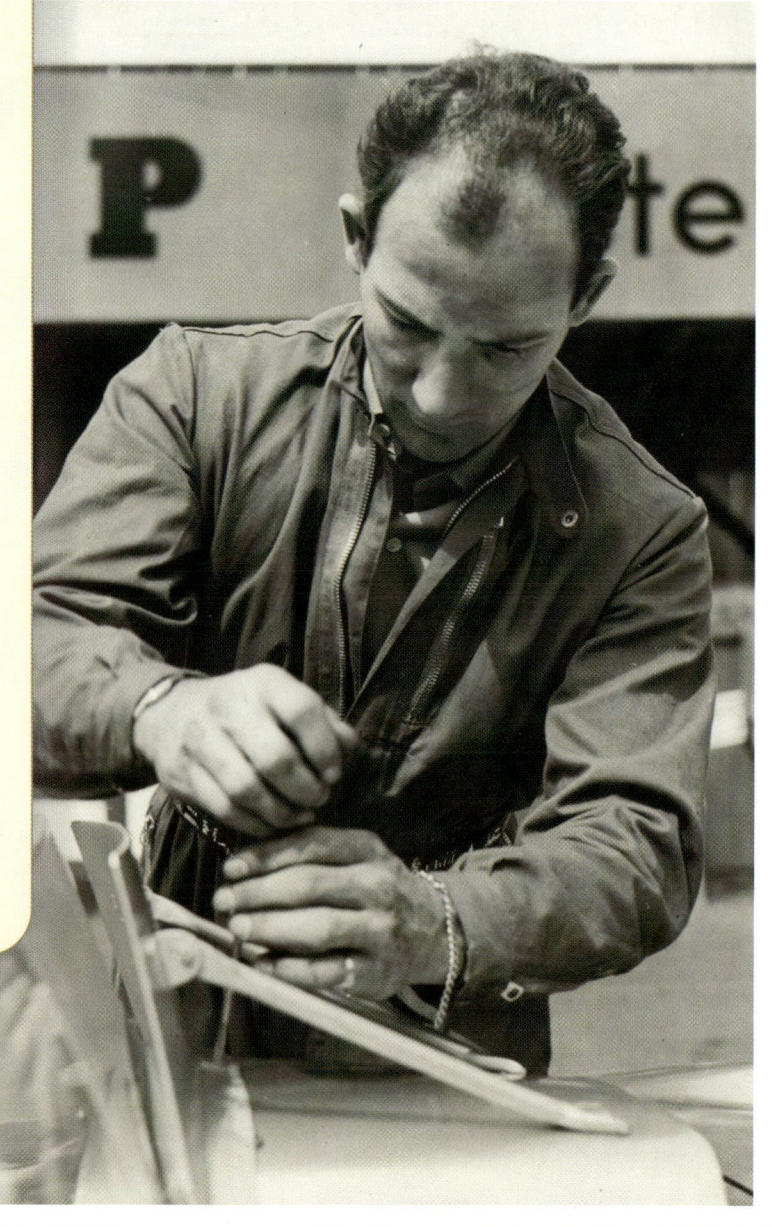

Stirling practices fitting the reserve steel windscreen they were to carry in the car in case of the glass screen breaking. Stones thrown up by other cars must have been a considerable hazard with some pretty poor road surfaces, especially in the mountains, and a lot of fellow competitors in slower cars to be overtaken.

SPORTING NEWS AND GOSSIP FROM ALL QUARTERS

MOSS, FANGIO DRIVE SOLO

TOP British driver Stirling Moss has set himself a stiff assignment this week-end in one of the world's toughest motor races—the Mille Miglia, 1000 mile sports car race across Italy.

In the past it has been compulsory for two drivers to handle each car in this race, but now one may elect to go through this 12 hour event without relief. At least two drivers are to do so—Moss and World Champion Fangio. Both will drive the new German 3 litre, straight eight, S.L.R. sports Mercedes, capable of 200 m.p.h.

Fangio and Moss have spent many months in Italy testing the cars, and familiarising themselves with the torturous course. More than 470 entries have been received for the race which starts on Saturday night, and finishes on Sunday.

Run on the open road, the course includes long stretches across the plains of the country where cars will exceed 170 m.p.h., and twists through the Raticosa and Futa mountain passes in Northern Italy.

'MERCS' MAY QUIT RACING

By COURTENAY EDWARDS

DAIMLER-BENZ, the German firm which makes the famous Mercedes cars, may withdraw from Formula One Grand Prix racing next year, according to reports from Stuttgart yesterday.

This is the firm that returned to Grand Prix racing last year for the first time since the war and caused a sensation by winning the world championship.

It is the firm for which Stirling Moss, Britain's champion racing driver, is driving this season.

A London spokesman for the firm said last night that the possibility had been known for some time, but no decision had yet been reached.

Daimler-Benz have spent enormous sums of money on racing during the past three years.

Daily Mail 23.4.55

Hand Signals ...

Having found it quite impossible to communicate by speech, Stirling and Jenks devised a system of hand signals. Basically, Jenks would stretch out his left arm as though he was pointing down the road ahead. The intensity of the signal was indicated by the speed at which he raised and lowered his arm. A gentle movement meant gentle braking would be needed ahead, but a fast action indicated heavy braking was required when they reached the bend or other obstacle. For these signals the hand would be flat (horizontal). If the hand was turned to be vertical, that meant flat out.

SM: "By the time we'd got it all worked out, it was pretty damned good I must say. Before the event, we practiced with the hand signals even driving around town and on every practice run."

PP: "So it became second nature?"

SM: "Exactly. But it was the interpretation; that was the difference. You see the signal was written on Jenks's 'toilet roll'. On that 'toilet roll' were little pictures and instructions, and the milestones to verify where we were. and that sort of thing. It was beautifully made and he just held it and read off it. You can see why he was once sick; he was looking down, reading this and there were fumes as well. I am glad to say he was sick out of the other side and not my side! He lost his glasses once but, thank God, he had got a spare pair."

Stirling Moss ...

THE 'TOILET ROLL' HOLDER

"It's a very special piece of gear. Don't forget when you are in the middle of the route you cannot afford for it to jam or anything. So it is spring-loaded to keep some tension on the paper as it is wound round. It had to be very well made. Jenks obviously had a lot of input on that."

IVe Grand Prix de Bordeaux

4ème Grand Prix DE BORDEAUX

23-24 AVRIL 1955   100 Fr.

BORDEAUX
23 & 24 AVRIL 1955
A 14 heures.
IVe GRAND PRIX AUTOMOBILE

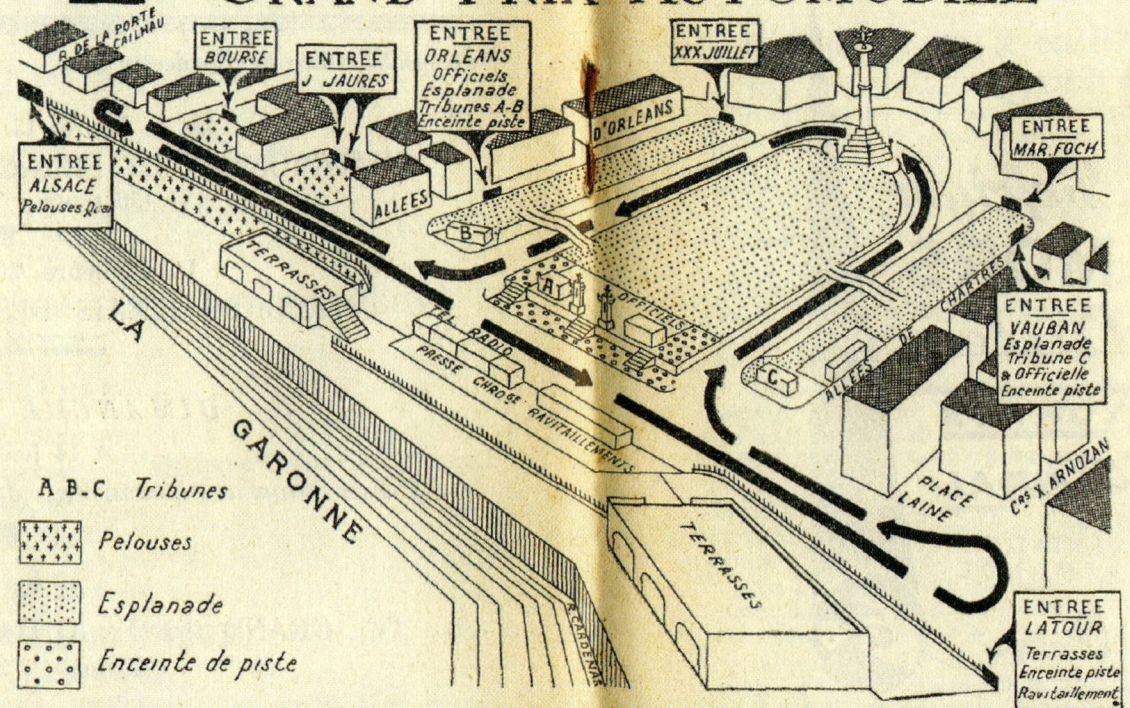

A.B.C Tribunes
- Pelouses
- Esplanade
- Enceinte de piste

IVe GRAND PRIX INTERNATIONAL AUTOMOBILE DE BORDEAUX

LISTE des ENGAGÉS
VOITURES COURSE (Formule 1)

N°	Pilote	Voiture	Nationalité
2.	MANZON	(Gordini)	Français
4.	BAYOL	(Gordini)	Français
6.	FARINA	(Ferrari)	Italien
8.	TRINTIGNANT	(Ferrari)	Français
10.	STIRLING MOSS	(Maserati)	Anglais
12.	ROSIER	(Maserati)	Français
14.	BEHRA	(Maserati)	Français
16.	MIERES	(Maserati)	Argentin
18.	MUSSO	(Maserati)	Italien
20.	SIMON	(Maserati)	Français
22.	Prince BIRA	(Maserati)	Thaïlandais
24.	Mis de PORTAGO	(Ferrari)	Espagnol

Note the BRDC (British Racing Drivers' Club) badge on Stirling's cardigan.

Uhlenhaut is seen chatting to Jenks and Stirling at Hockenheim. There appears to be a panel between the headrests which was probably one of the experiments to try and lessen the wind-buffeting.

The 'Gullwing' looked very dramatic with its doors open. It was so designed because of the high chassis members in the sill area.

MAY

1955 Calendar

1   Mille Miglia - 1st at record speed in 300 SLR (with Denis Jenkinson navigating)

7   BRDC International Trophy Meeting, Silverstone, England - Sports Car Race - ret'd in Beart Rodger Climax; Daily Express International Trophy - ret'd in Maserati 250F

22   Monaco Grand Prix - ret'd on 81st lap while leading in W196

29   Eifelrennen, Nurburgring, Germany - 2nd in 300 SLR

M ay 1st was the date for the start of Italy's most famous race, the tortuous Mille Miglia, which had only been won once by a non-Italian. Apart from the might of Italy in the form of works and private teams of Ferraris and Maseratis, there was Fangio driving solo in another 300 SLR. Stirling had chosen to take Jenks and, as mentioned, they had devised a system of route notes which Jenks communicated via hand signals. It was to be an incredible test of men and machine and would require super-human effort, bravery, stamina and determination.

"Up at 6am after a good night. To the start of the M.M. and off at 7.22am. At Pescara in 3 hrs. 2nd to Verona. 1st to Rome. Futa 1 hr 1. Av. Overall 157.7 [97.9 mph]. Cremona to Brescia 198 kph [125 mph]. Complete course in 10 hrs 7 mins. New records everywhere. Car went well. 7,700 [rpm] = 176 mph. Brakes fair. Pescara stop 28 secs, Taruffi 1 min, crowd booed. Rear tyres only at Rome."

Typically modest, and with true English understatement, Stirling makes no great mention of his and Jenks's extraordinary feat and wonderful triumph. Clearly Fangio had given him something to help him stay awake because, buoyed no doubt also by adrenalin and euphoria, he headed off into the night after the celebrations, as he records.

The Mille Miglia starting ramp. Kling had nearly stalled and Neubauer advised Stirling to use a load of revs., assuring him he would not bottom.

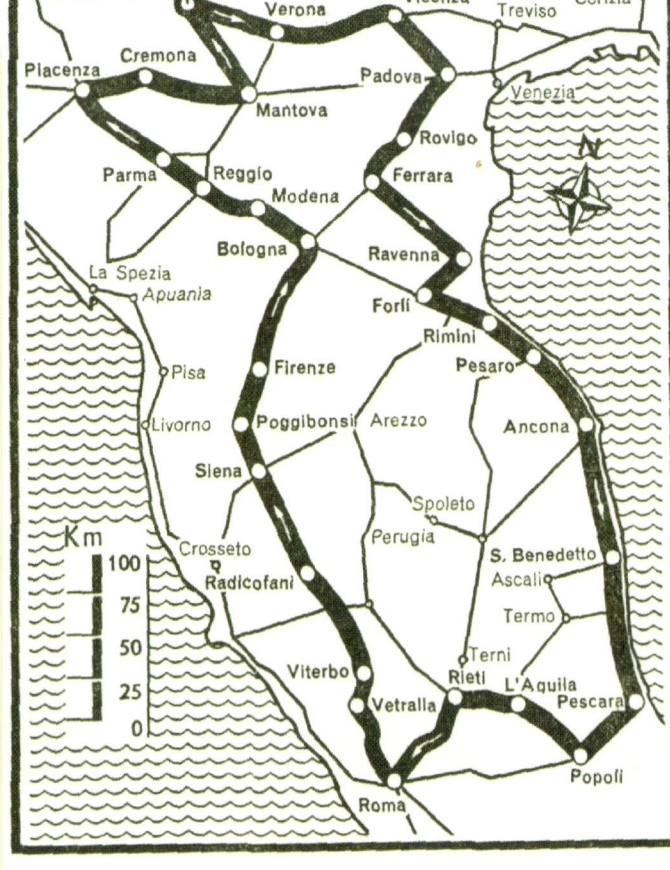

THE MILLE MIGLIA

Drivers

Moss on: PIERO TARUFFI ...

"Taruffi, I didn't drive against him much. Terrific sports car driver. He is, to me, the sports car drivers' answer to Alain Prost really. I think he was a forerunner, a man of considerable intelligence. A great thinking man does a really good job, not flash in any way but, my God, he brings home the bacon, so I rate him quite highly."

The duo near Popoli.

MAY 1955
Sunday 1
3rd after Easter (121-244)

Up at 6am after a good night. To the start of the M.M. & off at 7.22 am. At Pescara in 3 hrs. 2nd to Verona. 1st to Rome. 1st Rome. Futa 1hr 1. Av. overall 157.7 (97.9 ft) Cremona to Brescia 198 kpl. (125 mph) Complete course in 10 hrs 7 min. new records everywhere. Car went well. 7700 = 176 mph. brakes fail. Pescara stop 28 secs. Taruffi 1 min. crowd booed. Rear tyres only at Rome. Fangios pits are fantastic. I left Brescia at 12.15am & drove all night. Had a shunt at Pescara, & also Piacenza. Went into the ditch on the Radiocofani. Otherwise all o.k.. Took off on a bridge at 170 kph.

Mille Miglia

The Mille Miglia was one of Stirling's greatest races, if not his greatest. Run on a 1,000 mile course of ordinary public roads passing through villages, towns and major cities around Italy and over mountain passes, unbelievably he averaged just a shade under 100mph to take a brilliant victory. To help him in this gladiatorial contest, he chose motoring journalist Denis Jenkinson. 'Jenks', as he was affectionately known, was a fearless eccentric whose life revolved around racing, both bikes and cars.

For the race, they would have the new 300 SLR sports racer but, as we have seen, they had spent a considerable time practicing in various lesser Mercedes models. Obviously the challenge was even greater for non-Italians and so they devised the ingenious system of what today would be called 'pace notes'. Jenks's detailed notes of bends, blind brows and other obstacles were transcribed by him on to a 18 feet (5.5m) roll of paper. A small metal box with a Perspex window was made for him to be able to wind this through like a film. This clever ruse, and Stirling's superlative skills behind the wheel and extraordinary stamina, together with the implicit, and justified, faith he had in Jenks, enabled them to become only the second non-Italians to win the event in its 22nd running.

"Fangio's pills are fantastic. I left Brescia at 12.15am and drove all night."

He also mentions the more hairy moments during their epic run which would never be bettered.

"Had a shunt. At Pescara and also Piacenza. Went into the ditch on the Radiocafani. Otherwise all OK. Took off on a bridge at 270 kph." That is 168 mph!

Seemingly having had no sleep, Monday's schedule continued unabated. "Breakfast at Munich at 9.30am. Continued to Stuttgart. Arrived at 12pm (10 hrs). Had lunch with the Directors and SW with Miss Bauer. Had the seats fitted to the 220 and left at 5.15pm. Came to Koln at 9.15 (4 hrs)."

Next morning, he was on the road again at 9.35 and reached Ostend by 1.30. "No plane as I should have been at Le Touquet. Was picked up at 5pm. Came to Ferryfield at 6pm. Big reception. Left at 7.30 and to town in 1½ hrs. Dad took Ken, Ron, SW, Mum and I to the Colony. Unpacked and bed at 1.45am."

The indefatigable Moss was in his office early next morning and later saw *These Men Are Dangerous* (G). Leaving the office at 5pm, he went to Alexandra Palace "for TV Newsreel".

After working Thursday morning in the office, Stirling had a frustrating afternoon practising at Silverstone. "The Maser boiled after one lap and threw oil badly. Time 1.50. Roy [Salvadori] 1.48, Peter [Collins] 1.51, Fairman Connaught 1.51! Beart car [the 1,100cc sports racer] blew smoke, 2.01. Bueb 1.59. Alf worked on the Maser. We phoned the factory but they were not helpful!"

Next day was wet and SM's best with the Maser was a 1.57. "The baby Beart isn't good in the wet and did 2.16. Ftd 2.03 D-type." Later that afternoon, he did some filming for Pathé Pictorial. Graphically illustrating the ups and downs of motor racing, the BRDC International Trophy meeting at Silverstone was a disaster for the Moss camp. He raced the Beart "because the weather was OK. No good, down on power, etc. Lap 1.59. Bueb 1.57. Rotor broke. Later Maser. It was 800rpm down on the warming-up lap. Did a few laps and then it had had it - written off the engine."

Sunday is meant to be traditionally the day you wash your car and that is exactly what SM and SW did with the 220. That evening Stirling was in the television studios for a programme called 'What's My Story'.

Fangio (in cap) and Moss had a great relationship, based on mutual respect, generosity of spirit, fairness and trust. It takes a lot of trust when you are driving at racing speeds a few inches apart for two or three hours. In the current culture, Fangio would have considered Stirling a threat and would have kept him out of the team.

Stirling Moss ...

HAIRY MOMENTS

"As an example of Mercedes's thoroughness the entire team went with their cars to Hockenheim to have them, as it were, 'tailor-made'. In this our old friend Denis again proved to be of great value, because we found the original design of the SLR windscreen to be most unsatisfactory. The other cars, without a passenger, did not have the same problem, but Hans Hermann's car and mine had windscreens that protected our passengers and ourselves in one complete sweep from side to side. We found at speed there was a most uncomfortable rush of air into the cockpit from the back between the headrests.

"I shall never forget the experiments which followed, taking out first one side and then the other, and then the bit in the middle. Each time we tried something new Denis would pull some more hair out of his beard and hold it in the cockpit to test the air-stream!"

Cars

300 SLR

The prototype of the 300 SLR sports racing car, which was known at the works as the W 196 S, was first run at Monza in late 1954. The sports car closely resembled the GP car in all its main features. The track was as GP car but the wheelbase was increased to 93¾" (238cms). The GP tubular chassis was modified to take two seats and a larger fuel tank was fitted. The straight-eight engine was increased to 3-litres capacity and had an engine block cast in alloy. It produced 330/340bhp. The sports racer was 550-650lbs (250-295kgs) heavier than the GP car. Like the GP car, the 300 SLR employed Bosch fuel injection, desmodromic valve gear, twin plugs per cylinder, inboard drum brakes, torsion bar springing and a 5-speed gearbox.

The car made its competition debut on the Mille Miglia.

Moss racconta a Castagneto le sue impressioni sulla Mercedes 300 SLR.

Stirling chats with Renzo Castagneto, one of the four founders of the Mille Miglia.

Mille Miglia - The Race

What a fabulous scene - the colours, the cars, the setting - you can almost smell the atmosphere and the excitement.

Stirling Moss ...

METICULOUS PREPARATION

"We also practiced our own pit stops while we were in Hockenheim, changing wheels, plugs, fuel pumps, installing the spare metal wind-shield we carried and so on."

With the faster cars starting at minute intervals, their race number indicated a competitor's starting times. Fangio's was 658, meaning he left the starting ramp at Brescia at 6.58am. Kling was 701, Hermann 704 and Moss 722 with Castellotti in a 4.4-litre Ferrari a minute behind. Marzotto in another Ferrari left a minute later and the biggest threat and wily old fox, Piero Taruffi, departed in his Ferrari at 7.28am. It was clearly an advantage to leave after your rivals because you could know, en route, how you stood in relation to those ahead.

Though Moss and Jenks were pressing on and reaching around 170mph on the straights, they were disappointed when Castellotti caught them after one hour and 20 minutes. Then Stirling made a mistake, leaving his braking too late as he entered Padua at 150mph. He worked like crazy to slow the car and bounced off some straw bales. There was no damage but a grinning Castellotti nipped past. Stirling attempted to follow him but the Ferrari's acceleration (he was driving solo, had less fuel and an engine almost 50% larger in capacity) enabled him to pull away out of corners whereas the 300 SLR would gain again on the long straights and under braking. However, Castellotti was pushing very hard, driving wildly and really punishing his tyres. Stirling felt it could not last and was also worried he might get caught up in the accident Castellotti looked as though he was about to have at any moment. He dropped back slightly.

Sure enough, when they came to the first control at Ravenna, though Castelotti was leading the Brits by nearly two minutes, he had to change both rear tyres which negated his advantage. Taruffi was third, 41 seconds behind Moss. However, none of this was known to the intrepid duo.

Castellotti had effectively shot his bolt but now Taruffi began to press, using his local knowledge to full advantage. After the long run down the east coast of Italy with the glorious Adriatic on the left and the weather perfect, Moss stopped at Pescara for his first scheduled refuelling halt. "A Mercedes man in a white coat held a tray of cold tea, coffee, chocolate, bananas and anything else you could eat while the refuelling was going on. We had quite a meal in that 28 seconds stop," wrote Stirling at the time.

"Just out of Pescara I made my second mistake and again hit some straw bales. Again it was nothing serious and we were able to press on without stopping. Coming to Aquila, I found that Taruffi was 15 seconds ahead of me, as at Pescara. This was serious because we were coming to that section which would give Taruffi such an advantage - the mountainous drop into Rome."

At Pescara, Neubauer the tactician played his part. The Moss car would only need enough petrol to get them to the next fuelling stop at Rome, hence the quick stop. Taruffi, filled up which took 90 seconds and wiped out his advantage. Hermann, in third place, was now nearly 12 minutes adrift.

"Up in the mountains beyond Popoli," wrote Jenks in his report in Motor Sport, "Moss really showed his immense skill and the way he slid the car round corner after corner, never relaxing, never sliding too much or too little, was wonderful to watch." As they rushed down the mountainside, they overtook a Maserati and Stirling mouthed "Musso" to Jenks. By the L'Acquila control, Moss was averaging 114.6mph (184.4kp/h).

Taruffi's Ferrari was heavy with fuel as he tackled the mountains and by Rome Stirling had a 92 second advantage. They were also 27 minutes ahead of the record time to Rome. However, there was a well-known Mille Miglia legend that says, "He who leads at Rome, does not lead in Brescia".

As they approached Rome, the spectators virtually filled the road and Stirling weaved from side to side as he approached them at 125mph to 'encourage' them to give him more space. At Rome they were stationary for 60 seconds, while the rear wheels were changed, 60 gallons of fuel was added, the car was checked for damage and leaks, the windscreen was cleaned, Jenks drank some water but declined anything else and Moss relieved himself.

As they set off North on the return leg up the western side of the country, Stirling knew that this was where Taruffi would really push and use all his local knowledge. However, the skilful Italian's run came to an end at Viterbo with a broken oil pump. By this stage, Jenks was feeling totally exhausted, having been buffeted endlessly in the cockpit, weary from intense concentration and struggling with the immense heat in the car. "The cockpit had now become a raging inferno," he wrote, "with the heat from the rear axle and gearbox making the metal of the seat frames almost too hot to touch, while the mid-afternoon sun was still burning as only an Italian sun can."

On the Raticosa Pass, Stirling had a front brake lock which spun them into a ditch. Mercifully, Stirling, selecting first gear, was able to drive out of it, though he had to reverse twice to turn the car round in the narrow road. The rear bodywork was dented but there was nothing more serious. "Over the difficult Futa and Raticosa mountains, Moss worked like a maniac," stated his bearded companion.

In Florence, they passed Fangio, who was having injection problems, both Kling and Hermann having already crashed out of the race. "I thought," said Stirling, "that Taruffi was still in the race when we came to the fast stretch home of 300 kilometres. The highest reading I got on those fast stretches was 7,700rpm in fifth gear, which was about 177mph.

"We were taking the hump-backed bridges in fine style and Denis had not made a wrong move. Some of them we took flat out, at something over 170mph, and we would be completely airborne for more than 50 yards."

"On this fast run we caught up with the slower 1,500cc cars. This was most disconcerting because they were doing about 110mph, but we were travelling at about 50 or 60mph faster. The sun was in their eyes and I could not depend on them seeing us coming…"

Following the death of Nuvolari in 1953, the organisers created the Gran Premio Tazio Nuvolari for the competitor making the fastest time over the final Cremona/Mantua/Brescia stretch. Stirling and Jenks won it at 123.37mph (198.5km/h) to add to the Franco Mazzotti Cup for overall victory.

They had achieved one of the greatest motor racing feats of all time.

On Monday, work was interspersed with lunch with Dick Wilkins at the Savoy, a haircut, a visit to the tailor and, in the evening, he took SW to see *The Constant Husband*. "G. Food at La Rue's." Tuesday evening, the BRDC threw a special cocktail party in Stirling's honour and "Capt Eyston gave me a wonderful cig. case".

Next morning, he was woken at 7.00am when TWA phoned to say his plane would be delayed. Later, he flew to Frankfurt and then tried the Mercedes GP cars at Hockenheim.

Thursday, 12th: "Up at 1.30am and did 1½ hours in the SLR and bed again at 4am and up at 8am. To Stuttgart and tested the GP car (short test) on airport." He then flew back to London and saw *Dry Rot* (G). "Food at Ox on the Roof."

The following afternoon, he went to "Siebe Gorman with SW. Went in their tank with my aqualung and frogman's suit. V.G. Left later and more work. Phoned Alf who says Masers are co-operative. Good. Bed at 2.15am." Saturday morning Stirling visited the well-known London shops, Swann & Edgars and Lillywhites, and had lunch at the 'Wheel'. That evening, he dined at the Mirabelle and then drove down to Lympne C.C. [Hythe, Kent] Next morning, he flew to Le Touquet and drove to Paris, continuing south to Monte Carlo the day after. Tuesday was spent at the beach and trying his frogman's suit. "No fish."

On Wednesday, he went to Nice to swim. "NBG. Mistral. To Monte, noggin and food with Lance and Co." First practice for the Monaco GP took place the following afternoon. "My best was 3rd ftd, 1.43.4. Ascari 1.42 and Fangio 1.41.4! Old record was 1.45 (Carrac!) [Rudolf Carraciola]. The ratios are not good and are being changed. Poor Hans had an accident. He has hurt his leg and ribs."

For the Monaco GP, Mercedes-Benz took two new short-wheelbase W196s with outboard brakes which saved weight. Fangio's car also had the engine mounted further forward and handled better.

"Up at 5am after an awful night. Only 2½ hours sleep. In practice, I tried J.F.'s car to take a plug cut and did a 1.41.2! My own best was 1.43.8 in my car. His is better on the corners and faster. Mine was ftd. Called on my tailor Bienfay. Lance ran the Maser in. We all (Mercs) had food outside Nice and then a press 'do'. Later food at Oscars.

"Up at 5.45am. In practice, I tried lead in my car 1.42.8 and without 1.42.5. Cast 1.42, Asc

The famous roller map, otherwise known as the 'toilet roll holder'!

Mille Miglia - The Facts

652 cars entered
533 started
281 completed course
Capacities ranged from 250cc to over 4-litres
Roads closed for 20 hours
Smaller cars started first at 30 second intervals
Larger cars started at one minute intervals
Number of spectators estimated at five million
Field included 18 Ferraris, 19 Maseratis, 19 Porsches & 10 OSCAs
Mercedes had 84 personnel stationed around the course
Moss/Jenkinson averaged 97.88mph for 992 miles
Raised record average by 9mph, greatest ever increment increase
Record never broken
Finished 31 mins 45 secs ahead of 2nd placed Fangio
Finished 44 mins 59 secs ahead of 3rd placed Maglioli
Finished over one hour ahead of 4th placed Maserati
Finished over two hours ahead of 8th placed Porsche
Race abandoned after 1957 when 10 spectators (including 5 children) were killed

BRITISH DRIVERS AND RIDERS SCORE
BRILLIANT TRIUMPH BY STIRLING MOSS IN ITALIAN "CLASSIC"

IT was Britain's day yesterday in international car and motor-cycle racing. Britons won the classic Italian Mille Miglia, the senior event of the Spanish Grand Prix, and swept the field in the international motor-cycling races at Mettet, in Belgium.

These reports from the Continent tell of British triumphs:
BREDCIA (N. Italy), Sunday. Stirling Moss, 25-year-old British champion, driving a German Mercedes sports car, won the classic 1,000 Miles Italian Mille Miglia Road Race which ended today.

Yorks Observer 2.5.55

Jenks's Feat

SM: "The car was left hand drive, so Jenks would use his left hand to signal."

PP: "So he'd be holding the 'toilet roll holder' and winding it on with his right hand, reading it and signalling with his left hand, and putting up with all the vibration, G forces, the wind pressure at 170/180mph, the dust, the dirt and the fumes, and for over 10 hours. That must have been incredibly tricky!"

SM: "I would say. The other amazing thing is that he wrote an incredible story about it, without any notes at all, because he didn't have a hand free to write the notes with, or time to do them, or anything to write them on anyway. A very remarkable man."

"I really don't know what speed I could have done without Jenks but it would have been an enormous amount slower, because when I was coming up to the brow of a hill, I would probably pull only about 120/130 - with him I was doing 160/170."

"Club della Mille Miglia"

FRANCO MAZZOTTI

XXII MILLE MIGLIA

30 aprile - 1 maggio 1955

Arriving at the L'Aquila control.

1.41.1, and JF 1.41.1. Behra 1.42.5! Lance 1.49.4 [in Stirling's 250F] and not qualified. We have a do because Pollet is accepted with the same time. Lunch at Salon Privé and met Bella Darvi, star of *Racers*. Later saw the film and food and bed at 12.15am."

Alf Francis, who was looking after Stirling's own 250F at Monaco, got an insight into the Neubauer discipline. The hotel where the team's drivers were staying had been fully booked by M-B. All telephone calls to the drivers had to be vetted by Neubauer, otherwise the telephonist would not put them through. Finally, Francis managed to get through to Stirling but, before he could speak, Moss said quickly, "I am just going off to bed - right now". It was 10.30pm and Alf assumed Stirling must have thought it would be Neubauer.

"Up at 10am, mucked around, light lunch and then the race. Start at 2.45. I took the lead and waved JF passed, then Castellotti nipped by (½ tank of fuel). I repassed and from then on Fangio 1st, SM 2nd and we gained +30 seconds. Fangio then broke and I lead until the 81st lap, when I broke whilst 1 min 38 secs ahead of Ascari who went into the harbour! OK. Later called at the hospital, saw Hans and Alberto and then reception and Casino. Bed at 3am."

When Stirling rose next morning, he was feeling unwell and thought he might have flu.

However, he went for a noggin on Aristotle Onassis's yacht. "It's quite fantastic." That night he dined in San Remo. On Tuesday, he called at the Auto Club and "turned down £50 offered as expenses". He bought some food in Cannes and headed north, picnicing en route. Leaving Chagny where he had stayed the night, he lunched at Metz and headed for the Nürburgring where he bumped into John Fitch and Masten Gregory. He did two laps in an SLR in preparation for the Eifelrennen sports car race.

He began practice proper next day. "The circuit feels very slippery. My best was 10 mins 19 (4 laps only). Kling 10.19. Juan 10.16. Did one lap in the GP car. Later a lap with Uhlenhaut in my 220. The SLR is over-geared, 7,200 max, 2nd too high.

"Heard the awful news that Alberto Ascari was killed in practice at Monza."

On the Friday, practice began at 3.30pm. "I did 1st lap at 10.12, 2nd 10.05 but slowed due to yellow flag. (Jimmy Stewart's D-type crashed). Then sprinkle of rain and I went over the side

Rome control, where Moss was leading Taruffi by one minute and 52 seconds.

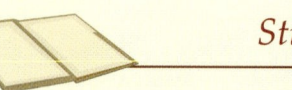

Stirling Moss ...

THE ISETTAS IN THE MILLE MIGLIA

"The roads were very steeply cambered in those days. I remember passing the Isettas because they were right in the middle of the road, when we caught them up near the end. They were chugging along, plonk, plonk, plonk! I had to pull over to the side to pass them and I recall looking in the mirror and saw them working like hell to try and keep them in a straight line. When a 300 SLR passes you at 175, boy, it makes a draught.

"I remember once blowing over a photographer. He said, 'Come passed me at high speed'. He'd parked his scooter and it blew it over!"

This superb painting by Nicholas Watts was done to celebrate the 40th anniversary in 1995. Jenks had great input into its detail and it was the only painting he ever deigned to sign.

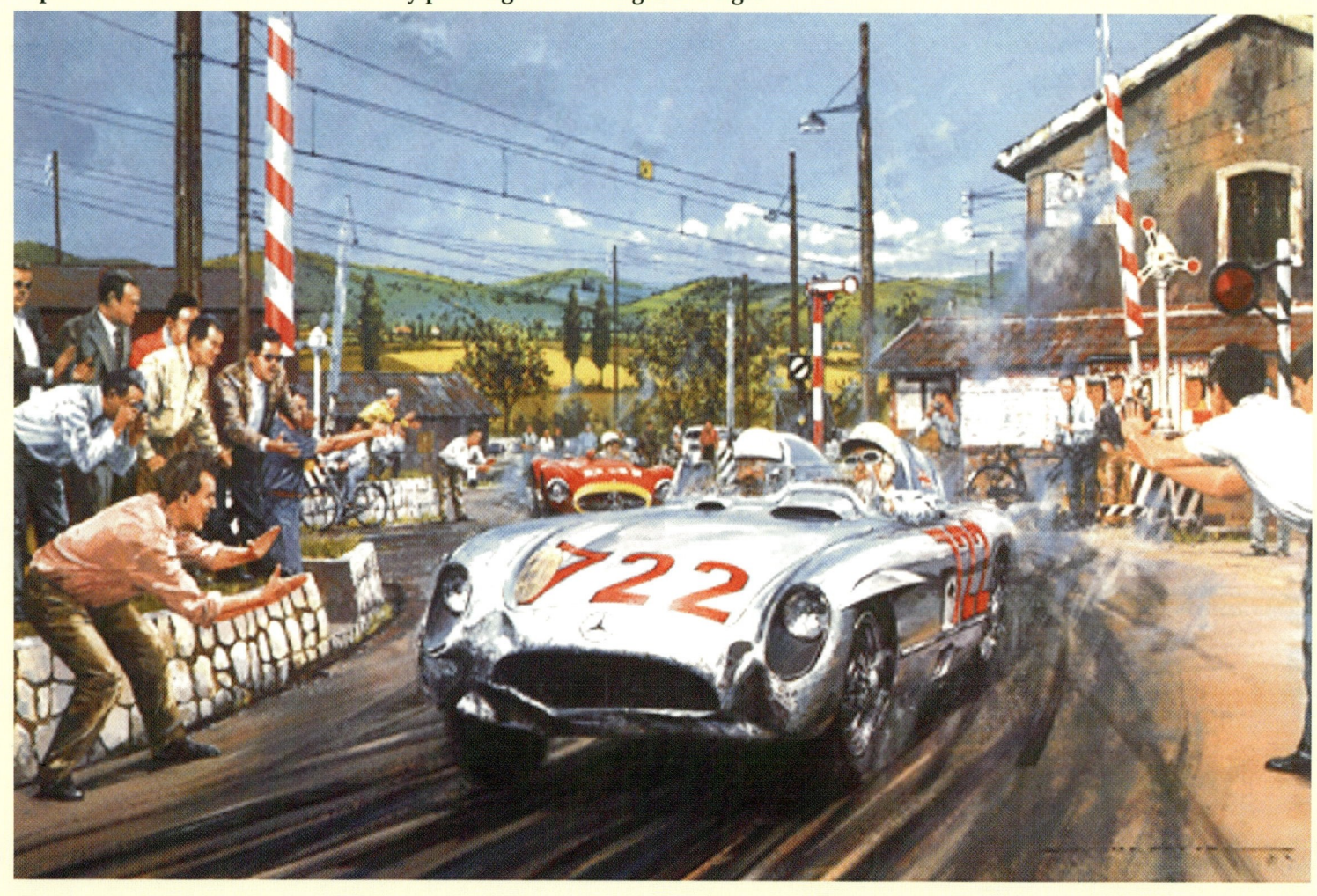

Stirling Moss ...

CALL OF NATURE

"Going for what we thought would probably be 12 hours, without stopping to spend a penny, is a big problem. So in the end, we decided we were going to do it when we get to Rome, which was halfway. We didn't know exactly where the Rome Control was going to be but in practice we had nipped round the back of somewhere. But when we came into the Control, they had built a grandstand for about 60/70,000 people, where we were going to do the stop, you see! So, I mean that was pretty awful in itself, so we had to get out and run round under the grandstand. In fact, it actually took me, I think, one minute and four seconds. We came back, having relieved ourselves, to find the car washed and polished and 58 gallons of fuel onboard and, you know, oil checked and everything else. Quite a unique event!"

Firenza control, where Moss was leading Hermann by five minutes and 48 seconds.

Mercedes 'power house' - from the right Dr Nallinger, Prof Scherenberg and Rudi Uhlenhaut with Artur Keser behind.

EDITORIAL

AN OUTSTANDING ACHIEVEMENT

To 25-year-old Stirling Moss go our most sincere and hearty congratulations on the finest achievement of his motor-racing career, for to win the classic Mille Miglia is a feat comparable with Seaman's winning the German Grand Prix in 1938. Enthusiasts in this country will warmly applaud his success, but their exultation may be tempered by the thought that it, like Seaman's, was gained in a German Mercedes-Benz car.

Is there any hope at all that this sobering thought will also occur to those who control Britain's motor industry? Stuttgart, it seems, decided to win the Mille Miglia and by dint of implacable thoroughness in all their preparations did that and more—for they also secured three important class victories—just as, in 1914, they announced that they would win the French Grand Prix—and gained the first *three* places. This is the way to go motor-racing, if one believes in competition successes to advertise one's wares. Daimler-Benz do, and they have steadily rising sales graphs, in such valuable export areas as the United States, to prove it.

One British manufacturer who shares this belief is Donald Healey, and he has every reason to feel pleased with the showing of his 100S model in the Mille Miglia. This is a production car in the truest sense of the term (one of the works models was driven through London traffic the day before leaving for Italy), but with it George Abecassis finished 11th, winning the special category for open sports cars costing up to two million lire and gaining fifth place in the unlimited sports class. His performance is an excellent one, which cannot fail to increase world-wide interest in the promising 100S Austin-Healey, but for the British motor industry as a whole it is not good enough that foreign cars should fill the first 10 places in such important—and widely publicized—events as the Mille Miglia.

Autosport 6.5.55

after the Karussel. Wow. Was I frightened! Got 7,000 on the straight. Poor Des Titt [Titterington] crashed… Broke his nose and shoulder. Both Ds have had it.

"Sent cable to Dad for his birthday. Practised in pouring rain. My best was 11.28, Kling 11.26, Juan 11.16!"

Sunday, 29th: "I was 3rd into the first corner, 2nd out of it. Fangio 1st, Karl 3rd. We continued and Kling fell back. Later slowed and changed positions, etc. After three laps my car developed a vibration and began sliding a lot (broken dampers?). On the 7th lap, Kling broke and spread oil <u>all</u> around the circuit. Juan and I continued to be 1st and 2nd, one metre apart. I got fastest lap in 10.10.8. Masten was 3rd. I won three cups, a suitcase and rug!"

Next morning, Stirling was at Spa by 11.45, where he dropped off some baggage and continued to Brussels where he checked in at the Palace Hotel. He met Mr. and Mrs Ickx (parents of future racing driver Jackie) and had an excellent meal.

The last day of May was a relaxing, low key one spent shopping and going to a "flick" (film).

Stirling Moss …

SIENNA

"When you come in to Sienna, it is quite remarkable. The whole place was just full of atmosphere. When you drive between the houses, the resonance is enormous and although it was a really dreadful din, the people, they loved it - the kids and the old ladies. It's fantastic!"

Moss sets record in Mille Miglia

BRESCIA, Sunday.

STIRLING MOSS drove his Mercedes Silver Bullet to a record-breaking victory to-day in the Mille Miglia (1,000 mile) road race. He is the first Englishman to win the race, and put almost 10 mph on the average speed.

The 24-year-old German racer roared the Italian route at an average speed of 97.95 miles an hour for the 992-mile route.

The old record of 88.3 m.p.h. was set in 1953 by Italy's Giannino Marzotto.

Clear lead

Moss's brilliant dash down the peninsula to Rome and back to Brescia, took him only 10 hours 7min. 48sec.

World champion driver, Juan Manuel Fangio, of Argentina, also in a Mercedes, finished second, but he was far behind.

The one-two finish for the Mercedes was a bitter blow to the Italian Ferrari and Maserati teams. Ferrari's ace, Taruffi, was forced out by a broken oil pump north of Rome after waging a close fight with Moss for the first half of the race.

Moss, smiling happily, said after the race: "This victory has given me the greatest satisfaction of my career. I didn't force the car too much in the first part of the race, but when, after Rome, I saw I was leading and the car was running beautifully, I let myself go."

At one stage, the British driver averaged just over 124 mph along the 56 miles stretch between Cremona and Mantua — the last checkpoint.

The race, begun in 1927, winds over the passes of the North Italian mountains.

Notts Guardian 2.5.55

La Gazzetta dello Sport

L. 25 - ANNO 59 - N. 104 — LUNEDÌ 2 MAGGIO 1955 - L. 25

DUE GRANDI IMPRESE IN UNA DOMENICA SPORTIVA D'ECCEZIONE

Moss (Mercedes) trionfa nella Mille Miglia
La vittoriosa Udinese a due punti dal Milan

Stirling Moss ...

TUSCANY

"The Tuscany leg was very twisty and very difficult because there were no open corners. You could see where the road was going but not the contour of it, because there were banks on the side and hedges and all that sort of stuff. If you can see through a corner, then that is pretty easy, then you have just got to worry about the surface changes and stuff, but when you can't see through, setting the car up is very difficult."

The last few yards, the last few seconds, the moment of sweet victory. Moss and Jenks have triumphed against great odds. The competition has fallen apart, attempting to match the electrifying pace. All records are smashed.

Slower Cars

PP: "It must have been hell passing all those slower cars?"
SM: "Half of them went off the road, all the Italian hairdressers with the go-faster tape. Half of those blokes were off in the first hundred miles."
PP: "That must have helped!"
SM: "It certainly thinned them down a bit. Then of course, we were catching drivers who were a bit better. Then, when they had been driving for 12-15 hours, they were getting a bit tired so they were still falling off."

Reflecting On The 1955 Mille Miglia

PP: "It has been called your greatest triumph."
SM: "I think now with hindsight it was certainly the most important race I ever competed in. It was certainly the most difficult race. It was a difficult race because on a proper race circuit you know exactly where you want to be for every corner - I mean I know when I go into, say Abbey [at Silverstone], I start here, I turn in there, move to the apex, etc. This is a race where there were no corners I could go into in this way, other than if I could see round them and that was very unusual because there were so many people lining the sides of the roads that you just couldn't see the full bend. Of course, in practice they hadn't been there and so I could see the bends. When you have got people inside a corner, of course, it makes it a wall, 6ft high, and therefore one has to drive with a different technique altogether. You are trying to go into every corner at 9/10ths and then build upwards if you can, without going over the maximum. It was quite a unique problem.

"It still staggers me that I could possibly achieve that average, just on 100."
PP: "Did you scare yourself at all?"
SM: "I am sure that I did because one does inevitably. I mean you even scare yourself when you know the road, so I am sure that I did. In fact, I know that I did because Jenks would shake his head in the Italian way whenever there was anything we both didn't expect.

"Once I made a mistake, because I thought I knew a corner and I didn't pay much attention to Jenks. It was in a town and therefore I had to go over a curb to get away with it. Didn't happen many times, not many mistakes.

"I think we were geared for something like 178-180mph. I knew it was quick, because I remember we were on one very fast section and a twin-engined aircraft was watching and we were actually overtaking it - so one knows it was a bit quick then!"

STIRLING MOSS WINS GREAT ITALIAN MOTOR RACE.
STIRLING MOSS THE WELL KNOWN YOUNG BRITISH DRIVER
BECAME THE FIRST BRITON EVER TO WIN THE GREAT MILLE
MIGLIA, THE MOTOR RACE OF ALMOST 1,000 MILES WHICH
COVERS HALF THE LENGTH AND THE WHOLE OF THE BREADTH OF ITALY.
DRIVING A GERMAN MERCEDES BENZ MOSS COVERED THE 992 MILES
COURSE IN 10 HOURS. 7 MINS. 46 SECS., AVERAGING 97.8. m.p.h.
a record for the race.
F.44323.   Stirling Moss being assisted in after his victory.

A dented car sets record

WHIRLWIND MOSS WINS THE CAR RACE OF HIS LIFE

ROME, Sunday.

STIRLING MOSS swept to victory in the greatest race of his career to-day when he out-drove and out-manoeuvred the world's best drivers in the 1,000-mile Italian Mille Miglia race to set up a record.

Moss drove his German Mercedes over the twisting route round Italy at an average speed of 97.95 m.p.h. and was the first Briton to win the race.

The old record of 88.3 m.p.h. was set in 1953 by Italy's Gian...

Moss led a pow... cedes team w... tinian world cha... Fangio and Ha... Fangio, who finished 30 mi... Moss, who course in 10hr...

A F...

The 253 st... out early an... fight between... and Merced...

Until M... Karl Kli... overturne... mark ou... Hermann... after wi... the fou... domina...

Mille Madness

PP: "Was it mad?"

SM: "Yes, of course, it was mad. I mean the only place you could do it was in a mad place like Italy where the people have such a passion for motor racing. The crazy thing was, it seemed to me, that if you parked before the start in the main square with a number on the side, you could take part. Literally, it seemed like all the Italian hairdressers with the go-faster tape on their cars. And on the first 100 miles you saw blazing wrecks on either side of the road. It was an absolutely unique event. It amazes me that, a) they allowed it and, b) I managed to go that fast. Every time I go round there now I am very surprised. I must have been very young!"

"Il Whisky di chi beve Whisky"

Above all, with their brilliant Mille Miglia win, Stirling and Jenks showed great spirit!

1955

Stirling Moss Scrapbook

ARTIE'S HEADLINE

"What do you think of S-T-I-R-L-I-N-G M-O-S-S, dear?"

Daily Express 4.5.55

After driving at an average of virtually 100mph through the villages, towns, cities and mountain passes of Italy, Stirling looks remarkably fresh (and unlike us mere mortals he did not have the supportive qualities of alcohol to sustain him in those days) and yet after this 'do' he would drive through the night to Germany.

The Isetta

The Isetta was the original 'bubble car' and manufactured by the Iso company from 1953 until 1955. The overall length was 90in (2.3m) with a rear track of less than 2ft. The rear-mounted engine was an air-cooled 236cc twin 2-stroke. Access was gained by the large swing-up front door to which the steering wheel and column were attached. The Suez crisis caused these very economical devices to be a great success and they were manufactured under licence by V.E.L.A.M. in France, Borward-Iso in Spain, Iso-Roma in Brazil and, most particularly, by B.M.W. in Germany who produced them until 1964. The B.M.W.-engined version was built under licence in the UK by Isetta of Great Britain Ltd from 1957 until 1964.

This remarkable victory alone should surely have been enough to seal Stirling's immortality, but he was not finished yet. There were more extraordinary victories to come in 1955, to say nothing of another six full seasons of brilliant endeavour.

RETURN OF A VICTOR

THE British racing driver, Stirling Moss, with his parents and manager on his arrival at Lydd Airport, Ferryfield, Kent, last night. He had flown home after his victory driving a German Mercedes sports car in the Mille Miglia, the classic Italian road race, which he was the first Englishman to win.

THE happiest sportsman I know is the racing motorist Stirling Moss. And since he *lives* his sport all the time, his intense pleasure is derived from it. "I experience great elation during actual races," he told me. "There is plenty of time to be happy while you are behind the wheel.

"But in the main I get my happiness from the fulfilment of personal standards.

"This is not the same as achieving *success*, as the public measures success.

"Obviously, I feel good if I win a race. But there are plenty of occasions when I don't get the cheers but I feel great satisfaction from my personal achievement in a race I have *planned*.

By ALLEN ANDREWS

AIMS

"I set myself a lap time, or a position to be maintained in a race. And my happiness springs from that sense of achievement over other people *and over myself* that comes with the fulfilment of these aims.

"If it's possible to give a general recipe for happiness, I'd say this: Happiness depends on achieving what you've set out to do. I think you should try to limit your ambitions — while keeping them high—to what is *possible*."

EAGLE SPORTS NEWS
● INFORMATION ● INSTRUCTION

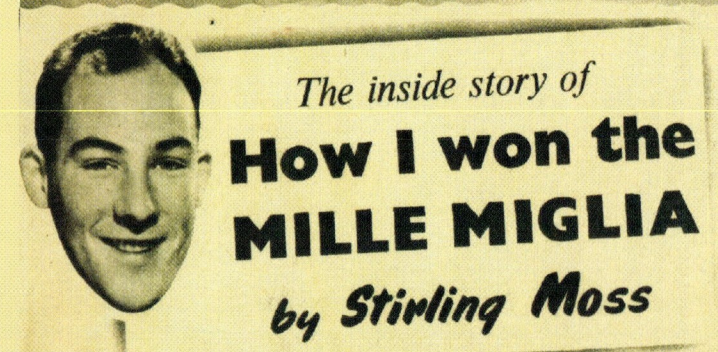

EAGLE 17 June 1955

The inside story of How I won the MILLE MIGLIA
by *Stirling Moss*

Stirling Moss, at the wheel of his Mercedes-Benz, reaches the Rome Control Point. Superstition said that the first driver to reach Rome never wins, and Stirling was just a little worried about this.

I LOOKED at my wrist-watch. It was coming up to 22 minutes past 7.0 on Sunday morning, 1st May. I glanced hurriedly at Dennis Jenkinson, who sat with me in the cockpit of the sleek, silvered Mercedes-Benz, and he gave me an answering smile.

It was dawn in Brescia, a picturesque town in Northern Italy, but already the tree-lined avenue ahead was filled on either side by hundreds of people.

We were on the ramp, ready to start the 22nd Mille Miglia, a thousand-mile race around the world's toughest and most dangerous road circuit, which circles the Boot of Italy through Padua, Ancona, Pescara, Rome, then up the East Coast through Florence, Bologna and back to Brescia.

A thousand miles of road, cleared as far as possible, with only two brief stops of seconds' duration for a bite to eat and to refuel.

No Englishman had ever won this race, and though we were in the much-fancied Mercedes entry, it was my team-companion, the World Champion Juan Manuel Fangio, who was favourite to win.

Dennis and I were placing a great deal of reliance on a small metal box, inside which was a roll of paper, some twelve feet in length. During our numerous practice laps, Dennis had plotted on this paper the whole course, noting every tricky bump and corner, and now he would be able to unwind the roll as we progressed, observing it through a plastic window in the box, and warn me of impending danger.

Seven twenty-two. Time for us to go. Already the smaller cars would be well on their way round Italy, for they had left at nine o'clock the previous evening.

Down swept the flag, and through the tree-lined avenue we roared. The crowds were just blurred splashes of colour as I stepped on the accelerator and the Mercedes responded. We soon left Brescia far behind and approached the tricky left and right turn bends that lead to Vicenza.

Through the tiny West Coast villages of Ferrara and Ravenna huge crowds moved slowly forward as each car flashed by, and it took some risky steering to avoid them.

Now we were hitting 170 miles an hour along the straights, and on the way to Pescara, a biggish town on the most southerly part of the circuit, we soared up and over a hump-back bridge—one we'd missed on our plotting – and went straight into the air.

One hundred and seventy miles an hour is an awfully fast speed at which to take such a bridge, and it seemed an eternity before we landed – surprisingly gently. Afterwards, onlookers told us we had travelled some sixty yards in mid-air!

We collected a dent on the right mudguard when the Mercedes sped into the straw bales marking the outside edge of the course, but luckily did not need to stop and waste precious seconds.

We took the lead soon afterwards, overtaking the Italian Taruffi in his Ferrari which was, unfortunately, developing oil trouble. On we thundered into blazing-hot Rome, the half-way stage, and now we were concerned, because we are both very superstitious and it is a well-known saying that in this race the first driver to reach Rome never wins.

Yet only five hours and one minute had passed since the start, and I knew that – provided nothing disastrous occurred during the next 500 miles – we had a wonderful chance of beating the record.

During a sixty-second stop, we loaded up with fuel, changed two wheels and grabbed some sandwiches. Then we tore away again, not knowing how close behind us Taruffi might be.

Actually, Taruffi's oil trouble worsened, and he was forced to retire.

The Appenine mountain range was crossed over La Futa Pass, just after Florence. Wonderful scenery here – I'm told. We didn't have time to see much of it; you don't when you're travelling at nearly 200 m.p.h.!

Nearing the finish, the crowds increased with every mile. Then, at last, after racing through Italy for just under 10 hours 8 minutes, we roared past the chequered flag.

Dennis threw both his arms high in the air, and the crowd responded by waving programmes and handkerchiefs. We had managed to do it. The superstition had been well and truly smashed. We were the first English, and only the second non-Italian, winners in the history of the Mille Miglia. What's more, our average speed of 97.95 m.p.h. was a new record, the previous best having been the 88.3 m.p.h. set up in 1953 by Italy's Giannino Marzotte.

Yes, it was my greatest achievement, and certainly the biggest thrill I've ever had. That goes for Dennis, too.

And I'm not forgetting my EAGLE insignia, proudly showing on my Mercedes. It certainly brought me good luck.

I always knew that it would.

STIRLING MOSS.

Fangio, Stirling's team-mate, overtaking in the early morning a car that started three minutes ahead of him. Just before reaching Rome, Stirling Moss overtook Taruffi, Kling and Fangio to gain a lead which he never lost. Fangio finally finished second.

Taruffi, in his Ferrari, chases the Mercedes, driven by Giardini, during the early stages of the Mille Miglia. Later in the race, Taruffi's car developed some oil trouble and he was forced to retire.

La voce dell'automobilista

MENSILE DELL'AUTOMOBILE CLUB BRESCIA — ORGANO UFFICIALE DEL *"Club della Mille Miglia"*

Anno V - Num. 5 Brescia, maggio 1955 Auto Club - Tel. 210-02

DOPO IL TRIONFALE ESITO DELLA VENTIDUESIMA EDIZIONE

Ancora una volta la Mille Miglia ha lanciato il suo insostituibile messaggio

Il primato di Stirling Moss aureo sigillo della corsa

Judy Noot

Stirling's office was manned by the indispensable Judy Noot (later Addicott), who had joined him in 1954 and would continue until 1958. "We had such fun. In the office there was a hatch between my office and his. He would open the hatch and say, 'Nootith....' I loved it. He had such a sense of humour, which is so important. It was fabulous. He had tremendous energy and we had a super working relationship. He's so loyal. He's so bloody normal.

"I went there on £6 a week and I don't think I ever got a rise. We had loads of fan mail. I had to make up all the scrapbooks - I hated it! It all took so much time. We had a cutting agency which provided all that. We had this funny little office in William IV Street, just off Trafalgar Square."

On the stylish streets of Monaco.

This is believed to be Sally Hindmarsh with Stirling on a yacht in the harbour at Monaco. Her father, John Hindmarsh, won Le Mans pre-War driving a Lagonda. Her sister, Sue, is married to Roy Salvadori and they have lived in Monaco for many years.

Crumpet In Monaco

In Ken Gregory's book he says that, during practice at Monaco, Stirling was waving to a Dutch girl on a balcony. He signalled each time he went passed and indicated they should meet later. They duly did so and were sitting in a bar late in the evening when Stirling was passed a note. "De Moss will be in De bed mitt aut de fraulein". He hastily turned round, worried that Neubauer would not be amused ... and saw a grinning Jenks sitting in the corner. Of course, he had written the spoof note!

Drivers

Moss on: ROY SALVADORI ...

"Roy was fast and competent, but not particularly clean. I don't think that he would try and drive you off the road, but I think he would be quite happy to take the piece of road you wanted. A good competitive sports car driver."

Superb study of Stirling at work in the 'office'.

Stirling Moss ...

DICK WILKINS

"Dick Wilkins was the Queen's stockbroker - very nice, rotund gentleman, very rich. Later on he bought the cars that I drove for Rob [Walker]. He was not the sort of guy who would want to figure at all. He was into horses - that was his scene."

Siebe Gorman

One of the most famous and longest-established diving apparatus manufacturers, Siebe Gorman of England have been producing diving dress dating back to the 1830s. Augustus Siebe was well-known for inventing the first deep sea helmet in 1830 and also patented the first Smoke Helmet.

Hospital Visits

PP: "Did most drivers visit the other drivers if they were in hospital?"
SM: "No they didn't. I think I was one of the few that did. I didn't know Alberto [Ascari] that well, but I respected him and he was a nice man and a bloody good driver and all that sort of thing, so I would go and see him, and also with Hans being a team mate. But I don't think it was general."

Stirling Moss ...

THE CIGARETTE CASE

"The cigarette case was a very nice silver one. I've still got it somewhere."

Speed Age
The Best in Racing and Hot Rodding

INCLUDING OFFICIAL AUTO RACING GUIDE

The Truth About the Chrysler 300

JANUARY 1956

A Champ Returns: Tim Flock's Story

Top Sports Car of the Year

Monaco is surely the most eccentric of the annual Grand Prix events and therefore loved for being so different. It is all about atmosphere and glamour, style and noise! Every enthusiast should go to the Monaco GP once.

Racers

Adapted from a novel by Hans Ruesch, in this Fox movie, directed by Henry Hathaway, Kirk Douglas plays an Italian bus driver who aspires to become a racing driver, somehow breaking into the European motor racing scene. However, his 'win at all costs' attitude alienates those around him and he only comes to his senses when he has all but lost his sweetheart played by Bella Darvi. Features racing footage; also stars Lee J. Cobb and Gilbert Roland. Also known as 'Such Men Are Dangerous'.

Bella Darvi

International actress Bella Darvi, led a tragic, tempestuous life. She was born Bayla Wegier in Poland but raised in Paris. Sent to a concentration camp at the age of 12, much of her adult life was ruined by gambling. In 1951, Darryl F. Zanuck, the head of 20th Century-Fox, cleared her debts and took her to Hollywood. Darvi made three films, of little distinction. She returned to Europe, appeared in mediocre movies, accumulated gambling debts again and, at the third attempt, succeeded in committing suicide in 1971.

Drivers

Moss on:
MAURICE TRINTIGNANT ...

"French 'gentleman' - always very charming and amusing. Competent rather than flash. He won Monaco which tells you he was a precise driver."

Alf Francis on SM at Monaco

Alf wrote in his book that he considered Stirling's driving that year at Monaco was "immaculate" and, had he been driving a works Maserati, he would have passed Fangio. Again and again in his book, Francis laments the fact that Stirling had chosen to drive for Mercedes and that he could have given them a run for their money had he signed up as No. 1 for Signor Orsi's Maserati team. "I am sure he would have had a brilliant year, although it must be admitted that he would not have gained such valuable experience [as he did as number two to Fangio]."

Drivers

Moss on:
EUGENIO CASTELLOTTI ...

"Castellotti was always quick. In the Mille Miglia Castellotti's was the only car that passed us I think, but when you see the way that he did it, he wasn't really a concern. It's rather like running a marathon. If you're going to run the marathon at the mile speed, you're not going to finish. There is no doubt that he had a lot of ability, a lot of speed, but at the expense of, I won't say intelligence, he was not unintelligent, but guile. I think he pushed both himself and the car too hard. I wouldn't think he was that easy on the car, but I think he wasn't that easy on himself. If you push both that hard, one of them is going to crack within a certain time frame."

The lock appears pretty restricted on the W196 and this hairpin, which has had several names over years as the adjoining hotel has changed its title, is extremely tight.

Monaco Grand Prix

In practice Hans Hermann crashed badly on the run up to the Casino and sustained internal injuries which put paid to his season. Fangio was on pole with Ascari, who clocked an identical time, and Stirling joined them on the front row. When the flag dropped a gaggle of cars fought for position at the famous old Gasometer hairpin but Fangio and Moss soon established themselves in an ever-increasing lead, while Behra's Maserati disputed third with the Lancias of Ascari and Castellotti.

Then, on the 50th lap, Fangio's axle broke and Stirling found himself in the lead with a one minute advantage over Ascari. Then, more drama, when a mere 30 laps from the flag and his first GP victory, Stirling's engine cruelly expired. Gregor Grant, Autosport's founding Editor felt that, with such a large lead, Mercedes should have slowed him down. Meanwhile, Ascari, who was being given Faster signs to avoid the ignominy of being lapped, over-did it at the chicane and famously plunged into the harbour!

These incidents gifted the race to Maurice Trintignant in his Ferrari and, though Castellotti's Lancia threatened towards the end, the Frenchman hung on to take a popular victory. For once, Mercedes had failed.

Aristotle Onassis's Boat

"Onassis's boat I remember very well. There was a mosaic sort of dance floor and if you pressed a button it went up and became a swimming pool, which really impressed me. I had never been on a millionaire's yacht in those days and to go on Onassis's was special and you could have anything you wanted. There were loads of staff floating around. It wasn't actually that big, but when you are that age, everything seems bigger and better. Yes, it was very impressive."

Stirling has always liked gadgets and was impressed that one space could be used for two purposes. Some years later he would create his home in Mayfair which was full of clever devices. Did such things always appeal to him? "Yes, yes, particularly and I seem to remember he had a map on which he could see where all his ships were - the entire the Onassis fleet and how many there were."

Alf Francis winds up Fangio's Mechanic

Francis reckoned that the World Champion had his own personal mechanic who was not in the employ of M-B but was probably paid by Fangio himself. He was an Argentinian of Italian descent. As Macklin had failed to qualify the Moss Maserati, Alf needed something to do during the race to avoid getting bored, so kept a stop-watch on Stirling.

This mechanic was standing in their pit and, on several occasions, Francis turned to him and said: "Fangio will have to watch out if he does not want Moss to pass him". Then: "Stirling gained a little there, you know". Today, we would say he was winding him up.

The guy started madly gesticulating at Fangio to go faster. When SM later retired from the race, Alf told him about his little game.

"That was the chap who was always waving him on," said Moss. "I never could make out who it was, especially as it was coming from your pit!"

Help in grooming

SIR:
I have been trying out some of the tips given by Stirling Moss in his Motoring Supplement (ILLUSTRATED, April 2). The most useful, I thought, were moving the windscreen wiper to the centre of the windscreen, where neither driver nor passenger is likely to strike his head on it, and widening the rear window to give better vision. But I wonder how many other readers had difficulty in identifying the dust-absorbing polisher used by Donald Sinden in giving his car a "star" grooming?

B. SELWYN BROWN
Wollaton Road, Nottingham.

₊ Sinden (pictured above) used the Nenette polisher. It cost him 13s. 6d.

Stirling Moss ...

ON FRIGHT

The incident at the Karussel: *"Just after the Karussel there is a very fast section. You go flat from the Karussel and there were a couple of corners which one ought to take flat and I seem to remember on one of the times I was going round I left a wheel on the side a bit, and it was quite exciting, I mean it didn't do any damage or anything else, but it let me realise that one has to pay considerable attention to the exit from the Karussel."*

Would you frighten yourself occasionally? *"Oh yes, sometimes, oh certainly, certainly. But you weren't frightened until after it had happened because you were trying to sort out the drama. You are trying to lessen the damage that is going to be done. After you would think, 'Shit, that was really quite bad'."*

KEYNOTES — **JUNE 4, 1955**

Sports-Page

Racing at Nürburg Ring

*To Keynotes
Very best wishes
to you all
Stirling Moss
29.5.55*

Stirling Moss just before the start of the race in his 3 ltr Mercedes SLR.

Stirling Moss came second to Fangio the Argentine Ace driver losing first place by only half a wheel's length.

The race was a continual struggle between Fangio, Moss and Kling, the Mercedes Team.

A WIN FOR MERCÉDÈS IN GERMANY: Juan Fangio, of the Argentine (left), races across the finishing-line less than 3 ft. ahead of Stirling Moss, of Britain, to win the sports car race for cars of over 1,500 cc., at the Nuerburgring Race-course. They are both driving the Mercédès-type 300 SLR car. The length of the course was just under 142 miles, and Fangio's average speed in the race was 81·02 m.p.h.

Drivers

Moss on: ALBERTO ASCARI ...

"Just notched out by Fangio. I think he was really excellent. I don't think he quite had the skill of Fangio but he was an exceptionally good driver. Very tidy, very complete, had quite good stamina, good car control, wouldn't throw it around unnecessarily. He has to be one of the best drivers of all time. I would put him in the top ten."

READER

WHEN I met Stirling Moss, that magnificent driver of fast cars, in Nassau recently he had a book under his arm.

The same book was still his sole spare-time reading matter in Monte.

Title of book: "How to ... and Breed Pigs."

Explanation—from Stir...

It is a sort of insur... You never know, ...icularly in my game, ...t your luck will be.

...feel it is a good ...g to have something ...behind you—like, say, ...g farm."

So when he is not talking about pistons and things, Stirling has a little chat about the Landrace. Yes—it's a pig.

Sunday Pictorial 22.5.55

Stirling Moss ...

LEARNING A CIRCUIT

"I'd go to a circuit like the 'Ring and I'd just drive round and round, just a lot, and things gradually began to fall into place. You'd think, 'I know this bit' and then you'd say, 'No, it's not that bit. I was thinking of another one.' I'd gradually piece things together. I would come to corners which were really faster than I thought they were and corners which were slower than they looked. I would concentrate on those particular ones and gradually I would assimilate the thing, I was younger and obviously this was my business and I could learn different circuits reasonably quickly."

MOSS BEATEN BY HALF A LENGTH

ADENAU, West Germany, Sunday.

Juan Fangio of Argentina and Stirling Moss of Britain finished first and second in German Mercedes in the international race for production and sports cars over 1,500cc on the Nuerburg-Ring track here to-day. There was half a length between them.

Moss led most of the way. Masten Gregory, American driver of a Ferrari, was third, followed by Germany's Karl Kling (Mercedes), fourth, and Italy's Giuseppe Farina (Ferrari).—Reuter.

Hawthorn's Close Second

Jean Behra, of France, driving an Italian Maserati, won a tremendous duel with Britain's Mike Hawthorn, in a Ferrari, to gain a narrow victory in yesterday's 1,000 kilometre sports car race at Monza, Italy, stated Reuter. He was 17 seconds ahead in a race lasting 5hrs 41mins 41secs. Third was Mieres, also in a Maserati.

Daily Telegraph 30.5.55

Eifelrennen

Due to at least three other clashing sports car races, the Eifelrennen, held at the Nürburgring, was not well supported. Fangio was quickest in practice and initially led the race. Then he and Stirling swopped places several times, with the British driver setting the fastest lap of the race, and breaking Lang's 1952 record, on his fifth tour. Fangio crossed the line one-tenth of a second ahead of Moss.

Stirling could probably have beaten the great Fangio at the 'Ring but as number two he treated him with due respect and played the team game.

JUNE

1955 Calendar

5 Belgian Grand Prix, Spa Francorchamps - 2nd in W196

11 Le Mans 24 Hour Race - Moss/Fangio leading after 9 hours when 300 SLRs withdrawn by Mercedes-Benz

19 Dutch Grand Prix, Zandvoort - 2nd in W196

On the first day of June, Stirling was up early and went to a cocktail party and luncheon in Brussels in celebration of the opening of a new Mercedes-Benz plant. "Later swopped my 220 with John Claes for his G.T. Lancia as I had scraped my car's side!" He and John Fitch then headed off for Spa where Stirling met up with Alf Francis. Referring to his troublesome 250F Maserati, he recorded, "Heard big ends have gone and no spares due to oversize crank!"

In preparation for the forthcoming Belgian Grand Prix, Stirling was out practising next evening in the W196 in the early evening. His best lap on the challenging Spa circuit was a 4.24 with the long wheelbase car and 4.25 in his own. Fangio was streets ahead on 4.18 but third fastest was Frère on 4.30. "I'm still learning the course. Got 8,900 on the straight. 4th a little low."

After an interview with Courtnay Edwards next morning, Stirling played golf and lost. Peter Garnier arrived with various things for him and Stirling 'phoned Sally Weston. Interestingly, practice was again in the evening, from 6pm till 8.30pm.

"Juan now has the practice car! Karl has the other long car! Self the short, brakes inboard." It is curious that Stirling, having surely demonstrably established himself by this stage of the season, was not more favoured. Fangio was, of course, very much the number one driver and Hermann and Kling were, of course, German! "I did 4.22 in Juan car of yesterday (1/10 faster than him!) and 4.19.2 in my car." Fangio was precisely one second quicker that day and Castellotti was a tenth faster still.

The Mercedes 'train' dominated the Belgian Grand Prix with Stirling finishing just behind his mentor.

GRAND PRIX DE BELGIQUE

Formule Internationale 1

★

5 JUIN 1955

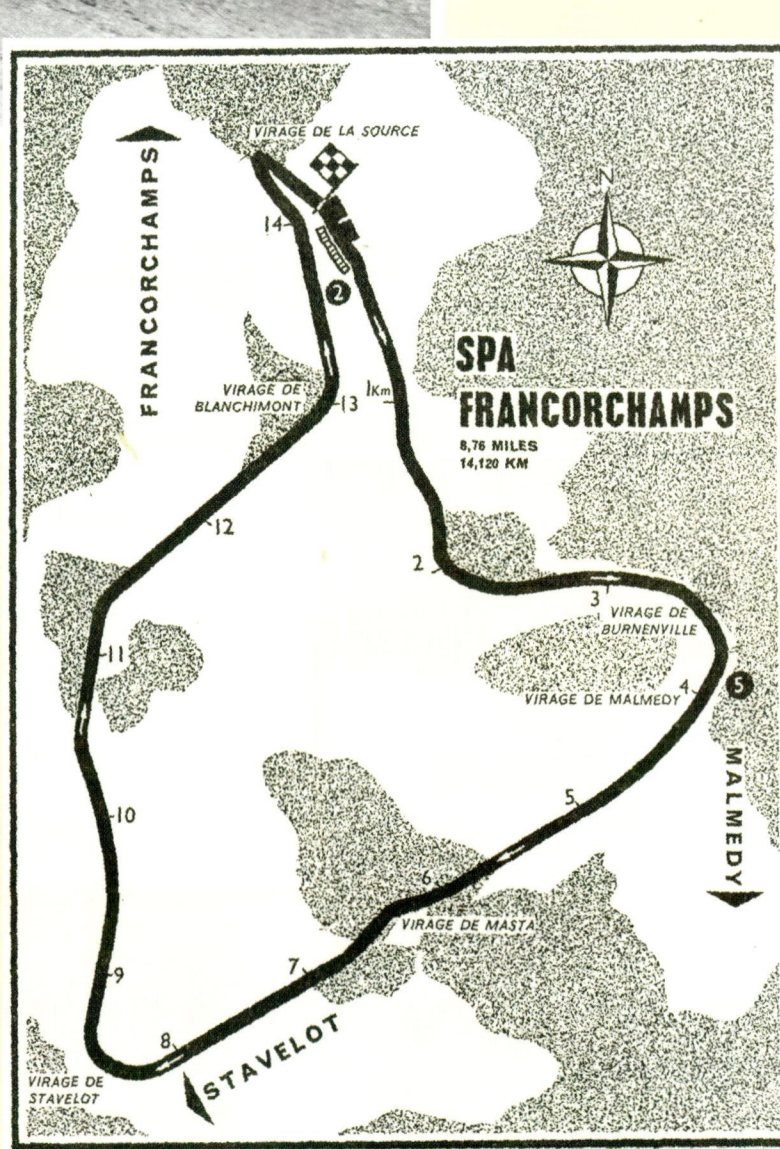

SPA FRANCORCHAMPS
8,76 MILES
14,120 KM

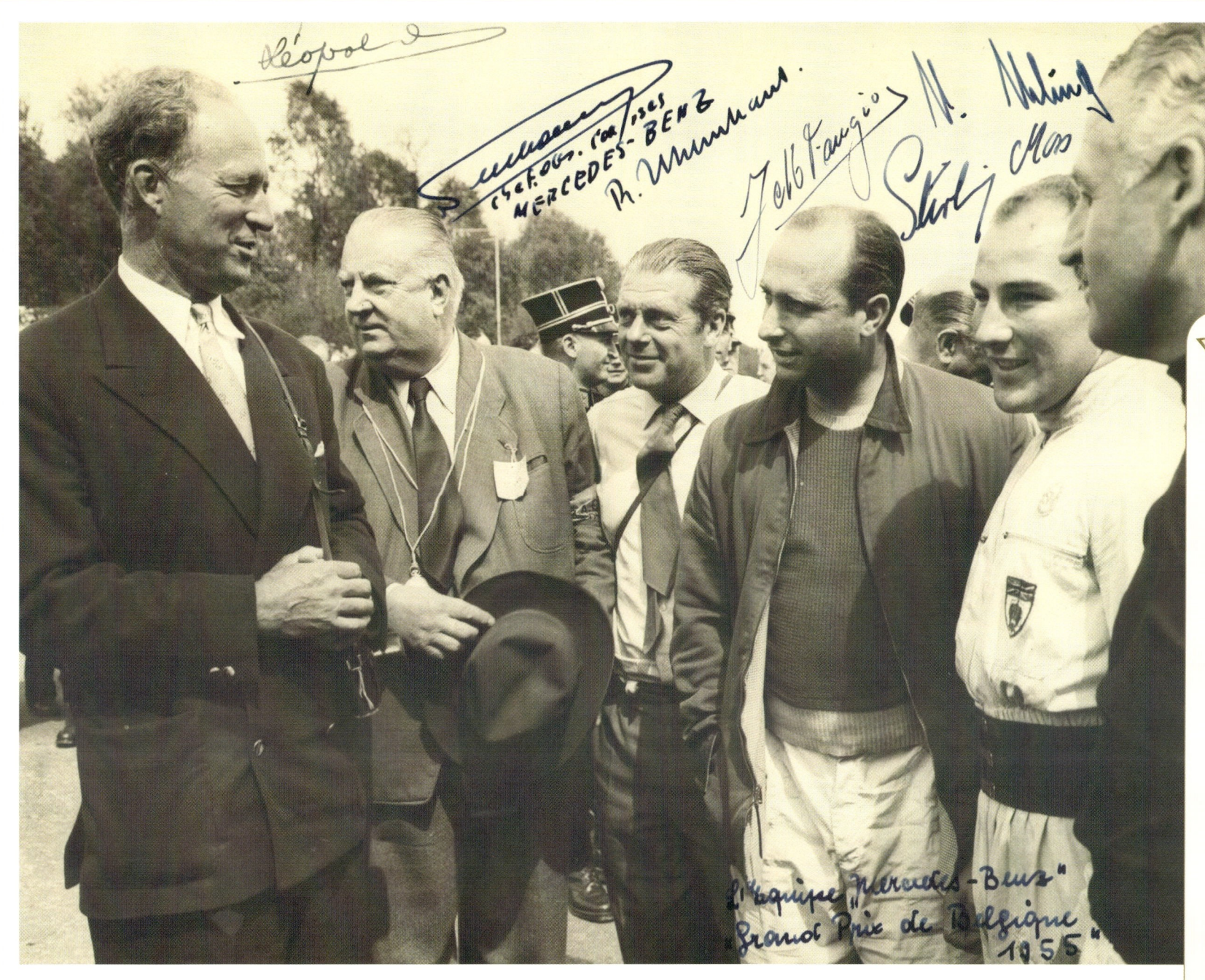

From left: **Prince Leopold, Alfred Neubauer, Rudi Uhlenhaut, Juan Manuel Fangio, Stirling and Karl Kling.**

Drivers

Moss on: Paul Frère ...

"Another who was very competent. Rather like Taruffi, he studied the art of driving. I don't think he ever had enormous flashes of brilliance but he was consistently very good. A thinking driver."

Drivers

Moss on: Hans Hermann ...

"Hans Hermann was a good polished driver. Very nice guy - good driver actually, quite fast and a fun guy. On high speed courses he was very quick."

Stirling Moss ...

DE-BRIEFINGS

"We usually had a de-briefing when we had been out practicing. We'd sit down all together with Rudi Uhlenhaut and Alfred Neubauer, but Neubauer was in the background rather than the foreground. If it was to do with running the team, he was in the foreground, but when there was a technical de-briefing it wasn't really much to do with him.

"We'd sit down and talk about how the cars were going and we'd have the practice times and I would say I could go a bit quicker if we did this or that and Fangio would usually follow what I would say, that sort of thing. At that meeting we had the chief mechanic there. It wasn't as it is today [each modern F1 driver having his own race engineer and mechanics]. The chief mechanic was the chief mechanic and then under him would be individual guys who looked after their areas.

"Fangio and I had a good relationship. Actually, contrary to many people's belief, Fangio, as far as I could see, was no engineer, anymore than I am. But I certainly knew if I wanted higher or lower gears, higher or lower ratio steering and so on and normally Fangio would follow what I'd chosen, which was quite interesting. I would say, 'Well listen, I would particularly like a higher third gear' and then he would say, 'Yea, me as well'.

STIRLING MOSS AGAIN

FRANCORCHAMPS, Sunday.— Stirling Moss, second to Juan Fangio in the Belgian Grand Prix motor race, today won the Winston Churchill Challenge Cup for the second year by being the best placed Briton.—Reuter.

Rather akin to the PR-fuelled life of today's Grand Prix drivers, Stirling spent the Saturday morning at a BP reception, followed by a Mercedes lunch. "Heard my b. Maser has thrown a rod whilst running in! Practice. They sent me out on bald tyres. 5.52 and I was frightened. Changed and did 4.55.2!" Judging by the times, the circuit must have been extremely wet so how very odd to send Moss out on 'bald tyres'. The thought of driving through the immensely challenging high speed Eau Rouge on virtual slicks in the wet is enough to frighten even the armchair reader!

The large crowds made getting to the circuit quite tricky - this was long before the days of the precious mega-stars being flown in by helicopter. "Met the ex-King who seemed most charming. At 3pm we started. I was 3rd into the first corner and 2nd after 300 yds. We continued this way all the race. Behra crashed but was OK. Kling had an oil pipe break. Reception and packed.

"Up early because Neubauer paid me." Later Stirling drove to Paris. "Poor John Lyons was killed today." John was the only son of William Lyons, the founder of Jaguar. His tragic death on his way to Le Mans would have a considerable impact on the future course of events with this great British company. It was a bad beginning to a cataclysmic week.

Wednesday was spent at Le Mans with scrutineering after lunch at Champagne. "Practice at night. I did one fast lap 4.24 (baulked). 7,200 on the straight. Juan 4.31. Jags 4.34 & Ferraris. On pulling away from the pits a Panhard hit my back and two persons. Neubauer waved me out. I received a Marvin watch today. The airbrake is fantastic. Coffee at Grubers. Bed at 3.15am."

Next morning Stirling visited Jean Behra, who was in hospital due to the accident in the pits the previous night, and bought some overshoes. The circuit was "dampish" but SM lapped in 4.15.3 in daylight and 4.16.1 in the dark. "Got 7,300, out-braked the D-types!! Juan 4.17.6, Ferraris and Jags 4.20 & 4.21. Food at Grubers. Bed at 2.15am."

Friday: "Up late and lunch at Faison d'Ore. N.G. Drivers' meeting for two hours & photos … to circuit. Only did a couple of laps and then fini."

The fateful Saturday began with Stirling rising late as usual. Fangio and Moss were paired together in a 300SLR. "Juan started and had a bad start. -30 secs at 1st lap. Caught it all up

by GERARD WALTER

STIRLING MOSS could earn £20,000 this year. That sounds a lot of money, but he would be lucky to keep £8,000 of it after he has paid taxes and met the expenses of his office and staff in the Strand, and his flat in West Kensington.

As a freelance racing driver in 1953 Moss earned £10,000, but he was able to bank only one-tenth of that sum.

The life of a racing driver is necessarily an expensive one. Moss, for instance, receives between five thousand and seven thousand fan letters a year, every one of which receives a personal reply, either from Moss himself or, during his frequent absences abroad—he reckons to spend only two weeks in England of the 52—from Ken Gregory, who runs the "firm" of Stirling Moss Ltd., and is empowered to make contracts and appointments.

a bore, but...

Correspondence alone swallows up £400 each year. Moss does not begrudge this money. He confided to me that letter-writing is a bore to him and that the autographing of thousands of photographs of himself is a "chore" which he tackles with reluctance. He appreciates, however, that this kind of thing is part of the payment for success.

"If a person is sufficiently interested in me to sit down and write to me," he says, "then he or she is entitled to get a courteous reply. The letters and requests for auto-

Moss—in a Jaguar—takes the Le Mans circuit at high speed

Picture: LOUIS KLEMANTASKI

He goes through life in top gear

Drivers

Moss on: Karl Kling...

"Kling, if he could have been a little bit slower, would have been better. He was inclined to crash it and people who are inclined to crash, hopefully, if they just go that little bit slower, then do well. I mean the best example to my mind is John Surtees. Following him, you would see more of the front of his car than the back, because he was so wild. But then he quietened down and became World Champion, and rightly so."

Belgian Grand Prix

Castellotti, Fangio and Moss shared the front row with the lone Lancia actually fastest by half a second. The tragic loss of Ascari and the absence of Villoresi were keenly felt by the Lancia team, and Ferrari and Maserati were just not competitive on the wonderful Francorchamps circuit. Following Ascari's sad demise, Gianni Lancia had announced that his team would be disbanded and Castellotti had to persuade Lancia to lend him a car to enter privately. Johnny Claes was supposed to be driving the Moss 250F but the engine expired during practice.

In front of a record crowd and the Belgian Royal Family, Fangio took an immediate lead and Stirling overtook Castellotti for second spot during the first lap. The Mercedes 'train' then remorselessly pulled away from the rest of the field who were left to squabble amongst themselves. At half distance, the game Lancia retired with a split gearbox. Neubauer joyously threw his hat under Fangio's wheels as he crossed the line, followed by Stirling a dutiful eight seconds behind.

Farina finished third and in fourth, and the only other car on the same lap, was local man Paul Frère in another Ferrari. This brought the crowd to their feet and the police completely failed to keep the crowd back. Autosport stated that "in next to no time the paddock area was like a London tube station in the rush hour".

Stirling was covered from head to foot in oil and the floor of the cockpit was said to be virtually awash with the lubricant. It was then discovered that a large nail had buried itself in one of Stirling's rear tyres and, as the mechanics pushed the car through the paddock, the tyre deflated. If the race had been a lap longer…

das AUTO MOTOR UND SPORT

EIFEL-RENNEN
GROSSER PREIS VON BELGIEN
SIE WOLLEN NACH SPANIEN?

HEFT 12
STUTTGART, 11. JUNI 1955
DM 1.20

Stirling Moss ...

BALD TYRES

"Normally 'bald' tyres on a formula car would not really matter, because they wouldn't be really bald. They would be very low tread and very low tread is when you've got fairly limited adhesion. The tyre change made a hell of a difference."

GO RACING WITH STIRLING MOSS

WHAT is it like to travel at racing speed with Stirling Moss in his Mercedes round the Nurburg circuit? Gerard Walter knows; he has done it. And he writes:

A roar and a splutter as of a hundred machine-guns and, with a swiftness for which one was not prepared, the stands were a smudge, the banners alongside the initial straight a flash as of a sword whipped from the scabbard ...

The STIRLING MOSS STORY by Gerard Walter starts in the News Chronicle on MONDAY

11.6.55

Playing Second Fiddle

PP: "Was it tempting to challenge Fangio when you spent so much time following him?"
SM: "Not really, no. I was very content being in second place to Fangio. It's difficult to describe but I was quite happy to be in second because it was such an easy race for me. I hadn't got to make the decisions, I'd got nothing to worry about, other than, well, just keeping within the rev. limit, doing all the things one needs to do. I felt if he was first and I was second, it was one-two, or it could have been two-one - does it really matter?

"I did not think, 'I could pip him here,' because he could probably have taken me somewhere else. What was the point? I was always there to back him up. We got known as 'the train' because we were so close. I really enjoyed being number two to Fangio."

and then there was an awful crash of Levegh's. Over 70 persons killed & 100 injured! I took over at 6.40 & lapped in 4 min 06. When I gave over, we had nearly three laps lead. Juan drove until 12.45, I drove for about 1 hour & then we withdrew. This was Fitch's idea & I disagreed. Big fight with SW. Bed at 4.30."

Sunday saw SM in Paris where he checked into the Miami and went to see *Battle Cry* (G) and ate at the Calvados (G). Bed at 4.45. Monday was pretty relaxed as well and he, SW, Fitch, Walt and Earl saw *Rear Window* before going to Walt's club. Bed at 5.00am. Tuesday he lunched with Fitch and Lance Macklin's parents at the Pam-Pam and took SW to see *Torch Song* (G). Later he and John Fitch went to Nouvelle Eve. Maintaining his average of a film a day, on Wednesday he saw *The Barefoot Contessa* (F).

Thursday was a more sombre day. "Met Neubauer & Co. Went to poor Levegh's funeral. It was ghastly. Film & cameramen in church!" He later drove from Paris to Zandvoort in Holland for the Dutch GP.

Next day he "had a test do" or what today we would call testing. "Time 1.42. Juan 1.44. Later real practice. I did 1.40.0 in Juan (practice that was) car & was baulked. I did 1.40.4 in my car! His has short chassis & outboard brakes & is better, but doesn't feel better!"

Saturday practice did not go well with Stirling's best being a 1.41.8, whereas Kling managed 1.41.2, Fangio a 1.40.0 and Hawthorn equalled his compatriot's time. SM went off to a cocktail party and dined with his father and SW.

For the Dutch Grand Prix, Stirling, "Had a bad start and was 3rd in 1st corner, Musso 2nd, pushed through behind pits & so Juan and I remained 1st & 2nd through the race & finished thus. Musso 3rd, Mieres 4th. Lapped Mike 3x! Big Merc party. VG."

On Monday Stirling and SW headed back to Paris. They had dinner and then he met Olga. Next day he drove to Cannes, doing the journey in bad rain in 9hs 50mins including lunch. He checked into the Oasis in La Napoule. When he 'phoned SW next morning, he found he had her passport. Having sent it off express, he drove to Juan les Pins and booked into the Hotel Provincal "800F!" He kept fit by doing some swimming and water-skiing and finished the day having "a noggin with Michael Pertwee". Michael was a writer and brother of actor Jon and cousin to actor Bill. All three were, at that time, involved in a BBC comedy series called 'Round The Bend'.

Cars

W 196 R

The W196, which was first used by Mercedes for the 1954 season, was based on a multi-tubular chassis frame, giving both light weight and good rigidity. The 2½-litre straight eight engine was front-mounted and to reduce its height was canted over at an angle. Fuel injection was used and a new type of valve operation developed. Known as desmodronic valves, this system eliminated the traditional valve spring. This positive control gave considerably improved acceleration values. The drive was taken from the centre of the drive shaft which had several advantages, including the elimination of a flywheel and the ability to run the prop shaft along the driver's seat to further lower the centre of gravity. Dry sump lubrication and a 5-speed gearbox were used.

Front brakes were initially inboard and used large finned drums of light alloy and cast iron construction. They were mounted inboard to minimise unsprung weight but were later moved outboard. A single-pivot swing axle with low pivot point was used at the rear with the drum brakes again being mounted inboard. Independent front suspension was by top and bottom wishbones and telescopic dampers.

An all-enveloping body was used for the high speed courses and known as the 'Streamliner'. The 1955 season began with a new version of the 'open-wheeler' with a shorter wheelbase - 88 ½"(224cms) instead of 92" (234cms). The power unit was now producing 280hp.

The Air-brake

At Le Mans, Mercedes employed an air-brake in an attempt to offset the advantage the Jaguars enjoyed with their disc brakes. It worked extremely well and though it was not really understood at the time, applied downforce to the rear wheels when raised.

These shots show Karl Kling operating the novel air-brake fitted to the 300 SLRs for Le Mans. The air-brake gave a retarding force of 0.27 G at 150mph. It was hydraulically operated by a lever in the cockpit.

Air-brake In Action

PP: "Practicing for Le Mans you out-braked a D-type, which was very impressive, with the 300 SLR with the air-brake!"

SM: "That's amazing. What you have to remember is that the air-brake is incredibly efficient at high speed. It was even efficient at relatively low speeds, but when you were coming down at 175, 180 and flick the whole thing up, it really would slow you up. At the same time, I would be just putting my foot on the brakes to warm them up so that they wouldn't fracture the drums. Because the problem with the big wide wheel drums, 5" wide or 4" or whatever, is that if you suddenly brake hard, creating a tremendous amount of heat in them, they were quite prone to cracking. So we would flick the air-brake up and more or less rest your foot on the brake to get the heat in, then start bringing it in, as the air brake reduced in efficiency. Then the foot brake would come in and the foot brake was really quite effective, except at very high speed.

PP: "Did it take much practice to get used to using the air-brake?"

SM: "No. Although we didn't realise it at the time, the air-brake was giving us downforce. Going into corners like White House was quite difficult in, say, an Aston or a Jag. With them you would come into White House, brake and then you would set the car up, drop down a cog and it was all quite a performance. With this thing, you just slipped the old air-brake up, lifted off, then bring the brake down and accelerate. It was really a very easy nice manoeuvre."

PP: "Was it fully up or fully down, or could you have it half way?"

SM: "No, it went fully up or down, I don't think that there was any way you could have stopped it. It was one or the other and I do remember once at Le Mans when I had been through the corners leading on to the pit straight, I put my foot down and thought, 'Oh Christ, I've broken the bloody engine,' because the engine note had completely changed. There was no power, it wouldn't pull, it sounded flat. I looked in the rear view mirror and I realised that the air-brake was still up. It made that much difference!"

Air-brake Dramas

"The brakes on the Jag were far better but the Merc was more powerful. On the straight, if we were behind a Jaguar, we could keep up with it. If we were alongside, we probably weren't quite as fast - but there wasn't much difference. But we had the air-brake. 'Lofty' England was the first to leap up and down say, 'You can't allow that'. 'Why not?' he was asked. 'Because if my drivers are following they can't see when this thing goes up'. So the next day we had windows cut in it, which I thought was very funny. But I could see his point."

'Lofty', however, flatly denied complaining about the device: "The scrutineers made them put windows in. How could a Mercedes driver see behind in his mirror with this thing sticking up?"

Did the airbrake create any problems for the other drivers? It has been stated that it caused turbulence and restricted visibility for those following.

"I asked Mike Hawthorn," said England, "about visibility and he said, 'No, I just have a look around the outside'."

Fangio's Poor Start

The reason Fangio had made a poor start was that the gear lever disappeared up his trouser leg when he jumped into the 300 SLR he was sharing with Stirling!

Thursday was spent indulging in more water-skiing and swimming before he drove to the Eden Roc. He then felt dreadful and had to go to bed. A doctor was called and administered some pills.

He was better by next day and went off to Monaco, visiting Lance Macklin's new villa. In the evening he went to the Casino and watched the show, finishing the evening at the Whisky A Go-Go in Cannes with friends Larry and Pauline, and Jackie. Saturday saw him water-skiing and swimming again. "Used my lung to 40ft at Eden Roc." That evening, he went to the Whisky A Go-Go again and danced until 5.30 before going for a final swim.

Sunday consisted of more of the same and in the evening he saw Joan Rhodes - not another conquest but a well-known 'strong woman' who performed a show on stage. The Riviera lifestyle continued until the end of the month.

The Marvin Watch

*The **Marvin** watch, which was first produced in 1850, had a glamorous past and they were particularly popular in the USA. Based at St-Imier, in the French-speaking part of the Bernese Jura mountains, Marvin watches were favoured by the rich and successful, including racing drivers such as Fangio and Ascari.*

Variations On A W196 Theme

It seems amazing how many variations Mercedes had of the W196. At different times, there were long, short and medium wheelbase versions of the open wheeler W196s, and the Streamliners. "Yes, they had quite a lot, but they would shuffle them around. Obviously the long car was beneficial at Spa with the long wheelbase and I had the short one with inboard brakes, which really was a bugger."

Stirling Moss ...

ONE SIZE DOES NOT FIT ALL

"When I was first told I was to drive with Fangio, I was thrilled but there was one snag. Fangio's 'rear' was five inches broader than mine. Mercs solved it by tailoring a special contraption. When I climbed in, I pulled a couple of straps and sort of bolsters hinged down and held me firmly in place. When Fangio jumped in, he just threw the straps aside."

Fangio pits in the car he shared with Stirling. By this stage, the pair had a lead of over two laps. Note the damage to the nose. One of the 'challenges' of Le Mans was the tremendous speed differential between the most powerful cars and what Roy Salvadori described as 'the creepers'.

HOW MUCH DOES A RACING MOTORIST EARN?

FOR sheer big money, motor racing takes some beating.

Aces like Mike Hawthorn, Stirling Moss, and Fangio can earn not less than £100,000 in 15 to 20 seasons.

Most of it comes in prize-money and retainers.

Crack racing car firms gladly give their aces the prize money. And Grand Prix awards alone can put £10,000 into the laps of the team which lands the chief laurels.

This year Hawthorn and Moss get top retainers. This will give them up to £20,000, varying, of course, with success.

Then there are handsome "perks."

These include publicity fees from all sorts of sales concerns, from oil to ginger pop.

FIFTEEN to twenty seasons of this kind of cash swells an ace driver's receipts to around £300,000.

But tax takes a huge bite. And, as with film stars, there's heavy office and secretarial expenses. The fan mail bill alone can take £550 to £800 a year in photo and mail costs. There may be 8000 requests a year for photos!

Then there's heavy insurance.

For the ace the cost is £25 per £1000 cover if he goes for only one or two big events.

For Fangio, Hawthorn, and the rest it is very much higher.

They take a specially-written, personal policy.

If they want to insure for £50,000— not an out-of-the-way sum for a man with a big earning future — their premium cost will be around £2000.

A few, like the great Nuvolari, have a lifetime's racing, and go into retirement as rich men.

Les Vingt Quatre Heures Du Mans

Before a record crowd estimated at 400,000, Castellotti in a 4.4-litre Ferrari led away, followed by Hawthorn, Maglioli's Ferrari and Walters's Cunningham. The Jaguars of Beauman and Swatters were next up and then came Levegh's 300 SLR and Salvadori in the first of the Astons. Rolt had had trouble starting his D-type and was working his way through the field, as was Fangio, who within a few laps had moved from 14th to fourth.

Hawthorn was closing on Castellotti and Fangio, soon up to third, was homing in on the Englishman. For 16 laps the red, green and silver cars circulated within seconds of each other, thrilling the crowd. Then Hawthorn and Fangio overtook the Ferrari, which struggled to maintain the pace as it hotted up, the lap record falling repeatedly. Hawthorn, by his own admission driven on by his anti-German prejudice, was driving flat out with nothing in reserve. Fangio told Hawthorn afterwards that he, too, was on the absolute limit. To Mike fell the final honour of setting the fastest race lap. Side by side much of the time, they sometimes even grinned at each other in enjoyment and mutual admiration. Then, at 6.27pm, it all came to a violent and tragic end.

The pit straight was unacceptably narrow which was the main culprit. As Hawthorn pitted, Levegh struck Macklin's long-tail Austin-Healey which had moved over, rather suddenly, to avoid Hawthorn's slowing D-type. The Mercedes became an airborne projectile and struck a concrete parapet opposite the pits. Levegh was thrown out and killed instantly. The car exploded and major components, such as the engine and front suspension, scythed through the densely-packed crowd, killing more than 80.

After the appalling accident, Fangio handed over to Stirling and Hawthorn to Ivor Bueb who was entirely new to this form of racing. Not surprisingly Stirling opened up a considerable lead. Then, at 1.45, the message came through from the Mercedes directors to withdraw the leading car and the Kling/Simon car which was lying fourth. The Ferrari challenge had petered out by this stage and the Hawthorn/Bueb Jaguar was left to take a rather hollow victory, in which no-one rejoiced.

'Lofty' On The First Two Hours

"Before the race I told Hawthorn to take it steadily for the first few laps. Fangio made a bad start so was behind Hawthorn, but when Fangio closed up the dice started. It was fabulous - the best Grand Prix I'd seen in a long time…"

Stirling Moss ...

FLAT BUT NOT QUITE

"The one thing people in the pits would always listen for was whether the drivers were taking it flat through the Dunlop curve at the end of the pit straight. You would want everybody to think you were taking it flat so you'd just roll back the throttle a little bit, way back before the pits. You'd go through the pits and then it was hard on the floor! Well, that isn't really flat. It was flat but," Stirling recalls with much amusement, *"you'd drop off two or three miles per hour. It was a bull-shit situation!"*

"Right, men—lunch"

Le Mans men race again so sadly

By TOM WISDOM   ZANDVOORT, Holland, Sunday

THE men from Le Mans went racing again today, in the Dutch Grand Prix, and a crowd of 50,000, about 15,000 more than at any other race here, turned up to see them.

Mercedes cars — it was a Mercedes that went into the crowd at Le Mans, killing 82 and injuring hundreds—were first and second, with Fangio and Stirling Moss driving.

The track here seemed to me to be more dangerous than the Le Mans circuit. In the pits area—where the Le Mans disaster took place—the road is only 35ft. wide, compared with 40ft. at Le Mans.

And in place of the 5ft. earth bank between cars and spectators at Le Mans, there was a single line of straw bales and a wire netting fence that looked as if it could not stop a runaway motor mower.

Bright spot

Either of these accidents occurring at the pits could have meant another disaster.

The only bright spot is the story the Dutch tell about the course and which the Mercedes team prefer to ignore.

It was built during the war by a Dutchman who fooled the Germans into believing it was part of the Atlantic Wall. They paid for it. After the war an extra half-mile of road and a grandstand was added and the Dutch had a course for practically nothing.

Results: Fangio (Mercedes), first at 89.64 m.p.h.; Moss (Mercedes) second, 89.63 m.p.h.; Musso (Maserati) third, 89.14 m.p.h.

In the Commons today the Minister of Transport is to be asked what he is doing to make road racing safer, and the Home Secretary will be asked about steps to lessen danger to spectators.

Stirling Moss ...

THE LE MANS ACCIDENT

"I think it was just one of those dreadful racing accidents that happen. There were ingredients that caused the accident. I think if it had been Fangio and not Levegh, it probably wouldn't have happened. He had a sort of sixth sense and the skill."

Stirling Moss ...

NEUBAUER'S SENSE OF HUMOUR

"An announcement came over the PA at Le Mans that everyone in the Pits must wear an official arm band. So Neubauer takes his handkerchief out and puts it round his arm, taking the piss out of them."

Stirling Moss ...

WHY WAS IT WRONG FOR MERCEDES TO WITHDRAW?

"Because, whatever happened, they could not remedy the loss. Obviously I was thinking of my own interests - I was leading by three laps in a car that was virtually bullet-proof. I thought I was going to win it with Fangio. I just couldn't see it did anybody any good. I thought this rather theatrical gesture came close to accepting some responsibility for what happened. As to the accident, I don't think you can lay blame on anyone."

Much has been written about the awful Le Mans accident, which involved the Levegh Mercedes seen here, and most of it was ill-informed. Stirling is of the opinion that no-one was to blame and it was just a freak series of factors that all came together on that tragic day. It was what is termed 'a racing accident'. Unfortunately, it caused a panic reaction in certain countries, leading to a number of events being cancelled which made the calendar look a little thin.

Drivers

Moss on: John Fitch ...

"He was driving the 300 SL in the Mille Miglia and did a really good job, a really credible job. He was a bit slow at the TT. John was an American and Americans aren't usually as fast as Europeans because, I suppose, of the upbringing, a lack of road racing there. So, considering he didn't really know what road racing was, I think he made a pretty good job of it, particularly in the Mille. He was a good consistent driver."

SPEED IS MY BUSINESS ... by STIRLING MOSS

Mr Smith, Mrs Jones, We Race at Le Mans for YOU

treacherous parts of the circuit like the palm of their hand.

For this year's Mille Miglia went to Italy some weeks in advance to practise with the 300 SLR Mercedes

He is worth millions to Mercedes and they know it

STIRLING MOSS says that if he succeeds in winning the world championship this ... come. Potentially, Stirling Moss must be worth millions of pounds to his masters, and they certainly treat him as if ...

Hands off racing

REACTION to the recent tragedy at Le Mans seems to be: "Curb motor racing in all forms." This is a wrong attitude and the whole position should be viewed in a sober light and not in a state of panic, writes Trevor Williamson.

Motor racing is a virile sport and the imposition of a "load" of unnecessary restrictions would do nothing but harm. It would be closing the door after the horse has bolted.

Motor racing is dangerous and everybody realises it. And as such precautions for the safety of spectators and competitors must be taken.

Nobody wants to see death or injury accompanying the sport, but any effort to curb cars performances must be resisted.

To remodel tracks on the lines of the old Brooklands track would rob the sport of much of its skill. It would very largely mean the race results being decided on top speed alone.

The thought of that appals me.

Let us have sound rules governing the sport but not a general clamping down so that unreal racing results.

Though in a different category, rallies—by no stretch of the imagination can they be called races—may come under the all searching eye of the public spotlight, and heavy and outmoded restrictions placed on them.

Rallies impose tests of skill of an entirely different nature from motor racing. The accent is on timing and navigation as opposed to speed on a track.

I learn that the Alpine rally, in which Stirling Moss was to have led the British Sunbeam team, has been cancelled by the French authorities. Here is an example of another panic move.

Let us temper our action with reason. Let remember that people watch motor racing at their "own risk." Let us play the game by the competitors and spectators alike and above all, let us not have any ridiculous restrictions imposed on a great sport.

Ilford Pictorial 30.6.55

Jenks On Fright

"With Eric Oliver, we often got into what we called a 'dodgy situation' and, while I was always fully conscious of what was happening, I often knew I could not have dealt with the situation had I been riding the motor-cycle. The same with Moss; I have been in situations that I knew I could not have dealt with, in all cases because of a lack of ability, but I have known in theory what should be done, so I have relaxed and thought: 'It's up to you, chum; if you cannot sort this little lot out then no-one can.' A childlike faith, but not an unreasonable one I feel, for they usually managed to cope."

A Point Is Proven

Interestingly, Alfred Neubauer, in his book 'Speed Was My Life', details a conversation between himself and Keser. After the horrific accident, the latter suggested M-B should retire from the race but Neubauer countered that it might be taken as an admission that there was some mechanical defect. With curious logic, Keser suggested, according to Neubauer, in that case the race should be stopped. Neubauer claimed to have warned race organiser Charles Faroux before the start that the narrowness of the track and the closeness of the pits, could lead to a dangerous situation when drivers were being signalled and reacting in such a small area. His comments were sharply dismissed, as was his request for a remote signalling tower half a mile from the crowded pits. Faroux now refused, quite rightly, to stop the race in order to keep the roads clear for the ambulances. Neubauer then suggested that if Jaguar would withdraw they would do likewise. Jaguar declined. Keser attempted to contact the M-B directors in Stuttgart, which was not easy as the telephone lines had been damaged. "Then around midnight he got their verdict. Mercedes had been in the lead for several hours. They could now afford to retire."

Stirling Moss ...

SHADOWS IN THE SAND

"Neubauer got a bit upset about me following Fangio so closely. He said, 'Well what happens if Fangio has an accident?' and I said, 'Well, he doesn't have accidents. The only place where he really, really did have something to say, which I can understand, was when I followed him at Zandvoort, because all the sand got in and of course wore the engine quite a bit, because I was right behind him. There was a lot of sand on the circuit, you know, and the cars would go by and whisk it around, but they could afford to put in new pistons so it didn't matter."

After the race, the Moss engine was found to have no piston rings left!

Moss sets up record

Stirling Moss, driving a Mercedes, set a new record time for the track at Zandvoort, Holland, yesterday on a practice lap for today's Grand Prix of Holland. He averaged 93.204 m.p.h. against the previous record of 87.612 m.p.h.

Daimler-Benz, makers of the Mercedes, will not decide until today whether or not to enter their cars.—B.U.P.

B'ham Gazette 18.6.55

ZANDVOORT

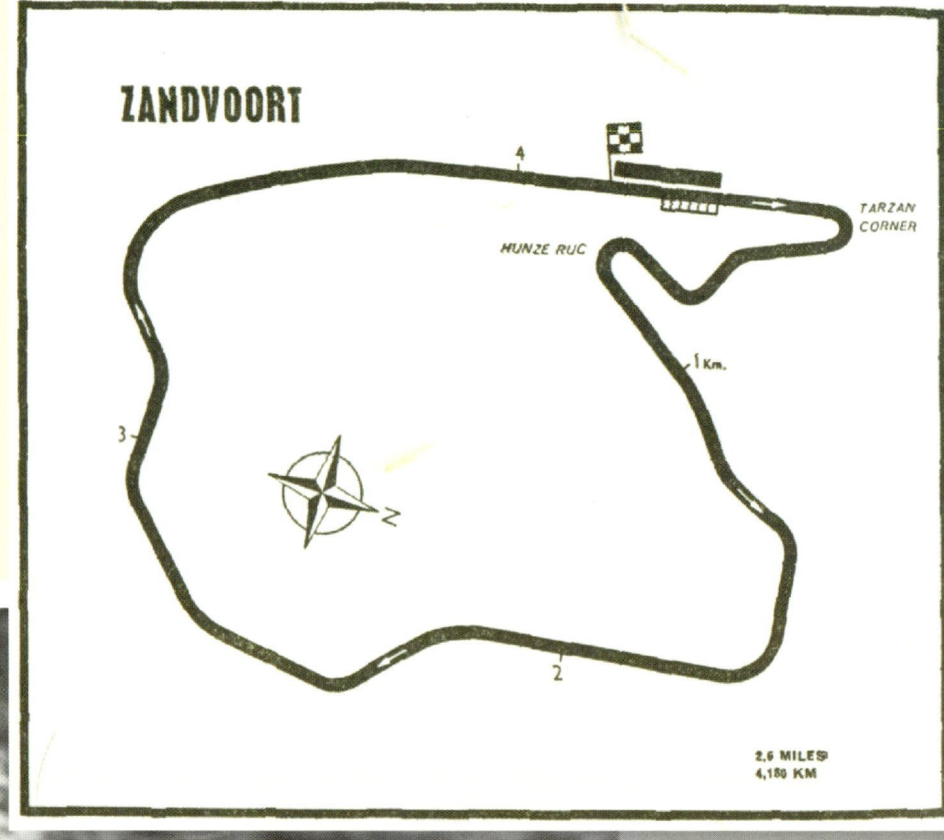

2.6 MILES
4,180 KM

This is a fine study of Stirling's relaxed, arms extended style. He has always given credit to Farina, whom he saw and admired early in his career, for influencing him in this respect.

Dutch Grand Prix

The Grand Prix of Holland took place at Zandvoort, amongst the sand dunes and close to a popular seaside resort. With a field of just 16 cars, including uncompetitive private entries, the Dutch GP was not a very thrilling affair for the crowd of 60,000. Prior to the event, Hawthorn had lost patience with the Vanwall and changed horses to Ferrari, for whom he had driven in 1954. Castellotti had also changed horses to the prancing variety but was far from happy with his Ferrari Squalo. Musso gallantly led the Maserati charge but by the end of the race would be the only competitor on the same lap as Fangio and Moss who finished in that order, with Stirling a third of a second behind at the line.

Luckily, the Dutch did not cancel their Grand Prix but, with Mercedes so dominant, it was not too thrilling a race. From a spectators' viewpoint, it is a pity that Fangio and Moss were not racing each other but Mercedes would hardly risk everything by encouraging this.

Rivalry With Hawthorn

PP: "There was a bit of friendly rivalry between you?"

SM: "Oh yes. Well, Mike was English - you were either a Hawthorn or a Moss fan, weren't you? Hawthorn was a tall, good-looking, beer-drinking, gay guy. I don't mean gay in the modern sense, I mean quite a character and I was only for the sport. I would give up anything and concentrate only on that. I didn't drink and, you know, appeared far less exciting. There was no doubt he was a very competent driver."

PP: "He varied a bit, didn't he?"

SM: "That was the problem. On his day he was terrific, but not terribly consistent. I don't think he was terribly fit. He was very fast in sports cars and could be very fast in Formula One, but not always. I actually lent him my car to race once! He was quite a good driver, nice bloke, careful with the car, so he was a good person to lend it to. I think people always felt, because there was a rivalry, that we didn't get along, which was not true."

Left to right: Jean Behra, Roberto Mières and Luigi Musso.

Walt Manarker

SM: "Walt Manarker was an American amateur. He worked for a big company in America selling carpet and was attached to the army, because he did all the carpets for the army. I will never forget, he had these creases in his overalls and he said, 'I may not be the fastest, but I am sure that I am the best dressed'. He was a real character, a really funny man. Now he is in a monastery."

Judy (Noot) Addicott: "Walt Manarker was going out with Eartha Kitt at one time."

Drivers

Moss on: Luigi Musso ...

"A bit like Mike Hawthorn, fast sometimes, really quite quick, never slow, but not a guy that one would be concerned about as a competitor. Good-looking bloke. Not quite as fast as Castellotti but a bit safer. He was only serious competition because he was in Maseratis and they were usually pretty good cars."

For the second time in a month 'the train' ran on time which must have chuffed them back at Stuttgart!

Eden Roc

The Hotel du Cap Eden Roc is set in a stunning Mediterranean pine forest at the tip of Cap d'Antibes, between Cannes and Nice. Built in 1870 in the elegant fashion of the era, it has long been a favourite of international stars and the 'jet set'. It is said to be the most expensive hotel on the Riviera.

Sally Weston is seen with Stirling at the post-race celebrations.

Crumpet Status

PP: *"You were away a lot at this time. There is little mention of any female company during the middle part of the year while you were away racing."*

SM: *"Well, I think one usually found it on the hoof. I can assure you, I didn't became a devout Catholic."*

Stirling Moss ...

WHY WATER SKIING?

"I was keen on water skiing because, 1. it gave me something to do on the beach, 2. it kept me quite fit, 3. I met some quite good-looking girls doing it and 4. it was a good outdoor thing to do."

Jenks On Art

"No doubt if I suggest that driving a car at high speed is an art, along with music, painting and literature, I should be greeted by some very cutting remarks from students of the accepted arts; but I really do consider fast driving as an art, an essentially twentieth-century art, and one demanding as much theoretical study, natural flair, learning and practice as any of the classical arts…"

Gregory On Neubauer

"Many analogies have been used to describe the remarkable Mercedes team manager, and during my association with the team he always gave me the impression of a mother hen looking after her chickens, taking his responsibilities down to the last minute detail.

"I am certainly one of the subscribers to the theory that 1955 was Moss's 'golden' year. I believe much of this was due to the fact that Alfred Neubauer was the only person in Stirling's long and brilliant racing career who ever had the personality and total authority to allow Stirling to give of his best. Such is the value of a team manager."

JULY

Calendar
1955

16	British Grand Prix, Aintree - 1st in W196
23	Civil Governor's Cup (non-championship sports car race), Monsanto, Portugal - 1st in Porsche 550

July began in frustrating fashion. Stirling spent two days driving to the Nürburgring to be told that practice was off because the German Grand Prix had been cancelled. On Monday 4th, he drove to Stuttgart where he left his 220 to have its tyres replaced and the brakes attended to while he shopped. That evening Rudi Uhlenhaut took Stirling and Jenks out for dinner.

After shopping for socks and ties, SM went to Daimler-Benz where "Fangio and I were presented with our victory pins. JF had 3! SM 1." Mercedes had also fitted Stirling's 220 with "a nicer steering wheel. Three spokes!" After lunch in Germany, he had dinner at Spa and then drove to Brussels to have a blown exhaust gasket replaced. He collected the car next morning to find, "A plug had come undone; it wasn't a gasket!" He did Brussels to Ostend in an hour, which was good going, caught a plane at Calais and was working in his office by 4.30pm.

He spent most of the week in the office, seeing Jean in the evenings. In fact, he was supposed to be leading the Sunbeam works team on the 2,000 mile Alpine Rally but the event had been cancelled, another victim of the knee-jerk reaction to the Le Mans disaster. On Friday, Stirling took Briggs Cunningham to lunch at La Rue's. On Saturday, he had lunch at Oscar Moore's with Jack Fairman before going to Tring and spending no less than three hours cleaning the 220. Sunday saw him at Brands Hatch and doing an article on Sunday driving!

After ordering a new sports jacket from his tailor on Monday morning, he had lunch at the

Back row from left: Rudi Uhlenhaut, Juan Manuel Fangio, Stirling, Karl Kling & 'Don Alfredo'. In passenger seat is Piero Taruffi and driving is Mort Morris-Goodall.

Cancellation Of Races

Following the Le Mans catastrophe, there was a great outcry in many quarters against motor racing. Autosport wrote very strongly in one editorial about "uninformed comment".

They said: "Although no-one would seek to minimise the gravity of the accident, so much rubbish has been published concerning it that it is little wonder the anti-motor racing section of the public has been given every opportunity to condemn, supported by 'by-line' fanatics in the daily Press.

It was reported at the beginning of July that the French GP, the Reims 12-Hour race, the Swiss GP, the Coppa Peronne in Italy and the Spanish GP had all been cancelled, as had the Rallye des Alpes.

A week later it was announced that the German GP was also cancelled. The German Minister of Traffic had instructed the Oberste Nationale Sports Kommission to ensure that the safety of the public at the Nürburgring was guaranteed. The necessary work could not be completed in time. Like Le Mans, the pit straight was far too narrow. Furthermore, it was felt there was not a "friendly atmosphere" toward the sport at that time.

Jean Clarke

Jean Clarke was a 22-year-old Scottish model who was to have a long career in television. She was ITV's 'Miss Televisual' in 1955 when Stirling met her. They went out for several months.

Stirling should have been on the Alpine Rally, his only rally of 1955, in early June but the event was cancelled as a result of the Le Mans disaster.

Steering Wheel Club with Jack Fairman. That evening he met Pat Scott, saw a film and thence to the Colony Club. Bed at 4am.

Wednesday began with Stirling cleaning the flat before meeting French motoring journalist and photographer Bernard Cahier and Roberto Mières for lunch at the 'Wheel'. Leaving at 2.30, he had a "noggin" at Tring before driving to Liverpool, being very British and having tea en route. After dinner at the Rembrandt, he continued to Southport and a party. It should be remembered that this was before the days of motorways.

With the British GP at Aintree at the end of the week, Stirling spent Thursday and Friday at the circuit practising. On Thursday, he was quickest with a "2.00.6 for ftd in short car & 2.01.4 in med. car. Juan did 2.01.8 & 2.02.4. 3rd was Behra at 2.02.8. Kling 4th in 2.03.6, Taruffi 2.04.4'" That evening he went to the Mayor's "do" and dinner with SW.

He spent Friday morning at the funfair with sister Pat and Alf Francis before going to the circuit after a light lunch. He did 10 laps setting fastest time again with 2.00.4. "Juan 2.00.6, Behra 2.01.2 (?) [actually 2.01.4 to be precise], Kling 2.02, Taruffi [who had been drafted into the M-B team, following Hermann's nasty accident at Monaco] 2.03, Shell in Vanwall 2.03.8! Cocktail party with Mrs Topham."

Saturday was to mark an important milestone. "Up late, breakfast & to circuit. Aston 1, 2, 3 & 4. Coopers 1, 2, 3, 4 also. Drivers' parade in Healeys (24) & start at 2.30. I took the lead in two laps due to Behra's proximity. Let Fangio lead later and at 29 laps took the lead to the end. Lap record on 89th lap, 2.00.4. Juan 2nd, Kling 3rd, Taruffi 4th, Cas/Haw 6th, Musso 5th. Two broadcasts & to Southport. Food & then a party at Mr. Holland's (toffee maker!). Bed at 2am."

Thus was recorded in diary staccato Stirling's maiden Grand Prix victory. To this day he does not know whether Fangio let him win. The official margin was two-tenths of a second. Photographs show it was one car's length.

Back down to earth on Sunday, he attended a christening, had tea with friends, took part in a photo session and ended up at La Popot with Ken Gregory and Shelagh. Next evening he saw *Kismet* (VG). A full Tuesday included hearing about the BRM from Harry [Mundy?] and cousin Audrey calling round to show Stirling her poodle! He met Jean that night and they watched sister Pat showjumping. Next morning

Stirling and the rest of the Mercedes team meet the Mayor of Southport!

The Moss Maserati

Stirling's own 250F, which was driven by a variety of people during the season with mixed results, was to be handled by Lance Macklin at Aintree. After Spa, Alf Francis and Tony Robinson had taken the car back to the Maserati works at Modena, stripped it and fitted a replacement engine. Back at their base at Tring, Alfred suggested painting the car a different colour. "After three blow-ups," he said to Alf, "it is about time we had some colour other than green."

Francis, who was Polish but had settled in Britain after demobilization from the 1st Polish Armoured Division after the War, suggested the Polish national colours of red and white, but Mr. Moss insisted on grey. However, John Morgan, the B.A.R.C. Secretary was not too pleased when they arrived at Aintree and asked them to "repaint it in some shade of green". Alf spent three hours "slapping green distemper all over the car, having paid a local garage hand £1 to help me".

Macklin, probably off-form after the dreadful Le Mans accident the previous month, was initially nine seconds slower than Stirling's lap record in a 250F and Alf Francis made the point that Moss, who would record the fastest lap of the race, was only two-tenths quicker in the W196 than he had been in the Maserati in 1954. In his book, he again makes the point that, in his opinion, if Stirling had been leading the Maserati team he would still have beaten Fangio in the race and by a greater margin. Having said that, only one of the four works Maseratis finished, plus Macklin.

British GP - The Entry

The 1955 race attracted works teams from Mercedes-Benz, Ferrari, Maserati, Gordini, Vanwall, Connaught and Cooper, plus privately entered Connaughts and Maseratis.

There was an interesting variation of engine configurations with Mercedes relying on eight cylinders; Maserati, Gordini and Cooper-Bristol six cylinders, and Ferrari, Connaught and Vanwall just four. Mercedes entered four cars (Fangio, Moss, Kling and Taruffi), Ferrari three cars (Hawthorn, Castellotti and Trintignant), Maserati no less than eight with privateers (works - Behra, Musso, Mières and Simon; private - Salvadori, Gould, Collins and Macklin in the Moss car), Gordini three cars (Manzon, Sparken and da Silva Ramos), Connaught some four cars (works - Fairman and McAlpine; private - Rolt and Marr), Vanwall a couple (Wharton and Schell) and Cooper just one (Brabham).

Stirling's father, Alfred, and sister, Pat, are seen at Aintree where they would have much to celebrate.

British GP - The Circuit

The third circuit to be used for a British Grand Prix was Aintree, some five miles from the centre of Liverpool. It was, and is, rather more famous for horse racing.

The first official horse racing took place there in 1829 and in 1949 the landowner, Lord Sefton, sold the course to the Topham family. They appointed ex-Gaiety Girl Mirabel Topham to manage it. In 1953, she had the idea of creating a motor racing circuit around the steeplechase course and five GPs would be held there from 1955, with the events alternating with Silverstone, apart from 1962.

The circuit was three miles in length and, according to Autosport, this was the first time the British GP would be run on a 'road circuit', though one publication described it as "flat and featureless". The lap record was held by Stirling in 2.00.6, driving a Maserati the previous October.

Stirling Moss does fastest practice lap

STIRLING MOSS, driving for the Mercedes-Benz team, put up the fastest time in yesterday's practice at Aintree for the British Grand Prix there tomorrow.

The official teams of Mercedes-Benz, the Ferraris, Maseratis, and Gordinis, and the British hopes—the Vanwalls, the Connaughts and a Cooper—were all at practice.

Moss, who holds the lap speed record at 89.55 m.p.h., which he set up last October in a Maserati, exactly equalled that time in the Mercedes yesterday (2min. 0.6sec.).

At first sight

His team mate, Juan Fangio, the reigning world champion, had a fastest lap of 88.68 m.p.h., and, in the team's practice car, did 88.24 m.p.h., although he had never before seen the difficult three-mile circuit.

The Maseratis of Jean Behra, Andre Simon and Roberto Mieres all did fast times, and Mike Hawthorn, in the fastest of the Ferraris, achieved a lap in 2min. 5.8sec.

Ken Wharton's Vanwall lapped in 2min. 8.4sec., and the best Connaught (Peter Walker) did 2min. 10.8sec.

M'chester Daily Desp' 15.7.55

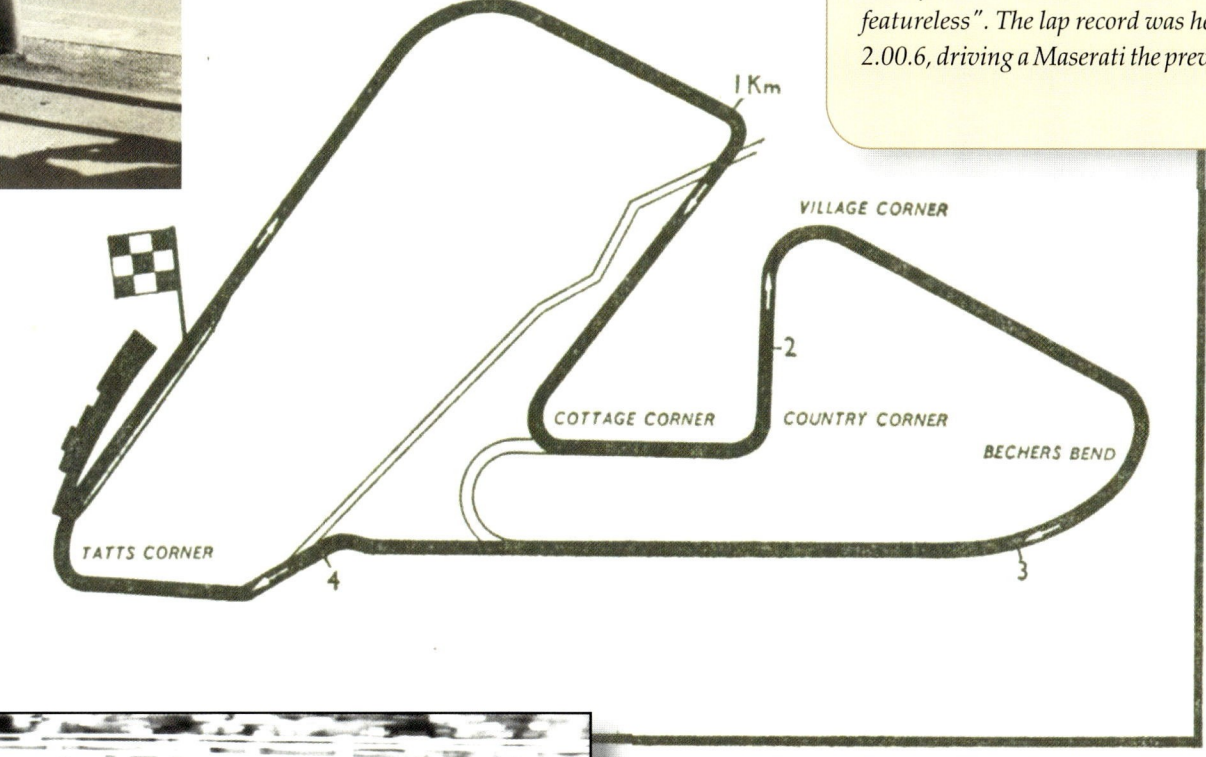

The Aintree circuit was three miles (4.84kms) in length and of generous width, which was a sensitive issue at that time. Indeed, Mercedes had sent Uhlenhaut over in late June to 'approve' the circuit before committing to a full entry.

he was up early and off to Crystal Palace "and did a TV film with Penny -". That night he and SW saw *Doctor At Sea* (VG).

On Thursday Stirling and SW flew from London Airport to Lisbon for the Civil Governor's Cup race at Monsanto Park in Portugal. He was to drive a small Porsche 550 but recorded in his diary, "Car too big for me".

A different seat was fitted next day and Stirling's fastest lap of 2.27 was seven seconds quicker than the next Porsche. "The 550 gives 7,000 rpm on the straight = 190kph. Brakes are inclined to lock. Car feels nice. Oil = 100°C. Max rpm 7,500 rpm. To cocktails by Maschranios and later … food and fairground."

After lunch on Saturday 23rd at the British Club, Stirling headed to the circuit. "Had a fair start but over-revved. Took the lead. All OK. Finished 1.05 ahead, media 131kph. Ftd lap in 2.25.6! Second was 2.29. Food with the Civil Governor at the Tennis Club and then Charles Laidly took … us out to do the town. Bed at 4.30am."

On the Sunday Stirling watched Masten Gregory win his race before attending a reception at the Autoclub. He then went to a nightclub. "Met Shani & danced. Bed at 5.30am."

After collecting his starting money, Stirling flew next day to Frankfurt and proceeded to the Nürburgring. Tuesday was to be the first of several days of testing with Mercedes. SM tried three different single-seaters - a medium length car with inboard brakes, a medium car with outboard brakes and a short car, also with outboard brakes. This last combination gave both Fangio and Moss their best times, with both under Lang's 1939 lap record. In each car, though, the Argentine master was a few seconds quicker than his British pupil. However, as soon as they changed to the 300 SLR sports car, Stirling was 2.1 seconds quicker than his team leader. He was also 22 seconds quicker than Kling. Chief Engineer Uhlenhaut was only 2.9 seconds adrift of Kling and almost eight seconds quicker than von Trips though, as Stirling very fairly noted, this was the first time he had driven an SLR.

"*Life* people have sent a photographer here for a colour shot for *Sports Illustrated's* cover!"

On Wednesday, Stirling circulated in a 190 SL (12.25) and 300 SL (10.45). "I think Mercs will give me an SL for Oulton & let me have it early." That evening Moss, Fangio and several other drivers went to the cabaret at the Park Hotel in

British GP - The Scene

In the course of a few weeks in which Britons took the World's speed record for solo motor cycles, raised the sidecar record and Donald Campbell set a new water speed record, Stirling won the British Grand Prix.

The crowds were unprecedented and estimated at 145,000. Liverpool had never seen such traffic jams and the famous tunnel was packed solid for hours. Many people missed the supporting races and, when they did arrive, the facilities sounded excessively primitive. The paddock surface was a loose ash surface which is hardly conducive to keeping engines and components clean.

Instead of the tradition of drivers walking behind their cars as they were pushed on to the grid, the organisers, the B.A.R.C. (British Automobile Racing Club) thought up a novel innovation. The drivers were taken round the track in a parade of white Austin-Healeys. When the drivers were announced, Fangio, Moss and Hawthorn received a thunderous roar of support.

Autosport reckoned that, with a profusion of flags fluttering in the glorious weather, Aintree was blessed with something close to a genuine Grand Prix atmosphere. "Hot-weather dress was the rule everywhere, and practically every woman wore sun-tops, brightly hued skirts and, of course, sun-glasses and plenty of lipstick. Some of the men wore pyjama tops that looked like shirts, and others donned shirts that looked like pyjama tops. There was even a Scotsman in the paddock area wearing a kilt, no shirt, and a broad sombrero."

As many of the spectators arrived with their cars boiling, shirt-sleeved policemen asked people blocking the view of those in the grandstands to move further back. It was said that the spectators on the inside of track "became as black as sweeps from dust set up by cinders". Within 30 seconds of 2.30pm, 'Ebby' Ebblewhite, the famous Brooklands handicapper, raised his flag as a signal to start their engines.

Stirling in pensive mood before the start. He had looked set for his first Grand Prix win at Monaco when bad luck robbed him of the spoils. Where better to open his GP account than his home race?

Drivers

Moss on: JEAN BEHRA ...

"A really good tough competitor. Wouldn't give an inch. Not dirty, but hard. A lot of ability and once you had passed him, you couldn't discount him. With a lot of people, once you passed them, you discount them because they were not 'racers'. Mike [Hawthorn] was a bit like that, you know, and Fangio. In fact, many drivers were. Jean was what I would call a 'racer' and there were very few racers ever.

"I don't mean he was one of the great drivers, but he would always really have a go. It wasn't easy being a racer."

Stirling discusses his scooter with Lance Macklin who was to drive the Moss Maserati, seen on the left. Stirling has always favoured scooters as a great way to get around and rides a modern variation to this day.

STIRLING MOSS GETS HIS BIG CHANCE

By DEREK HARRIS,
Our Motoring Correspondent

BRITAIN'S No. 1 motoring marvel, Stirling Moss, stands his best chance ever of being the first British driver to win the British Grand Prix on Saturday at Aintree.

Moss will be driving one of three Mercedes cars which are now "favourites" for the Grand Prix after a brilliant season so far this year.

He knows the Aintree circuit intimately, while the only man likely to beat him — world champion Juan Fangio — has never yet raced there.

Moss holds the Aintree lap record of 89.55 miles an hour, but this will almost certainly be smashed on Saturday. The Mercedes team, who travel to their Southport headquarters on Wednesday, will begin practising on Thursday to give Fangio, Karl Kling and reserve driver Piero Taruffi a knowledge of the circuit.

There will be five other strong works teams in the Grand Prix — from Maserati, Ferrari, Gordini, Vanwall and Connaught — as well as a number of brilliant independent entries.

M'chester Eve Chron' 11.7.55

JULY 1955

Sun rises 4.0 **Saturday 16** Sun sets 8.11
(197-168)

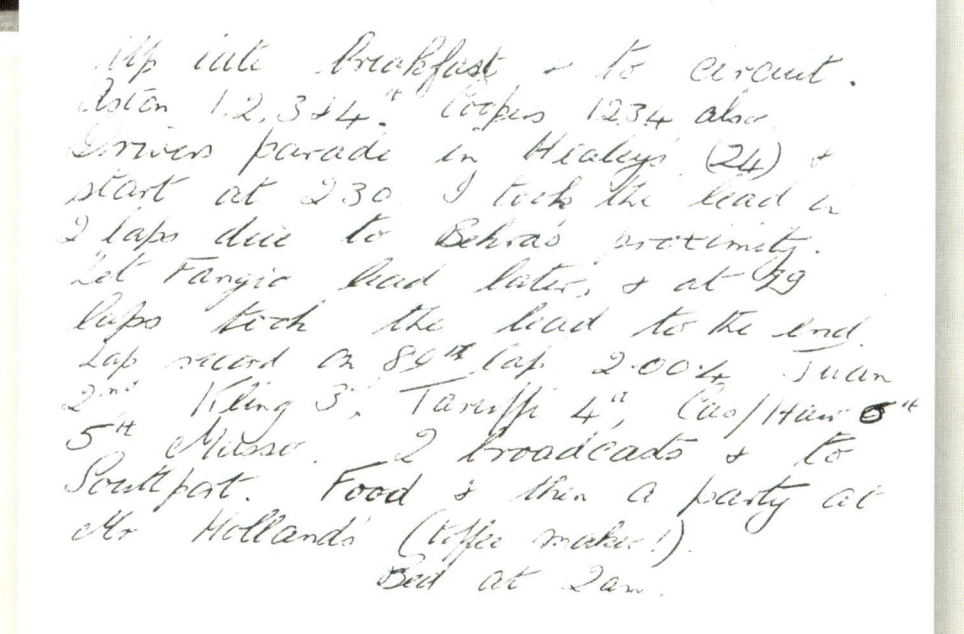

Up late, breakfast + to circuit. Aston 1,2,3+4th Coopers 1,2,3,4 also. Drivers parade in Healeys (24) + start at 2.30. I took the lead in 2 laps due to Behra's proximity. Let Fangio lead later, + at 49 laps took the lead to the end. Lap record on 89th lap. 2.00¼ Juan 2nd, Kling 3rd, Taruffi 4th, Cas/Haw 5th 5th Musso. 2 broadcasts + to Southport. Food + then a party at Mr Hollands (toffee maker!). Bed at 2am.

Weisbaden. He danced and noted the name of Cecille Adrienne! Bed at 5.45am.

Thursday was a day off and he visited the "Kenkell Champagne house for lunch & a gander". Friday - "SLR broke so I had no work" and thus he flew back to London.

On the last Saturday of July, Stirling was a spectator with Jean at Crystal Palace where he saw Mike Hawthorn take the Moss Maserati to victory over Schell's Vanwall. On Sunday he headed for Bourne in Lincolnshire and "thence to Folkingham to see the BRM. It certainly looks nice."

Mort Morris-Goodall, who is driving the Healey with Stirling's number appropriately on the side, was a fascinating character who had a very long and distinguished career which embraced everything from racing at Le Mans to team management. His name will be forever associated with the Aston Martin marque.

British GP - The Cars

There were rumours that the Formula One Lancias, which had been passed to Ferrari when the company ran out of money, would appear but they did not. Similarly, it was hoped Gordini would have his new eight cylinder car ready in time, but he did not.

The W196s had a modification applied to the rear suspension. A central, floor-mounted hydraulic lever in the cockpit allowed the drivers to disable a coil spring at the front end of the torsion bar. This action altered the camber by 2° and softened the rear springing to compensate for a lighter fuel load as the race progressed.

The drivers were instructed by Neubauer from the pits when to throw the lever. Apparently, he signalled this instruction by taking off his hat and twirling it around several times!

Alfred Neubauer briefs his young English charge. They had an excellent relationship and Stirling would later write the foreword for Neubauer's book.

Is it luck—

Do racing-car drivers train themselves to do the right thing when a crash is inevitable, or are they just born lucky?

KEN WHARTON was doing nearly 100 m.p.h. when his Vanwall crashed in flames at Silverstone. His was one of three bad crashes—there were several smaller ones—yet no driver was killed. Wharton himself escaped with burns and a suspected wrist fracture.

Every year on the roads of Britain hundreds of drivers die in smashes. What does the average driver lack?

—or judgment?

I asked the race drivers. Like war-time fighter pilots who "got away with it," they would admit to no predetermined emergency action. Their main advantages over us—apart from open cars with no large windscreen: quicker reaction and acute instinct.

As STIRLING Moss told me yesterday: "You can't say exactly what you'll do. You must judge the right moment to jump clear and get well away from the car.

"But when it's obvious you'll crash, perhaps in flames, there are no rules.

"In the end it's instinct and experience of reacting at high speeds which saves the racing driver."

I imagine that, unlike most motorists, the racing driver's mind is subconsciously prepared for emergency action.

Daily Mail

How interesting it would be to know what Fangio and Moss were discussing just before the off. Unfortunately, Fangio spoke no English and Stirling had no Spanish, so they conversed in the little Italian Stirling had.

Fangio (10) and Moss leave the line for what was to be a genuinely exciting race, especially for the partisan British crowd.

British Grand Prix

The Race

As the flag dropped, Fangio took an immediate lead, closely shadowed by Moss who was followed by Kling. Behra was making rapid progress in the Maserati and flew passed Kling. The leading Mercedes duo opened a slight gap and then, on lap three to a roar from the crowd, Stirling slid into the lead.

He immediately pulled away by a couple of seconds and after just five laps they began lapping the slower backmarkers. Behind Behra came Kling, Mières, Taruffi, Musso, Hawthorn and Collins. The last-named was driving brilliantly, having passed eight cars on the opening lap.

After nine circuits, Behra's race was run with a broken oil pipe. Meanwhile, it appeared as though the two leading Mercs were genuinely dicing. On lap 13 Collins passed Hawthorn. Schell's Vanwall, which had stalled on the line, was also threatening the Ferrari. Lap 18 saw Fangio regain the lead. Schell's noble charge came to an end when the throttle pedal broke. Moss retook the lead on lap 26.

Stirling then began to draw away from the World Champion. "I got away from Fangio by leaving him a slower car to pass just before a corner." With 40 laps gone, he had a lead of almost 11 seconds. Autosport described Stirling's driving as "absolutely perfect. Every corner - same line - same smooth braking. A master driver indeed!"

Meanwhile, Kling was surprising everyone by keeping it on the road for once and Taruffi finally passed Musso to make it an all-conquering 1-2-3-4 for Mercedes-Benz.

In the final laps, while Stirling was being given the 'PI' (Piano - take it easy) signal, Fangio either upped his tempo or Moss slowed in deference to his instructions. Whichever, the gap tantalisingly closed. Not surprisingly, the partisan crowd were on the edge of their seats.

"I don't know whether he let me win or not. But I do know I went like hell. At the last corner, on the last lap, I pulled right over and waved him on but my foot was flat on the floor with 300 horsepower doing its stuff. I thought if you've got any more, you'll pass me but of course he couldn't."

Moss, with a slight lead on Fangio, passes Leslie Marr in the Streamliner Connaught.

Stirling, proudly displaying his Union Jack flag, had one of the best days of his long career on July 16.

By the standards of the 1955 season, this is quite a lead for one of the two top Mercedes drivers to have over the other. According to contemporary reports, the duo appeared to be genuinely dicing and Stirling set the fastest lap, showing great maturity and coolness under pressure from the World Champion. Indeed, he dominated the weekend from first practice until the chequered flag.

Drivers

Moss on: JUAN MANUEL FANGIO ...

"One of the first to congratulate me after becoming the first Brit to ever win the British GP was Fangio.

"I had respect and a sort of love for Fangio but he was quite naughty. Fangio had quite an eye for the ladies. In fact, I have a feeling that he took a fancy to Sally Weston, who spoke Spanish. Regrettably, we didn't have a social life together. Fangio was with Fangina most of the time; that was his lady. I don't think he actually married her but she was known as his lady. In modern terms, she would be known as his partner.

"He had quite a presence and a lot of charisma around him and, therefore, when we had interpreters, he fell quite easily into a warm relationship, let's put it that way. I don't know, and one doesn't brag anyway, but certainly Fangio was one of the most humble men one could meet.

"As a driver, he was the tidiest, least ruffled, fastest on corners and most consistently successful, yet always modest. A man of genius, for me he was the very best."

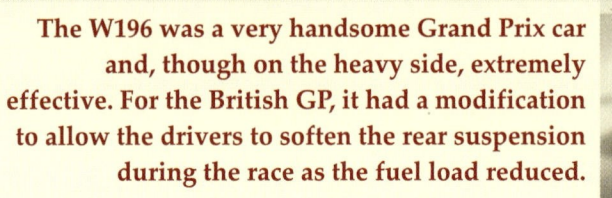

The W196 was a very handsome Grand Prix car and, though on the heavy side, extremely effective. For the British GP, it had a modification to allow the drivers to soften the rear suspension during the race as the fuel load reduced.

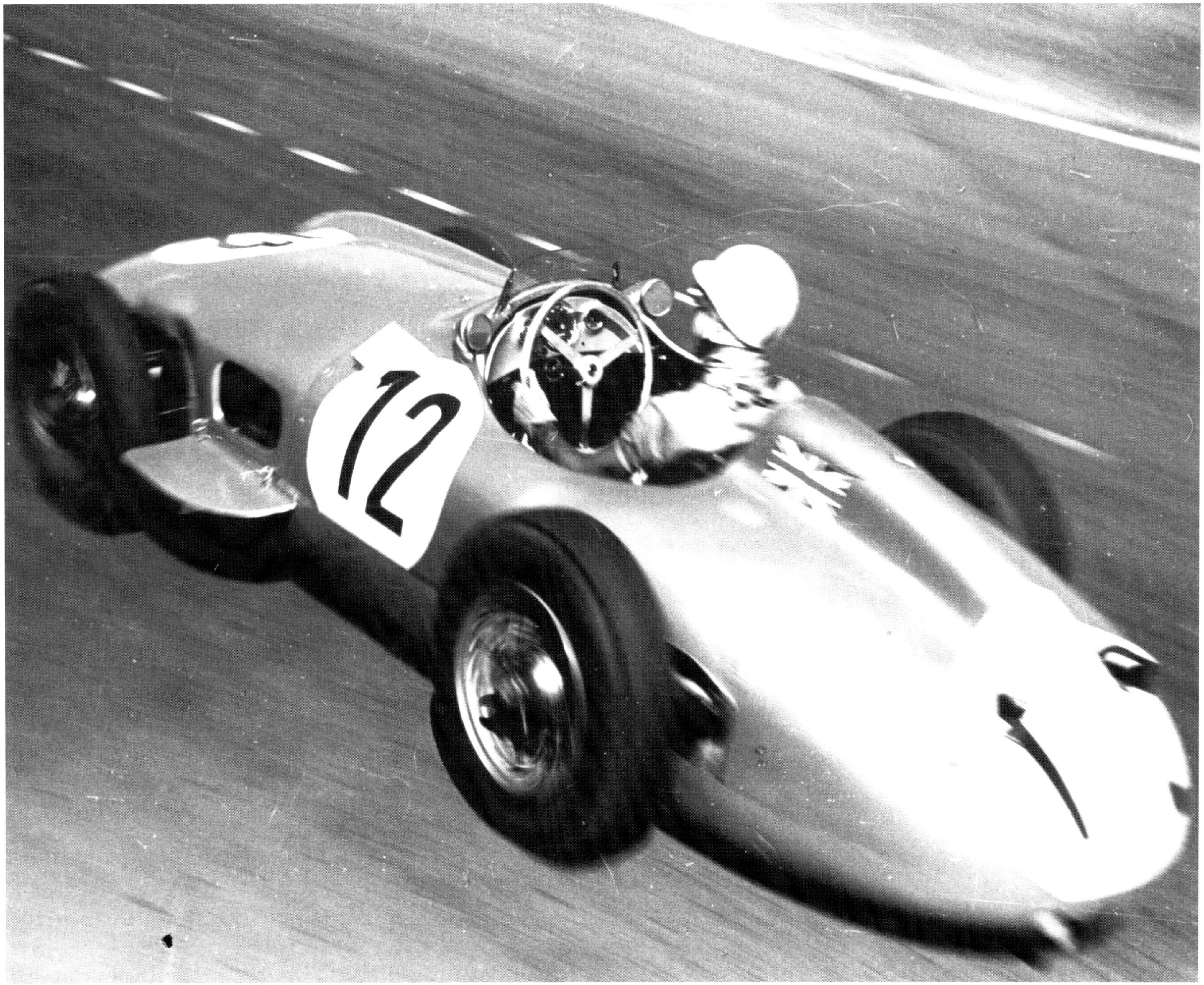

What wonderful publicity the 'Silver Arrows' were for Mercedes-Benz. Fangio had triumphed in his homeland and now young Stirling Moss, the darling of the British public, was on the verge of doing the same. No wonder the British motoring press berated their motor industry for not doing more to uphold British prestige by building competitive Grand Prix cars. In the early fifties, the Jaguar and Daimler-Benz companies were the same size. The same cannot quite be said today!

In the closing stages, Neubauer signalled Stirling to ease up and Fangio closed in. Did Moss slow down or did the Maestro up his tempo to catch his British team mate. The fact that Stirling took the fastest lap logically suggests that he slowed rather than the alternative scenario. It would be interesting to see their relative lap times!

Did Fangio Let Moss Win?

No-one will ever know the answer to that question. It is curious that Moss, while leading, was given the Slow sign but Fangio, seemingly, was not. That may, however, be explained by Neubauer's love of close, formation finishes.

One thing that is incontrovertible is that Stirling was fastest in practice and set the fastest lap in the race. If Fangio had been minded, or instructed, to gift the race to Stirling surely he would have made a point of making the fastest lap. Furthermore, when he was pushing hard to close the 11 second gap Moss had opened up, surely he would have set the fastest lap if he could have done so.

It will always be one of motor racing's most intriguing questions!

SUNDAY MERCURY, July 17, 1955. Page Twenty-One

MERCEDES SWEEP GRAND PRIX

Moss achieves his greatest ambition

IN a thrilling finish to the British Grand Prix at Aintree, a crowd estimated at 150,000 saw 25-year-old Stirling Moss flash across the line in a German Mercedes only four feet and a f….… of a second ahead of his team-mate, world champion Juan Fangio. By his win, Moss became the first Briton to win a British Grand Prix.

After Moss had received the awards to the winner, he paid this tribute to his team-mate: "Fangio is the greatest driver in the world. He could easily have come up and made it a different story, but being a sportsman he allowed me to realise my greatest ambition."

By finishing second Fangio retained his world title.

The race was a triumph for Mercedes, who filled the first four places.

There was drama in every mile of the gruelling 270 miles, 90-lap race with Moss and Fangio setting a scorching pace under the blazing heat of the sun. The surface was slippy and tricky, but by superb driving and cornering the leaders tore on, building up faster and faster speeds as lap succeeded lap.

Long way behind

First Fangio and then Moss led with the rest of the field a long way behind.

Moss took the lead in lap 27 and stayed there, but always with Fangio close on his tail.

So it went on until the race reached its powerful climax three laps from the end.

Fangio crammed on pressure. His Mercedes crept to within inches of Moss, who accelerated still keeping his lead.

Into the last lap streaked the two silver-grey German cars. The crowd rose to their feet as the two Mercedes sped into the corners, Fangio closing up then slipping away as Moss accelerated on the straights.

Looked over shoulder

The finishing post was in sight. The chequered flag was already swinging as Fangio shot to the right of the leader. Moss looked over his shoulder.

lap record which he had set up last year in a Maserati. The old record was 89.55 m.p.h. The new one is 89.70.

Nine finished

Of the 24 cars which started, only nine finished.

It was thought that Jean Behra, in a Maserati, would provide a challenge to the German Mercedes, but in the eighth lap, smoke poured from his car. He drove on, but shortly after he had roared into the ninth lap the smoke increased. Behra drew up sharply and leapt from his car. It was later stated that the car had a broken oil pipe and that Behra had retired.

'Greatest moment'

As Moss and his victorious colleagues drew up in front of the grandstand for the presentation of awards, the crowd, believed to be the biggest to attend motor racing in Britain, broke through the barriers and swarmed over the track. Broadcast appeals were made to them to keep off the road as the race was still on.

As Moss received his award he described his win as: "The greatest moment of my life."

Works entered Aston Martin cars were in the first four places in the race for sports cars over 2,000c.c.

Jim Russell, driving an official Cooper Norton, won the 500 c.c. scratch race at an average speed of 78.19 m.p.h.

BRITISH DRIVER WINS AINTREE GRAND PRIX

Stirling Moss, driving a Mercedes-Benz, about to cross the finishing line at Aintree on Saturday to win the British Grand Prix. Behind him is J. Fangio, also driving a Mercedes, who was second.

One of the first to congratulate Moss was Fangio.

1955

Stirling Moss Scrapbook

Left: sharing in Stirling's moment of glory were Earl Howe (far left), Alfred Moss (in glasses, looking down) and sister Pat (far right).

The great John Bolster, the original 'man in the pits'.

INTERVIEW: John Bolster (with microphone) introduces Stirling Moss to the listeners at the end of the race and asks him to "say a few words".

NEW LAP RECORD

Moss' average speed was 86.47 and he set up a new lap record at 89..7 m.p.h., beating the one he had set up himself last year.

So we had an Englishman winning the British Grand Prix for the first time. After the race, when Moss received his victor's garlands and trophies, he grinned through the oil and blisters and said: "Fangio is the greatest driver in the world. He could easily have come up and made it a different story. But being a sportsman, he allowed me to realise my greatest ambition."

Speaking in Spanish, Fangio said: "Moss is a brilliant young driver. I have enjoyed very much following him."

The results were:
1.—Stirling Moss (Mercedes-Benz), 3hr. 7min. 21.2secs. Speed 86.47 m.p.h.
2.—Juan Fangio (Mercedes-Benz), minus 0.2sec.
3.—Karl Kling (Mercedes-Benz), minus 1min. 11.8sec.
4.—Pierro Taruffi (Mercedes-Benz), minus one lap.
5.—Luigo Musso (Maserati), minus one lap.
6.—Hawthorn and Castelloti (Ferrari), minus three laps.
7.—Mike Sparken (Gordini), minus nine laps.
8.—Lance Macklin (Maserati), minus 11 laps.
9.—Ken Wharton and Harry Schell (Vanwall), minus 18 laps.

Southport Visitor 19.2.55

Newcomers to the Mercedes team during the season were American John Fitch (far right) and Frenchman André Simon (second chap from right).

AUTOSPORT

JULY 22, 1955

1/6

EVERY FRIDAY

Vol. 11   No. 3

BRITAIN'S MOTOR SPORTING WEEKLY

The British Grand Prix at Aintree

SOUVENIR NUMBER

Autosport, the motor sport enthusiasts' weekly 'bible' from August 1950, was rightly proud of their young countryman and, in tribute, forsook its normal red cover for a patriotic green one.

Evening News, 24.7.55

FIONA... Stirling stopped for a chat.

Fiona's back

I spotted the unmistakeable titian hair of London's most famous model, Fiona Campbell-Walter in Park Lane Steering Wheel Club.

Fiona went with her father Rear Admiral Campbell-Walter when he became Flag Officer in Germany, and London expected to see little of her for two years.

But visiting London she was that night and looking just as beautiful as ever—although the face was obscured for a time by the broad back of an acquaintance who stopped to talk to her.

I recognised the shoulders as those of Stirling Moss. There must be something about driving a Grand Prix car which gives you the biceps of Marciano.

No give-away

Incidentally, don't believe the story that world champion driver Fangio "gave" Stirling his recent British Grand Prix win in recognition of Stirling's brilliant team work for Mercedes.

Mercedes are that sure of themselves these days—and Moss who was leading close to the end got the slow-down signal from his pits too late. Fangio just could not catch Moss—and for once team discipline came to naught.

AUTOSPORT, July 22, 1955 — p. 65

BRITAIN'S No. 1 RACING DRIVER
—and now
1ST BRITISH GRAND PRIX
Subject to official confirmation

STIRLING MOSS

Says—

"Every driver should fit the **TRICO AUTOMATIC Windscreen WASHER"**

It's power operated by the car engine. Just touch the button and twin jets of water clean your screen as you drive.

ONLY 49/6

Get your local garage to fit one to your car TODAY!

LTD • GREAT WEST ROAD • BRENTFORD • MIDDLESEX

Sunday Graphic, 24.7.55

Driven home

PERHAPS Stirling Moss is right when he says women drivers have little sense of anticipation — but what a woman lacks in foresight she more than makes up in patience and tolerance, two qualities so noticeably missing in male motorists.

HILARY NORRIS (Miss)
Whetstone, N.20.

AUTOSPORT, July 22, 1955 — p. 85

Esso first at the finish!

British Grand Prix, July 16th

WON BY
MERCEDES

1st S. MOSS		**2nd** J. M. FANGIO	
3rd K. KLING		**4th** P. TARUFFI	

Using ESSO FUEL

SPORTS CAR RACE

OUTRIGHT WINNERS
David Brown's ASTON MARTINS

1st R. SALVADORI	**2nd** P. COLLINS
3rd R. PARNELL	**4th** P. WALKER

2,000 c.c. CLASS
1st D. HAMPSHIRE Lotus-Bristol
2nd A. BROWN Cooper-Maserati
ENTERED BY ALLBRO ENGINEERING
3rd C. DAVIS Lotus-Bristol

1,500 c.c. CLASS
1st C. CHAPMAN Lotus
2nd K. McALPINE Connaught
3rd I. BUEB Cooper-Climax

All using ESSO EXTRA

(Subject to official confirmation)

For your car you can't beat
ESSO EXTRA
THE FINEST PETROL IN THE WORLD

Feud Rumours Demolished

It was not certain whether Stirling would be back from Germany in time to race his Maser and so Ken Gregory decided to offer the car to Mike Hawthorn. Gregory reasoned that, as Hawthorn was available, "it seemed a fine opportunity to secure his services, at the same time scotching those silly rumours about a feud between Moss and Hawthorn".

Success on the track brings other bonuses, literally, and Stirling was one of the first, assisted by Ken Gregory, to begin to exploit the potential for sponsorship and personal endorsement that has so mushroomed today.

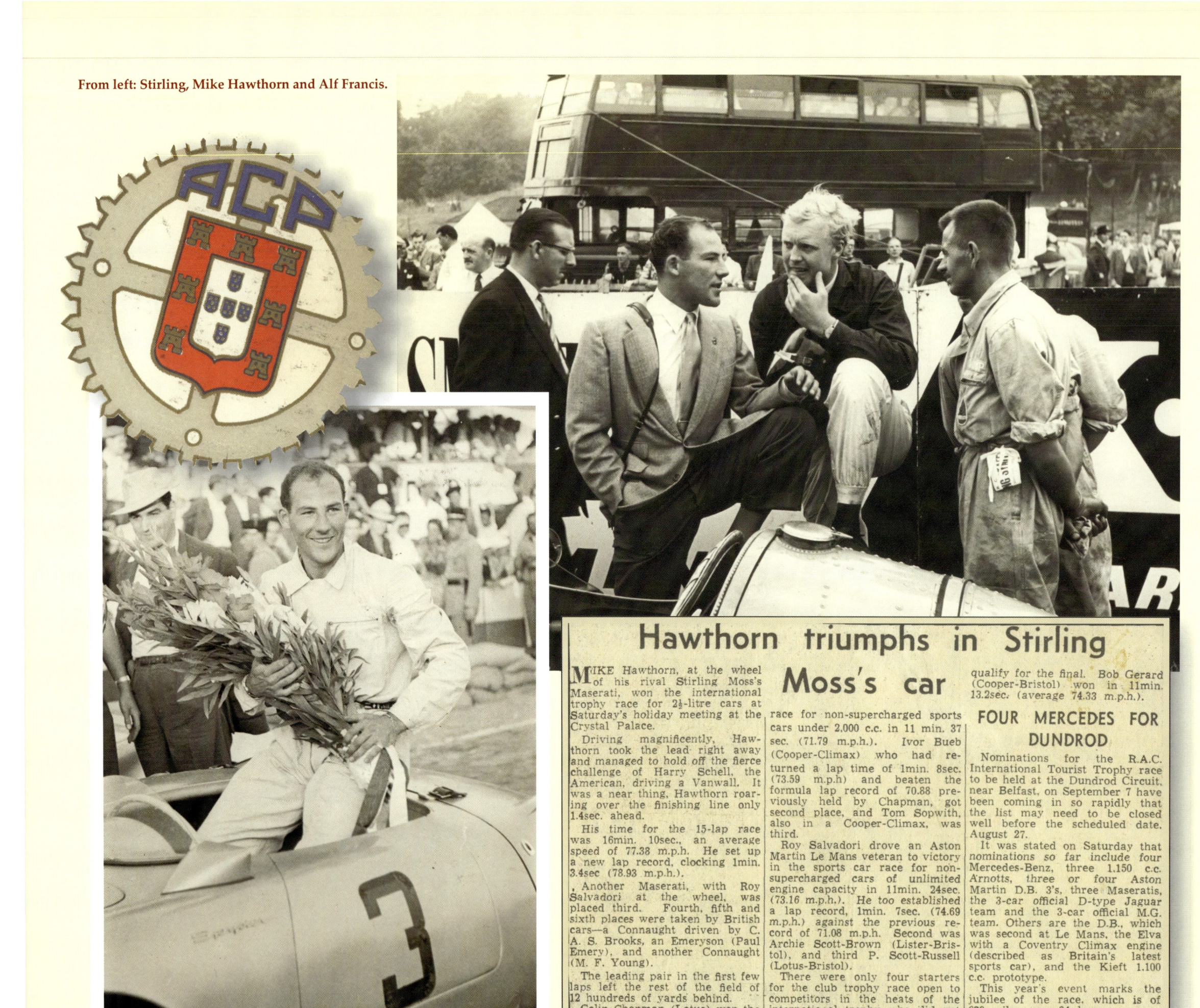

From left: Stirling, Mike Hawthorn and Alf Francis.

Hawthorn triumphs in Stirling Moss's car

MIKE Hawthorn, at the wheel of his rival Stirling Moss's Maserati, won the international trophy race for 2½-litre cars at Saturday's holiday meeting at the Crystal Palace.

Driving magnificently, Hawthorn took the lead right away and managed to hold off the fierce challenge of Harry Schell, the American, driving a Vanwall. It was a near thing. Hawthorn roaring over the finishing line only 1.4sec. ahead.

His time for the 15-lap race was 16min. 10sec., an average speed of 77.38 m.p.h. He set up a new lap record, clocking 1min. 3.4sec (78.93 m.p.h.).

Another Maserati, with Roy Salvadori at the wheel, was placed third. Fourth, fifth and sixth places were taken by British cars—a Connaught driven by C. A. S. Brooks, an Emeryson (Paul Emery), and another Connaught (M. F. Young).

The leading pair in the first few laps left the rest of the field of 12 hundreds of yards behind.

Colin Chapman (Lotus) won the race for non-supercharged sports cars under 2,000 c.c. in 11 min. 37 sec. (71.79 m.p.h.). Ivor Bueb (Cooper-Climax) who had returned a lap time of 1min. 8sec. (73.59 m.p.h) and beaten the formula lap record of 70.88 previously held by Chapman, got second place, and Tom Sopwith, also in a Cooper-Climax, was third.

Roy Salvadori drove an Aston Martin Le Mans veteran to victory in the sports car race for non-supercharged cars of unlimited engine capacity in 11min. 24sec. (73.16 m.p.h.). He too established a lap record, 1min. 7sec. (74.69 m.p.h.) against the previous record of 71.08 m.p.h. Second was Archie Scott-Brown (Lister-Bristol), and third P. Scott-Russell (Lotus-Bristol).

There were only four starters for the club trophy race open to competitors in the heats of the international trophy who did not qualify for the final. Bob Gerard (Cooper-Bristol) won in 11min. 13.2sec. (average 74.33 m.p.h.).

FOUR MERCEDES FOR DUNDROD

Nominations for the R.A.C. International Tourist Trophy race to be held at the Dundrod Circuit, near Belfast, on September 7 have been coming in so rapidly that the list may need to be closed well before the scheduled date, August 27.

It was stated on Saturday that nominations so far include four Mercedes-Benz, three 1,150 c.c. Arnotts, three or four Aston Martin D.B. 3's, three Maseratis, the 3-car official D-type Jaguar team and the 3-car official M.G. team. Others are the D.B., which was second at Le Mans, the Elva with a Coventry Climax engine (described as Britain's latest sports car), and the Kieft 1,100 c.c. prototype.

This year's event marks the jubilee of the race, which is of 623 miles over 94 laps.

Moss lapped every single car, bar the second-place man, to win the Civil Governor's Cup in Portugal.

HAWTHORN WINS IN MOSS' CAR

By THOMAS WISDOM

AN enthusiastic but disappointingly small crowd saw some magnificent racing, in which all the lap records were shattered on the little Crystal Palace course on Saturday.

Highlight of the meeting was the race for the International Trophy, which went to Mike Hawthorn, at the wheel of Stirling Moss' Maserati.

In the final the front line-up was Hawthorn, Harry Schell (Vanwall-Special) and Roy Salvadori (Aston-Martin). As the flag fell, Hawthorn streaked into the lead, and as in other more important Formula I events this season, the race proved somewhat of a procession.

INTERNATIONAL TROPHY

HEAT 1.—1, J M Hawthorn (Maserati), 11min 0.6sec, speed 75.75 m.p.h.; 2, R Salvadori (Maserati), 11min 2.2 sec; 3, H Gould (Maserati), 11min 15sec. Fastest laps—Hawthorn and Salvadori, 1min 4.2sec—77.94 m.p.h. (new record).

HEAT 2.—1, H Schell (Vanwall Special), 11min 4.4sec, speed 75.33 m.p.h.; 2, P Emery (Emeryson), 11min 39.8sec; 3, J Brabham (Cooper-Bristol), 11min 58.6sec. Fastest lap—Schell in 1min 5.2sec—76.75 m.p.h.

FINAL.—1, J M Hawthorn (Maserati), 16m 10sec, speed 77.38 m.p.h.; 2, H Schell (Vanwall Special), 16min 11.4sec; 3, R Salvadori (Maserati), 16min 42.8sec. Fastest lap—Hawthorn in 1min 3.4sec—78.93 m.p.h. (new record).

500 C.C. SENIOR.—1, J Russell (Cooper-Norton), 11min 26.2sec, speed 72.92 m.p.h.; 2, I Bueb (Cooper-Norton), 11min 26.25sec; 3, C Allison (Cooper-Norton), 11min 27sec. Fastest laps—Allison and D Parker (Kieft-Norton) in 1min 7sec—74.69 m.p.h. (new record).

500 C.C. JUNIOR.—1, I E Raby (Cooper-Norton), 11min 49.6sec, speed 70.51 m.p.h.; 2, J Brown (Martin-Norton), 12min 1.8 sec; 3, T Bridger (Kieft-Norton), 12min 27.2sec. Fastest lap—Raby in 1min 9.2sec—72.31 m.p.h.

SPORTS CARS (A).—1, C Chapman (Lotus), 11min 37sec, speed 71.71 m.p.h.; 2, I Bueb (Cooper-Climax), 11min 40.6sec; 3, T Sopwith (Cooper-Climax), 11min 42.6sec. Fastest lap: Bueb in 1min 8sec—73.59 m.p.h. (new record).

SPORTS CARS (B).—1, R Salvadori (Aston-Martin), 11min 24sec, speed 73.16 m.p.h.; 2, A Scott-Brown (Lister-Bristol), 11min 32.6sec; 3, P Scott-Russell (Lister-Bristol), 11m 52.6sec. Fastest lap: Salvadori in 1min 7sec—74.69 m.p.h. (new record).

CLUB TROPHY.—1, R Gerard (Cooper-Bristol), 11min 13.2 sec, speed 74.33 m.p.h.; 2, M Keen (Cooper-Bristol), 11min 56.6sec; 3, J H Webb (Turner), 1 lap behind. Fastest lap: Gerard in 1min 5sec—76.98 m.p.h.

Leo Roman ran a successful water skiing school in the French Riviera, the playground of the rich and famous, the glamorous and the successful. One thing that both driving racing cars and water skiing have in common is, of course, balance. It was also a great, fun way of keeping fit.

AUGUST

1955 Calendar

7 Swedish Sports Car Grand Prix, Kristianstad - 2nd in 300 SLR

13 Redex Trophy, Snetterton, England - 3rd in Maserati 250F

20 Nine Hours Race, Goodwood, England - ret'd after accident in Porsche

27 Oulton Park, England - Sporting Life Trophy - 5th overall & 2nd in class in Standard 8, Daily Herald Trophy - 7th overall & 1st in 1,500cc class in Connaught ALSR

After a swim at the Hurlingham Club in Fulham and lunch with Jean, Stirling had tea in Eton and went on the River Thames in an "electric canoe". Next day he went to see *Teahouse of the August Moon* (G). Demonstrating his fetish for having everything very clean, he devoted time for the third day running to cleaning the flat. "Engagement to Jean in Mail, etc! X! Called on Jack Dunfee re. Claudia. Met SW and saw *East of Eden* VG. Food at La Rue."

Next day, Stirling and his father flew from Heathrow to Malmö and then travelled on to Kristianstad where SM was to race in the Swedish Sports Car GP. "Up early after a bad night. Looked at circuit which is bumpy & narrow but interesting. Lunch & practice. SM 2.22.8. JF 2.22.4. My brakes weren't too good so I stopped. 3rd Behra 2.30. Frère turned over, OK except for kneecap broken. Merc dinner."

On Saturday 6th, Stirling did a 2.21.0 in the practice car and a 2.20.7 in his own car, while Fangio clocked 2.21.0 in his own car. Castellotti, in the Ferrari, was a good four seconds slower but only did a few laps.

The race took place on the Sunday and Stirling led off the line and was pulling away during the first lap but deferentially waved Fangio by. He remained in second place but was then hit by something which smashed his goggles and hit him on the forehead, cutting

● Gorgeous Jean Clarke, who, as "Miss Televisual," will model British fashions on commercial TV, is having driving lessons from Stirling Moss in his 110 m.p.h. Mercedes.

Britain's top racing driver Stirling Moss bruised his elbow when his Mercedes car was in collision with another car in Kensington early today. Miss Claudia Hall, a 20-year-old American, whom Moss was driving home from the West End, received a bump on her head. Here they are in Kensington this afternoon.

Evening Standard 11.8.55

Good Friends

"YOU might call him my steadiest date," laughed Miss Televisual (Jean Clarke) when I asked her about the engagement rumours between herself and racing driver Stirling Moss.

"We are just good friends," she continued. "We both have wonderful times and great fun together, but he hasn't said anything . . . yet."

Jean is 22. She met 25-year-old Moss in the south of France when

Miss Televisual

he was there on holiday and she was on a modelling job. Later in London she suddenly saw him sitting at a fashion show watching her work. They arranged to meet and have gone out regularly ever since.

"We shall see very little of each other during the next four months," she added. "He is going to Mexico, New Zealand and hundreds of other places and I shall be abroad a lot, too."

Evening News 3.8.55

Flying from London Airport on the same plane to Scandinavia were screen star Patricia Medina and racing motorist Stirling Moss. Miss Medina was bound for Copenhagen on the first lap of her journey back to Hollywood over the North Pole air route. Stirling Moss was off to Stockholm for Sunday's Swedish Grand Prix.

Stirling Moss ...

JUST GOOD FRIENDS

"I was certainly never engaged, that's for sure. It was obviously one of those press stories."

Engaged soon?

IS STIRLING MOSS, Britain's No. 1 racing driver, going to become engaged soon? Many friends say he will.

For the past month he has been seen at theatres, nightclubs, horse shows with MISS JEAN CLARKE.

This 22-year-old Coventry-

MISS JEAN CLARKE
Today at the top.

born winner of several beauty competitions came to London to try her luck at free-lance modelling two years ago.

Today she is at the top; has been elected Miss Televisual for a Commercial TV programme; is to represent England at the fashion show at the British Trade Fair in Copenhagen at the end of September.

There she will be entertained at dinner, with her colleagues, in the royal yacht Britannia as the guest of the DUKE OF EDINBURGH.

Daily Mail 3.8.55

STIRLING MOSS IN CAR CRASH

Stirling Moss has first road crash

By Daily Mail Reporter

STIRLING MOSS, 25-year-old British motor racing ace, was taken to hospital shaken early today after his first accident on the highway.

His new Mercedes saloon—he races for the firm—was in collision with another car at the junction of Earl's Court-road and West Cromwell-road, Kensington.

Daily Mail 11.8.55

Stirling Moss ...

CLAUDIA HALL

"Cute little thing. She was only five foot and half an inch."

Moss—'No romance'

Daily Sketch Reporter

BRITAIN'S ace race driver Stirling Moss denied last night that there is a secret romance between himself and beautiful blonde American TV star Claudia Hall, who was in a car crash with him early yesterday.

Daily Sketch 12.8.55

Stirling runs to kiss

By ELIZABETH HICKSON

IN his track clothes, racing motorist Stirling Moss whipped across the road in first gear last night from HIS hotel to HERS. And there SHE stood in the doorway, one of the prettiest little blondes ever to come out of America, 20-year-old starlet Claudia Hall.

She was all ready for an enthusiastic bearhug from "my favourite race driver."

"Let's drop this corny stuff about how we're just being friends," said Stirling, leaning down to kiss her on the forehead. "Let's say she's just my mascot."

Stirling is staying at Snetterton, near Norwich, for to-day's motor races. Claudia, who arrived from New York on Wednesday, was in a London car crash with him early next day.

He told me that he met Claudia at a party given by a New York racing fan. "If that wasn't enough, we had to meet on 42nd street," added Stirling.

GUESS WHAT?

"She was in a Sunbeam Talbot, and I was in a cab. She flashed her indicator at me, and ever since we've been great friends.

Is there to be an engagement? Both denied it. Joked Claudia: "I'm a rolling stone, and I gather no . . . guess what?

"It would be bad for my career to announce an engagement. Why, I've even kept my baby under wraps."

Claudia's marriage is dissolved. She has a daughter aged two.

She added: "It doesn't do to have a fiancé if you are my size and play ingenue parts—much less a baby."

Stirling cut in: "Playing ingenue parts she looks as ingenuous as Marilyn Monroe."

Said Claudia: "Coupla years ago I used to take M.G.s around the mountain tracks. These days I'm just a race-track fan."

What induced her to come to England? She glanced at Stirling quickly, and her eyes twinkled.

"If you think I'll come right out and say it, I'm not so dumb," she said. "Let's say it was to do with my future."

"As a matter of fact this screwball here borrowed my car in New York and parked it in a no-parking area. Then he quit town, leaving me to explain to the judge.

"I had to part up with 15 bucks, and I came over to collect."

him quite badly. Fangio and Moss made equal fastest lap. Stirling finished just three-tenths of a second behind the maestro. Afterwards, Moss had to go into the town, to a hospital, to have some metal removed from his left eye. He still managed to go the dinner dance in the evening, though!

By mid-week he was back in London and took Claudia to the Colony Club on Wednesday evening. "At 1.25am returning, an [Austin] A50 hit me at Earls Court Road." It happened at the junction with Cromwell Road and Stirling was in a 300 SL lent to him by the factory to race at Oulton Park later in the month. The police completely exonerated SM from any blame. Thursday saw him at Snetterton testing his 250F Maser and next day he went "To hospital & doc checked my eye as it troubled me last night. Claudia had her hair done. To circuit. Lap 1.44.6. Wharton 1.43.8. My axle ratio is too high."

Saturday: "Up late, to circuit in rain. Car was awful. Cooper 2.2 faster on straight. I got 6,900rpm! Schell 1st, Ken W. 2nd, SM 3rd. Found plug electrode had dropped in the motor…" That night, back in town, he ate at La Rue's with Ken Gregory, Claudia and her young daughter Sherry. Next day he took Claudia and Sherry to Tring and did some riding.

Back in London, on Monday afternoon he saw Claudia and later collected Sherry from a nursery. They went to see *Reluctant Deb* (VG) before eating at the River Club. Bed at 5am.

On Tuesday he collected Claudia and took her to a police station, presumably in connection with the accident. After work at the office and a haircut, he lunched with Keith Challen of the *News of The World* newspaper. He dined that night at Rules, London's oldest restaurant. Wednesday was a day at the office interspersed with a recording for Italian radio, seeing Jean "for a cuppa" and playing canasta with Kay Petre. "Won 3/- [15p]" They were joined by Jean for supper.

"Up latish as I was disturbed by a radiophone for Claudia." That afternoon, he went to Goodwood where he was to share a Porsche with Huschke von Hanstein. Stirling was the quickest of the 1,500cc cars but five seconds slower, not surprisingly, than Hawthorn's 3-litre Ferrari. Next day, he took both Jean and Claudia out together for a drive before

EYE TROUBLE SENDS MOSS TO HOSPITAL

By BASIL CARDEW

STIRLING MOSS, 25-year-old car-racing champion, went to Norwich Hospital yesterday to have urgent treatment for sudden eye trouble.

He is due to drive his 250 h.p. Maserati at Snetterton, Norfolk, today.

Yesterday morning his right eye was angry and infected. A specialist at the hospital gave him treatment for an hour and he was able to see with it again.

Moss was then able to drive slowly to Snetterton to put in his necessary practice laps on the 2¾-mile airfield circuit.

SPLINTERS

Red-eyed Stirling, who had spent the night in Norwich, said: "The trouble may have been the result of my goggles breaking and splintering glass on me in the Swedish Grand Prix last week. It was jolly painful, and I had very little sleep."

Fascinating Claudia Hall, 20-year-old American TV starlet who crashed with Moss early on Thursday after a London party, is staying at an hotel in Norwich with her two-year-old daughter.

Said Stirling: "They say I must not take my girl friends to my race meetings. It causes too much romantic publicity and speculation."

Daily Express 13.8.55

40,000 share the thrills of Scotland's greatest race

Bob breaks the record and hoodoo too

By Bill Knox

A NEW lap record shared by two drivers, the apparent end to a "hoodoo," the greatest moment in the life of an American race fan, and the most despondent day in the career of a French driver—Charterhall saw all of these on Saturday in the "Daily Record" sponsored international race meeting, Scotland's biggest motor sports event of the year.

Forty thousand spectators lining the two-mile circuit, saw veteran Leicester ace Bob Gerard, driving a foreign-built car —a Maserati—for the first time in his long career, roar home to victory in the 20-lap formula one race at an average speed of 83.29 m.p.h.

Maseratis also came second and third steered by French star Louis Rosier and Bristol driver Horace Gould.

And Stirling Moss, who had loaned Gerard the car for the race, must have shaken his head and wondered when he heard the result.

In his heat of the formula one race he equalled the track lap record of 1 min. 24 secs. set up by Ken Wharton in the B.R.M. in 1953.

Then came the final. Gerard took the lead from the start, and before the halfway mark in the 40 miles distance smashed the record, returning 1 min. 23.8 secs.—85.92 m.p.h.

Only once did the engine falter, in the 13th lap. But the grey car slowed only for seconds before sizzling away again. It was just at the halfway mark that Rosier, then lying fifth, made his effort.

His blue car went faster and faster, moved into fourth position, then in a tremendous burst, which equalled Gerard's record time, shot into third place behind Gould.

Thus the race finished, with it a new lap record, Gerard's first win on a foreign machine and perhaps, for Stirling Moss the beginning of a new streak of racing luck.

Daily Mail 11.8.55

Fangio is revenged—by third of second

JUAN FANGIO, the world champion racing driver, had his revenge yesterday.

In the British Grand Prix at Aintree three weeks ago Stirling Moss beat him by 4ft.

But in the Swedish Grand Prix at Kristiansand yesterday it was Fangio who won, 10 yards ahead of Moss.

As at Aintree, both drove Mercedes.

Moss had roared ahead at the start, but Fangio caught up after two laps and the two drivers hurtled round the track side by side.

Moss was clocked in at the finish at .3 of a second behind. Fangio was timed over the 32-lap, 130-mile course at 1hr. 18min. 13.7sec.

Eugenio Castellotti, of Italy, Ferrari, was third and Jean Behra, of France (Maserati) fourth.

Manchester Dly De'patch 8.8.55

Stirling Moss...

CRASHED GULLWING

"As far as I know, that 300 SL was unique. Later they fitted a swing axle to the 300 SL Roadsters, but this was the only Gullwing with this axle. I said to Uhlenhaut, 'We're never going to beat the Jaguars with a 300 SL with the standard back axle.' So Rudi suggested I try this one. Then this guy came through a traffic light on red and hit us, and really wrote it off."

STIRLING MOSS would not have been blamed for being a non-starter at Snetterton after a road accident. However, Stirling is not one to disappoint organizers, and, although still suffering from after effects, pluckily drove his Maserati.

AUTOSPORT, AUGUST 19, 1955

Blood blinds Moss racing at 140mph

From TOM WISDOM

KRISTIANSTAD, Sweden, Sunday

A STONE smashed Stirling Moss' goggles as he raced at 140 m.p.h. here today. Blinded by blood, he swerved off the track in a cloud of dust. But he kept going—and came second.

Moss, Britain's No. 1 driver, was driving a German Mercedes in the Swedish Grand Prix. He was lying second to Juan Fangio, also in a Mercedes, when the stone hit him.

"It must have been quite a size," he said as he showed me his shattered goggles after the race. "I was lucky to get away with it."

Stirling Moss...

TEAM ORDERS

"Only once in the whole time I drove for Mercedes did they say they would like Fangio to win, which I quite understood."

STIRLING MOSS ready for practising at Snetterton yesterday for today's International Formula I Trophy race.

Daily Express 13.8.55

BOOST FOR BRITISH GRAND PRIX HOPES

New Vanwall And Connaught Win At Snetterton

By THOMAS H. WISDOM

BRITAIN'S two chief Grand Prix hopes gained their first victories on Saturday in the international meeting held on the Snetterton (Norfolk) circuit.

Sporting Life 15.8.55

Tony Vandervell saw his Vanwall Special, driven by the Franco-American Harry Schell, score its first success, while another of his cars, driven by Ken Wharton, was second, and Stirling Moss, with a "sick" engine, third on a Maserati.

In the 67¼ miles "free-for-all" race, victory went to Peter Walker with the new Grand Prix Connaught. The B.R.M. lasted one lap, one Vanwall failed to start and Schell's blew up. Moss was a non-starter.

Walker and Roy Salvadori (Maserati) fought out the issue, passing and re-passing each other in a bitterly fought race.

On the last lap the two cars collided at the hairpin turn on the 2.7 miles aerodrome circuit, but Walker stayed on the road and won by 50 seconds from Salvadori.

In the sports car race the one-armed driver Archie Scott-Brown, winner of many races, overturned, but escaped injury. In the 500 c.c. race, won by J K Hall (Cooper-Norton), champions Ivor Bueb and Stewart Lewis-Evans collided, and both retired.

All these drivers, with Mike Hawthorn and the leading drivers from ten nations, have entered for the "Daily Herald" meeting at Oulton Park, Cheshire, on August 27.

Stirling Moss ...
AN ARRESTING MOMENT IN SWEDEN

"During practice, I overshot a corner down an escape road, whilst doing all I could to stop. A policeman stepped out and put his hand up!"

Drivers
Moss on: Ken Wharton

"A very good serious hillclimb driver, not really a racer. A good all-rounder with his rallying as well."

MOSS DRIVING IN NINE-HOUR EPIC

Kay Petre

Diminutive Kay Petre (she was just 4ft 10ins) had been a very successful racing driver at Brooklands before the war. Being very pretty, she was a favourite of the Press. She raced an Invicta, a Bugatti and, with her ex-Cobb 10 ½ litre Delage, held the Women's Outer Circuit lap record at 129mph, later raising it to 134mph. Before a serious accident caused her retirement, she was a member of the famous Austin 750 works team.

practicing at Goodwood. That night he stayed in a caravan and had a bad night due to the heat. As to the race, the flag dropped at 3pm. "Bad start but 1st at handover at 5.10. 3 min stop. Took over in 4th position at 7.15. Drove & 1st by 9.15. Fuel & tyres at 9.35 & continued. At about 10.20 Crook [Tony Crook of Bristol fame] spun off & came back & hit me whilst I had seven laps lead."

Next day, Sunday 21st, he flew from London Airport to Milan and had dinner with Bettina. "Up at 8am & to Monza. The new circuit is very bumpy & dodgy. Kept the speed down on the banking as our new tyres aren't ready yet. Av. 200kph. In the afternoon, we used the old circuit. SM 1.47.4 in the Streamliner, 1.47.8 in the long & med. & 1.48.0 in the short. JF 1.46.8 in S. Liner & 1.48 in others. To town, shower & to food with Alberta & then saw a comedy show. Bed at 1am."

After collecting some Maserati spares early next morning, Bettina drove Stirling to the airport where he caught a plane for London, spending the entire flight in the cockpit. That night he and Claudia and Mackay Fraser (whom Stirling was coaching) went to the 'Wheel' followed by The Colony.

Next morning Mac went off to collect his car with Stirling's truck while SM spent an hour with Mrs Tollit, Sally Weston's mother, and an hour and a half with Mrs Earl, her aunt, regarding SW's mysterious apparent disappearance. He then went to see *Seven Year Itch* (G) on his own, which was most unusual as Stirling hated to be alone, but took Jean to L'Epicure later for a meal.

Next morning he phoned Princess Chelita, the wife of Siamese racing driver Prince Bira, with whom SW had seemingly been staying in the South of France, and found she was OK. He then drove up to Chester for that weekend's meeting at Oulton Park. "Up early and to practice. I did 2.33.4 in the Standard which was excellent & then tried Berry's D-type. Only did five laps but the car felt awful & unsafe. Returned and we went surfing on the Dee with Mac & Mike."

"Had a bad start in the 8 due to vaporisation. Finished 5th and 2nd in class to a D.K.W. Used Leston Connaught in the sports car race. Started at the back & had a good getaway along the pit counter! Car went well, except the No. 4 cylinder jammed full bore. Also I had no seat &

MOSS ENTERS A STANDARD

Stirling Moss has entered a works Standard Ten—kind of car the family man takes out at weekends—in the production saloon car 41-mile race during the international trophy meeting at Oulton Park, Cheshire, on Saturday. His opponents include Ken Wharton, Alan Brown, Les Leston and Peter Collins.

Moss will switch from the Standard to the high-powered German Mercedes car for the main event, the 221-mile international trophy race for sports cars, in which 30 leading drivers from nine countries have entered.

Meeting the powerful foreign challenge, including eight Italian Ferraris spearheaded by the works team leader, Mike Hawthorn, will be the Aston Martin team of Reg Parnell, Roy Salvadori and Peter Collins.

B'ham Eve Despatch 18.8.55

Standard Eight

Stirling's Standard Eight was not exactly standard! It had a Ten engine, which had been tuned at Barwell Engineering, two large Solex carbs, lowered suspension, a Panhard rod, competition linings, Borrani wire wheels and, not too surprisingly, an interior full of gadgets.

Stirling's Standard Eight seen parked in the paddock at Goodwood. Note the Borrani wire wheels!

Stirling Moss on Snetterton track

DRIVING this Maserati in the Formula I event at Snetterton circuit on Saturday is Stirling Moss who, after a hard struggle, came in third.—

Suffolk Free Press 17.8.55

Judy (Noot) Addicott

"Sally Weston was a long-time girlfriend, but he had plenty of girlfriends. She was very possessive but he had girlfriends wherever he went. They came and went quite a lot. He kept his private life under wraps."

GERMANS PUT ALL ON MOSS TO WIN

By TOM WISDOM

THE German Mercedes firm last night decided to give all-out support to Stirling Moss against the might of the Italian Ferrari team in next week's *Daily Herald* International Trophy race.

So this 221-mile sports car race, to be run at Oulton Park, Cheshire, on August 27. will now be a full-scale battle of the giants.

There will be eight Ferraris, the most ever entered for a race in Britain.

Four are "works" cars, captained by Mike Hawthorn, friend and great rival of Moss.

Moss' car was damaged in a London road accident last week.

It was this upset coupled with the great Ferrari challenge that caused last night's decision by Mercedes.

Susie Palethorpe, as she is today, claims to have been Stirling's first fan and he remembers her well. Today, she attends *XK Club* events with her brother Peter Vale (aka Lord Vale of Evesham!). This photo was probably taken in 1954 as Stirling is sitting in a D-type Jaguar.

STIRLING MOSS is the driver, Miss Susan Vale the girl helper, polishing the windscreen of his racing model at Oulton Park, Cheshire, yesterday. He competes today in the International Trophy.

Daily Mail 22.8.55

Today's profound question
BUT WHAT'S THE USE OF A MINK?

"WHAT'S the use of a mink coat?" ... That sums up the philosophy of Pat Moss, Stirling Moss's 20-year-old sister.

Her first love is horses, her second is cars, and between the two she has probably carried off more prizes than any other girl in Britain.

Stirling is seen here in the Connaught ALSR, which he drove to win the class at Oulton Park. He had also raced the car, owned by Peter Bell, at Montlhéry in October 1954.

my back ached. 1st in class & 7th overall." He headed for Tring for the night. Next day he was helping Mac with his Ferrari.

On Monday Stirling spent four hours with Mrs Tollit & Mrs Earl talking about SW. He then borrowed a Bond Minicar three-wheeler, met David Haynes at 7pm & saw Norman Wisdom at the London Palladium (G).

On Tuesday Stirling picked up Claudia in the Bond, which must have impressed her no end, and they had a sandwich at the 'Wheel'. After working at the office, he had tea with Jean. He ate at the Ox and called on Claudia. A separate note at the bottom of the diary page says simply, "SW came home".

Next day, rather ironically, Stirling saw *Love Me Or Leave Me* (F). "Phoned SW. She seems different."

You mustn't wish the driver luck

Peter London's Journal

IF you ever meet STIRLING MOSS in the pits before a race, do not venture on any polite platitudes. If you wish him good luck, he will take it as a bad omen. Even if you suggest that the weather looks like holding you will get a baleful glare.

For Stirling is very superstitious. "That accident I had in the Mercedes would happen when I didn't have my lucky clown mascot with me," he told me.

He attaches enormous significance to the number seven. His Standard Eight carries the registration number SFM 777. Before that his Jaguar was also 777, and once, at Aintree, he won at 77.77 m.p.h.

It is a constant grief to him that Grand Prix rules prevent his having seven as his number of the racing Mercedes, but he was careful to choose instead 14—two sevens.

Similarly, he mistrusts the official British racing colour—green. When his Maserati carried that livery, it never won a race. So he decided to paint it dove-grey, with a green patch only on the bonnet, as a concession to authority. In its next race, the car came in seventh. Defiantly, he removed the green patch—and the car won.

Ace British racing-car driver Stirling Moss, on the latest of his succession of Vespa models, chats with fellow driver Lance Macklin

---

A SURE CURE FOR PARKING TROUBLES

Says STIRLING MOSS

SPEED is money to me—both on and off the track, and for skating around town in these traffic-jammed times it is manoeuvrability that pays in time and money.

For two years now I have done my running around on a Vespa — I claim mine as the most travelled scooter in the world.

That Vespa has travelled with me to every motor racing circuit in Europe and is now on its way across the Atlantic to Nassau.

Economical

It costs little to run—something like 100 miles to the gallon—and it takes up no room. When I am in town I usually take it up to my office on the first floor for safe parking.

In Italy, where the scooter has become a national tradition, I have drawn some pretty funny looks from the Italians buzzing along with my British registration and G.B. plates.

CHEAP... AND EASY TO PARK

In Britain the weather can be a drawback, though on a scooter you are better protected than on an ordinary motor-cycle.

If you want scooter economy and complete weather protection, then a three-wheeler such as a Bond Minicar is the job.

I have tried one of these, too, so I know what I'm talking about.

It does about 80 to the gallon, and the economy of the car goes deeper when you consider how much easier it is to find parking space when you have a three-wheeler.

I rate ease of parking the Minicar's greatest asset. Its front wheel swivels through 180 deg. and allows the car to squeeze into a gap little more than its own length.

In my trips the Minicar has proved to be a lot faster and nippier than I expected.

When its little 197c.c. engine is warmed up it will touch 50 m.p.h.

Thanks to being able to park it smartly, I have managed to clock as fast a door-to-door time from my flat to my office with a Minicar as with a Mercedes.

The Bond Minicar (the name pre-dated BMC's famous Mini by about 10 years) was a three-wheeler designed by Laurie Bond and announced in May 1948. It was intended simply as a local runabout and economy was its raison d'être. Powered by a 125cc single-cylinder, two-stroke motorcycle engine which drove the front wheel, it was of very advanced stressed aluminium construction but had no rear suspension. With a very light weight of just 195lb (88kg), the car achieved 100mpg (35km per litre). In 1952, the under-bonnet kick-starter was replaced by an electric starter (luxury!) and from '53 rear suspension and a front brake were added.

Two great fifties characters: the extraordinary Spanish nobleman, the Marquis de Portago (left) and the 'other' British hero, Mike Hawthorn. They shared a works Ferrari for the Goodwood Nine Hours. Sadly, both would be dead by the end of the decade.

The Marquis de Portago (also famous as a horseman) and Mike Hawthorn standing

"I think there's a distinct element of doubt about the possibility of a pre-arranged finish here today...."

3-NATION HUNT FOR GIRL
Stirling Moss's friend

Scotland Yard have asked police in France and Italy to try to trace Jennifer Clare Tollitt (aged 22), who disappeared about a fortnight ago.

Miss Tollitt, also known as Sally Weston, left Blue Mist Farm, West Burton, Bury (Sussex), with an aunt on August 9 and flew to Nice. Two days later she went to visit friends in Italy and her family have not heard from her since.

Miss Tollitt, who is interested in motor racing, has been a friend of Stirling Moss, the racing driver, fo[r]

Miss Tollitt pictured last year at London Airport when seeing Stirling Moss off on a trip to the United States.

several years. In December, 1951 she was his guest at the annual dinner of the British Racing Drivers Club. She has often been seen with

RACE DRIVER'S FRIEND DISAPPEARS

INTERPOL have been asked by Scotland Yard to join in the search for Jennifer Clare Tollitt, aged 22, who disappeared a fortnight ago.

Miss Tollitt who is also known as Sally Weston, is a friend of Stirling Moss, the British racing driver.

A year ago she wore a diamond engagement ring, but both she and Moss denied that they were engaged. "We are just good friends," they said.

HIS GUEST

In December, 1951, she was his guest at the annual dinner of the British Racing Drivers' Club. She has often been seen with him at motor racing tracks.

Miss Tollitt left Blue Mist Farm, West Burton, Bury (Sussex), with an aunt on August 9 and flew to Nice. Two days later she went to visit friends in Italy and her family have not heard from her since.

The Star 25.8.55

SUSSEX GIRL DISAPPEARS IN ITALY

Scotland Yard are called in

Missing girl is friend of Stirling Moss

SIR HAROLD SCOTT, former head Scotland Yard, has been called in help trace 22-year-old Miss Sally Tollett, Bury, near Pulborough, who has d appeared from an Italian resort.

Miss Tollett, a close friend of racing driver, Mr. Stirling Moss, had been holidaying in France and Italy with an aunt, Mrs. C. Earl.

They left England at the beginning of August.

Mrs. Earl has returned to Miss Tollett's home at Blue Mist Farm, Bury, but her niece decided to remain on the Continent longer.

That was two weeks ago.

Since that time she has not written or contacted her home in any way.

Last night her grandmother, Mrs. Bishop, who lives at Blue Mist Farm with Miss Tollett's mother and aunt, told how the absence of any news for nearly two weeks made them decide to telephone Sir Harold Scott, personal friend of the family.

"He promised to look into the matter immediately, and informed Scotland Yard," said Mrs. Bishop.

Through Interpol, the international police organisation, they are making extensive inquiries in Italy and France.

Miss Tollett's mother also telephoned friends on the Continent where she may be visiting.

Mrs. Bishop continued: "Although we are rather anxious about Sally she is quite capable of looking after herself, and we can't imagine she has come to any real harm.

"Perhaps she has run short of money, and is staying with friends

"She has several in France and Italy. We have heard a report that she has been traced to a French hotel where she is supposed to have registered as Sally Weston."

S. Weekly News 26.8.55

HUNT FOR STIRLING MOSS' GIRL FRIEND

SCOTLAND YARD have asked the police in France and Italy to try to trace Jennifer Clare Tollitt, 22-year-old friend of race-car ace Stirling Moss.

Miss Tollitt, who is also known as Sally Weston, left Blue Mist Farm, West Burton, Bury (Sussex) with an aunt on August 9 and flew to Nice.

Two days later she went to visit friends in Italy and her family have not heard from her since.

Scotland Yard were asked to help and messages were sent through Interpol, the international police organisation, to Rome and Paris.

'Only Friends'

Miss Tollitt is interested in motor racing. In December, 1951, she was Stirling Moss's guest at the annual dinner of the British Racing Drivers' Club.

She has often been seen with him at motor racing tracks.

A year ago she wore a diamond engagement ring, but both she and Moss denied that they were engaged. "We are just good friends," they said.

Liverpool Dly Express 25.8.55

DARTS FINALS

Finals of the Stirling Moss four-a-side darts tournament take place at the "Rothschild Arms," Aston Clinton, tomorrow.

Miss Pat Moss will present the prizes. The tournament drew 71 entries.

WHY ALL THE FUSS? ASKS 'LOST' GIRL

From JOHN TOMICHE: Paris, Thursday

MISS SALLY WESTON, aged 22, who had been reported missing by her mother to Scotland Yard, was today lunching with Prince Bira, the Siamese racing motorist, and his wife, at Mandelieu, on the Riviera.

Miss Weston refused to come to the telephone. But Princess Bira relayed this message from her: "I cannot understand what all the fuss is about. I am very surprised, since everybody knew perfectly well where I was.

"Anyhow, I have immediately telephoned my mother to reassure her and I shall be flying back to London tomorrow."

Friend of Moss

Miss Weston, whose real name is Jennifer Clare Tollitt, lives at Blue Mist Farm, Bury, Sussex. She went to Nice on August 9 and then to Italy.

She has been a friend of Stirling Moss, the racing driver, for several years, and has often been seen with him at meetings.

FRENCH AND ITALIANS IN GIRL HUNT

Interpol And Yard Search For Missing Sussex Girl

Police seek girl friend of Stirling Moss

SCOTLAND YARD have asked police in France and Italy to try to trace Jennifer Clare Tollitt, aged 22, who disappeared about a fortnight ago.

Miss Tollitt, who is interested in motor racing, has been a friend of Stirling Moss, the racing driver, for several years.

In December, 1951, she was his guest at the annual dinner of the British Racing Drivers' Club.

She has often been seen with him at motor racing tracks.

A year ago she wore a diamond engagement ring, but both she and Moss denied that they were engaged. "We are just good friends," they said.

Miss Tollitt, who is also known as Sally Weston, left Blue Mist Farm, West Burton, Bury (Sussex) with an aunt on August 9 and flew to Nice.

Two days later she went to visit friends in Italy and her family have not heard from her since.

Scotland Yard was asked to help and messages were sent through Interpol, the International Police Organisation, to Rome and Paris.

Belfast Telegraph

Cars

Porsche 550 Spyder

The Porsche 550 Spyder was powered by a flat-four 1,498cc engine which produced 110nhp at 7,800rpm. Due to its light weight, it could reach 60mph in 7.8 seconds and had a maximum of 125mph (201km/h). Examples won both the 1,100 and 1,500cc classes at Le Mans in 1955.

That Stirling was trying in the Porsche can be seen by his use of every inch of the road, and more. Being a 'racer' this situation of having first one handicap (his delayed start) and then a second (the pedestrian von Hanstein) must have given him a challenge he relished.

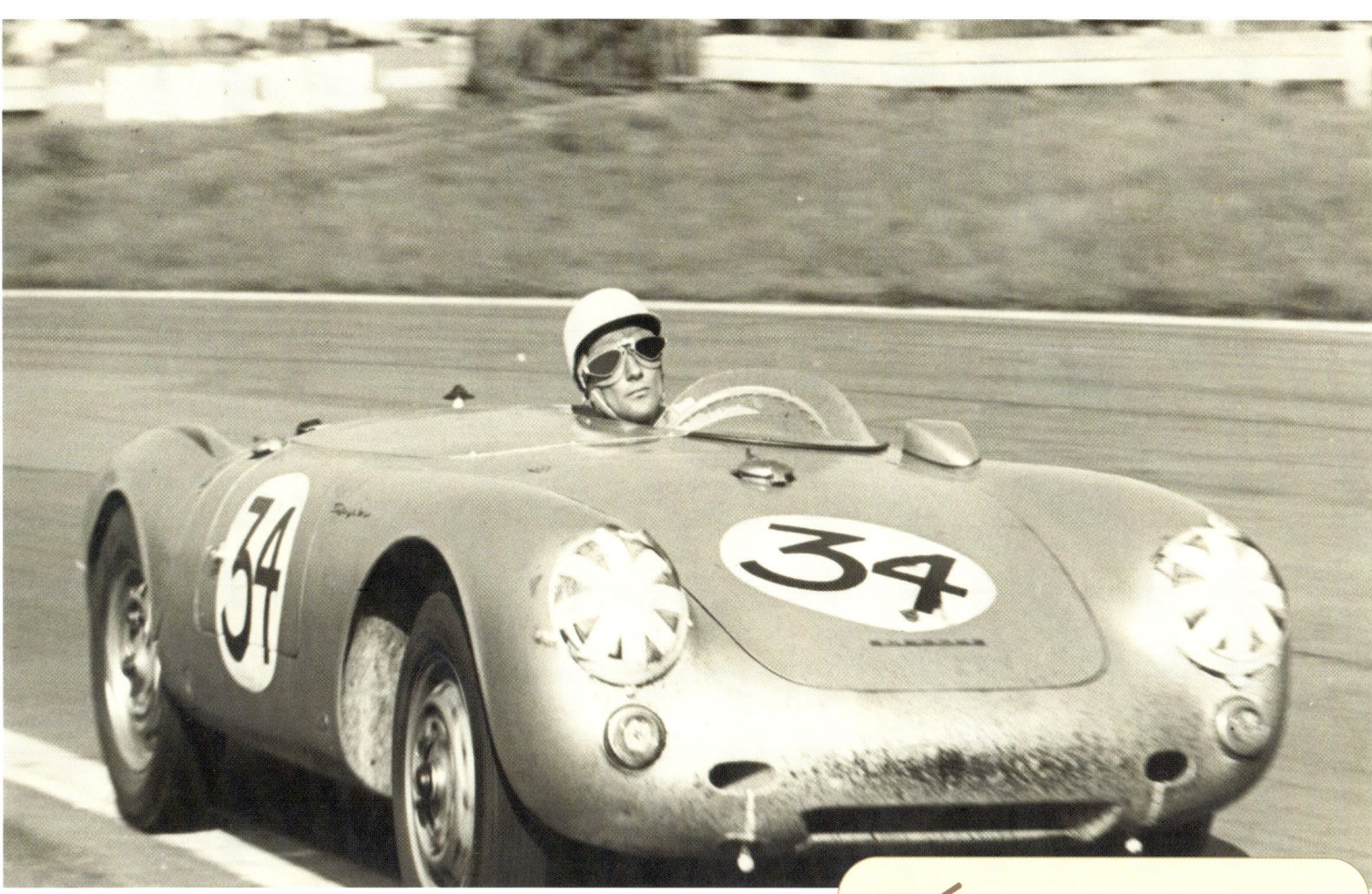

Goodwood Nine Hours

Stirling's bad start was a result, according to Autosport, of him stalling the Porsche but this is a curious statement as the start was of the Le Mans type, with drivers running across the track to their cars, jumping in and pressing starter buttons. Les Leston led the 1,500cc class, initially, followed by Colin Chapman in his Lotus-MG. When von Hanstein took over from Stirling, he was 10 seconds a lap slower, which dropped them well behind Chapman's rapid Lotus who was now followed by Arche Scott-Brown in the Leston Connaught. With Chapman replaced by Peter Jopp, the brilliant Scott-Brown led the class and was now fifth overall amongst the DB3S Astons, D-types and Ferraris. "One could see that Moss was just itching for von Hanstein to come in, in order to do something about the 1,500cc section," wrote Gregor Grant in Autosport. When, at 7.15pm, he finally took over, Stirling was fourth in class.

However, Stirling was pressing on and managed to retake the class lead and was now placed sixth overall. Then Crook spun in front of him and Moss unavoidably rammed him, deranging the Porsche front suspension. He "walked back to the pits fuming".

SEPTEMBER

1955 Calendar

3	Daily Telegraph Trophy, Aintree - ret'd in Maserati 250F
11	Italian Grand Prix, Monza - ret'd in W196 Streamliner
17	RAC Tourist Trophy, Dundrod, Northern Ireland - 1st Moss/Fitch in 300 SLR
24	Gold Cup, Oulton Park, England - 1st in Maserati 250F

Following the phonecall to SW on August 31st, they had lunch at No. 8 next day. "Later Ken and I went to the Radio Show (bad). At 6.20 to Dorchester for cocktail party. Met some S.A.S. hostesses, etc. Later to Tring with David Haynes & Jean."

Next morning Stirling and David drove up to Aintree where SM was to race the recalcitrant Maser. "Practiced but car didn't feel good. Slow from corners. Lap in 2.06.4 (ftd!), Les Leston 2.13.0 but only a few laps. Water leaked thru to three rear cylinders badly. It was a slow day. To town and Adelphi. Food at the Corn Market. G. My gold Omega broke today.

"Up late & breakfast. To circuit & race. Good start, but Parnell's Connaught was much faster & took the lead. I followed for some 15 laps, one sec. behind, but couldn't pass. The car held back & smoked. I stopped."

The following Tuesday Stirling flew to Milan where he was met by Betina and they saw a film in Italian. Next morning it was raining hard so he looked around town before heading off to Monza in Betina's 1100 (presumably a ubiquitous Fiat, as this was Italy!). "I tried the long Streamliner 2.49 (damp). JMF (later) 2.46. Karl 2.53. The med. Streamliner was impossible. Used the med. open car, did 2.53 but baulked. Felt 2.51 OK. Behra & Mieres 2.53.5, Collins 3.03. Returned to town. Cabled home for 6in bandages & re. Mac's Ferrari. Had food with Mac, Denis & Bettina." Separately on the page is written, "SW came over!" Woops!

Sport mag puts the accent on speed

SPEED features in the special 56 page, September issue of *World Sports*.

"Crashing the sound barrier" by Neville Duke, "The age of speed" by Stirling Moss are but two of the many top rate articles by speed stars.

Other big time sporting events, including Russian athletics are also contained in this big "all the sports" issue.

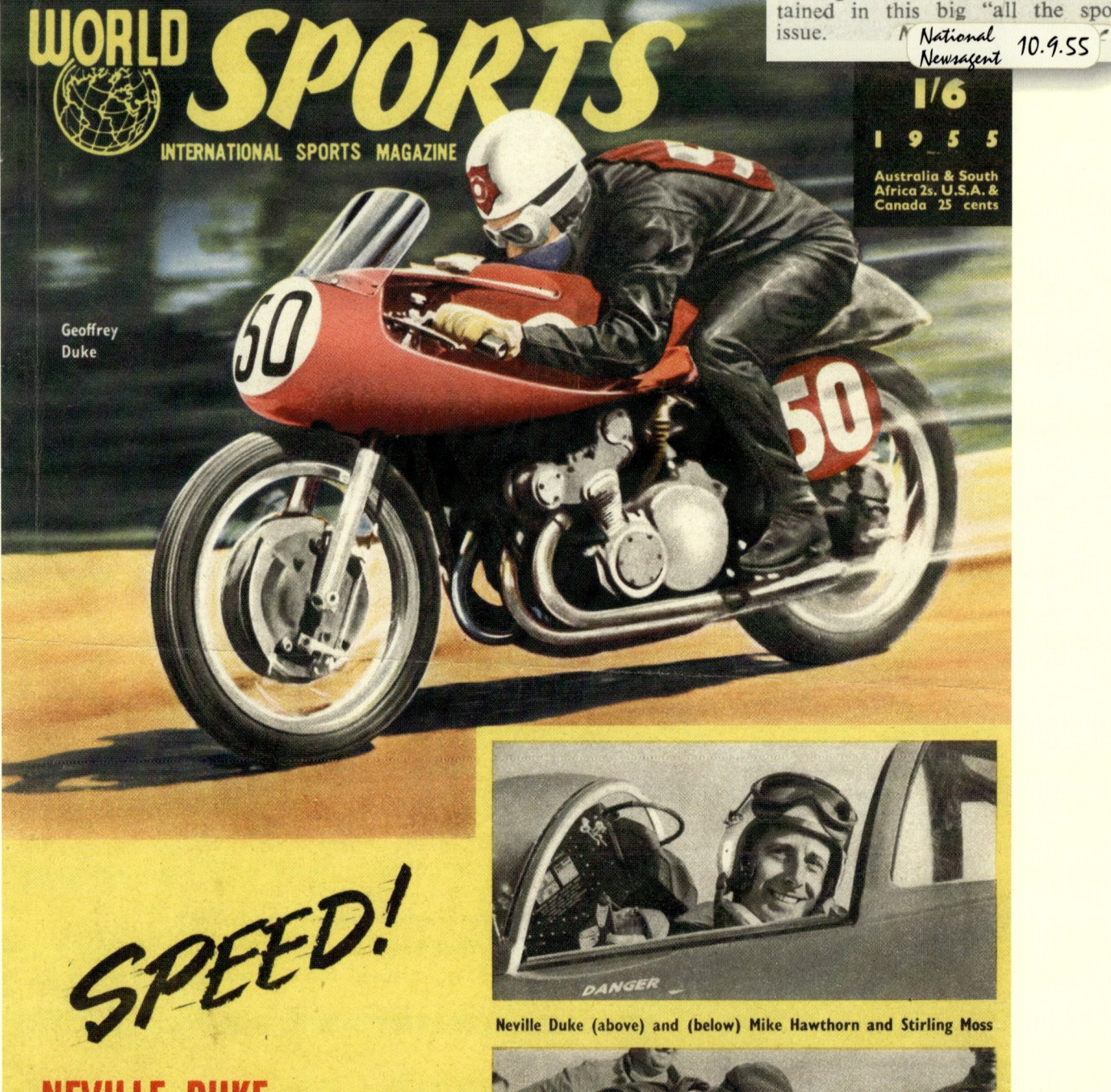

National Newsagent 10.9.55

WORLD SPORTS
INTERNATIONAL SPORTS MAGAZINE
1/6   1955
Australia & South Africa 2s. U.S.A. & Canada 25 cents

Geoffrey Duke

SPEED!

NEVILLE DUKE on *Breaking The Sound Barrier*

DENZIL BATCHELOR asks— *Where Will It All End?*

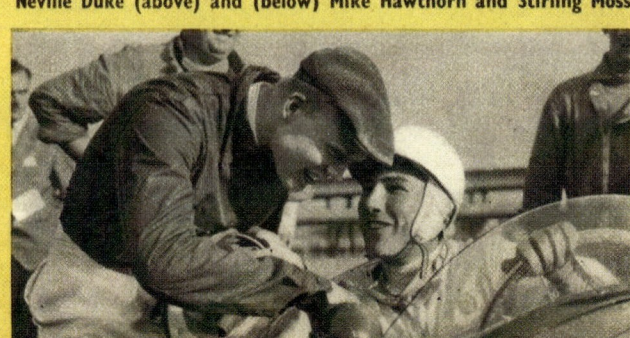

Neville Duke (above) and (below) Mike Hawthorn and Stirling Moss

XXVI GRAN PREMIO D'ITALIA

Stirling Moss, the famous racing driver, arriving at Southend Airport with his Mercédès-Benz sports car. The aircraft is a Bristol Freighter.
(Photograph courtesy Air Charter, Ltd)

City Press 1.9.55

Frustrating Aintree

Reg Parnell, who was driving the works Streamliner Connaught, immediately took the lead and, as Alf Francis put it, "went like a dingbat". Stirling hung on for 13 laps but, with just four to go, the Maserati expired with a burned piston. This necessitated Alf and Tony Robinson catching the night ferry from Dover as they had just five days to reach the Maserati works at Modena, rebuild the engine and get the car to Monza in time for John Fitch to drive it in the Italian GP.

Drivers

Moss on: Peter Collins ...

"Collins was a consistent Mike [Hawthorn] really - very good. I got Pete to drive with me in the Targa, a good choice, because he was good. I mean he did go off the road, so did I, so he was going fast enough. The point is he was fast enough to make mistakes, but he was also fast enough to be forgiven for making them. Some you can't forgive because they weren't going that quickly, but Pete would be going that quickly, and therefore that is why I chose him. Other times one would take Jack Fairman who was steady and reliable."

Italian Grad Prix

The organisers had decided that there would be a mandatory stop between the 20th and 30th laps to change all four tyres. However, Mercedes objected and the rule was dropped. The Lancias, now being run under the Scuderia Ferrari banner, had to be withdrawn before the start as their contracted Belgian tyre supplier did not have a suitable tyre for the heat generated on the banked sections of the track.

The start was delayed by more than half-an-hour due to the presence of the Italian President. The race finally got under way but was considered a pretty dull affair as the Mercedes domination was becoming rather tedious. Fangio led from start to finish in a Streamliner. Initially Stirling shadowed him in the usual way but then, around the 20th lap (contemporary reports vary), a stone shattered his windscreen making the car extremely unpleasant to drive. He pitted and had a new screen fitted. The time given for this stop, again in contemporary reports, ranged from 25 seconds to one minute and 40 seconds!

Stirling was now down in eighth but, being a 'racer', was determined to catch up the leaders. In that attempt he repeatedly set the fastest lap, leaving it at an average of 134mph (215km/h) (all contemporary reports agree on this one!). All was to no avail, for on the 27th lap he was forced to retire with axle problems, or piston problems, or gearbox problems, or ... Just take your pick!

Prior to this, the crowd mistakenly thought there was something amiss when Moss and Fitch indulged in much arm-waving as the former passed the latter. However, John Fitch was driving the Moss Maserati and Stirling was merely enquiring after the health of his car!

On the penultimate lap 'Don Alfredo' hung out the 'naughty-naughty' sign to Taruffi when the Italian had the presumption to try and pass Fangio on the pit straight.

MOSS DENIES ROMANCE

ACE racing motorist Stirling Moss yesterday denied rumours of any romance in his life. Told it had been reported that he was secretly engaged to Miss Audrey Lambert, a Londoner, he said:—

"That brings the score to three 'engagements' in a month. There is not a grain of truth in the reports of any of them."

Sunday Dispatch 4.9.55

Next afternoon, SM and SW went to Monza. "I only did 10 laps slowly. JF did 1.00.0 on the piste, but on the long car. I didn't try it. The short was impossible. To Como & I skied. Friday afternoon, Albertina took SM to Monza. "My car hadn't come. I did 2.51.1 in an open mid wb. JF 2.46.6 in closed special med. I only did a couple of laps (4 or 5). Returned to Milan, met Mum & Dad. SW out with Maglioli.

"Up early & pissing down with rain. To Monza, but my car wasn't ready. Lunch & practice. My car is an old heavy one. I was ftd in 2.46.8 (still damp at Lesmo). Full bore on the banking. 2nd Kling 2.48.8, 3rd Farina 2.51.4, etc. JM yesterday 2.46.5. To town & food with SW."

The Italian Grand Prix took place on the Sunday. "Met President & race began at 3.30. H.M.S. Forth gave me their mascot. After about 20 laps, I was 2nd, about 0.3 secs. behind J.M., & Kling & Tar 3rd & 4th. Then windscreen broke. Stopped in 1.40 (VG!). Continued & ftd 2.46.7. Then a piston. J.M. 1st, Tar 2nd, Cast 3rd. My Mas finished OK. To town (took 2 hrs) & food with SW with Mercs. VG."

Next morning Stirling collected his starting money for the Maser which, at 1650 lire to the pound, worked out at £500. He paid Alf Francis, leaving himself a surplus of £242. "Walt decided to marry Alberta! Saw him & SW off & Alberta took me to Malpensa. Travelled over with Louis K, Bas & Courtenay. [photographer Louis Klemantaski, Basil Cardew of the *Daily Express* & Courtenay Edwards of the *Daily Mail*] Dave Haynes met me with 220."

Next morning Stirling spent no less than five hours cleaning the flat before a Miss Chester of the *Picture Post* "came & took photos, etc. To office & work. More flat cleaning & then SW came & we had a big fight. Made up & to Colony & joined Ken & Pat (on me)."

On Wednesday Stirling flew to Belfast for that weekend's Tourist Trophy at the dangerous Dundrod circuit. Before leaving "Mary B. brought a cake round. VG." That night he ate with Pete Collins and Graham Whitehead.

"Up early & scrutineering & medical. Shopping with Trips, Fitch & Simon. Lunch with John & to Dundrod. Three laps in saloon 4.53. My car 4.49.1. Wrong gears & many cars. Reckon 4.40 is possible! 3rd ftd. Mike in 4.55, etc. Gendebien crashed in a Ferrari & broke an arm. Fitch & Trips 5.00, Kling & Simon 5.10+. Ferraris 5.05+. Long discussion & to town & food with Alf & NAM. SW phoned."

Magnificent sight of, from left to right, the Fangio and Moss Streamliners and Kling's 'open-wheeler' on the front row of the grid at Monza.

START OF THE MONZA GRAND PRIX

The start of the Monza Grand Prix yesterday. Fangio, driving a Mercedes, the winner, is ... The others in front are Stirling Moss and K. Kling, both in Mercedes car...

MOSS CUP DARTS

The "Stirling Moss" four-a-side darts tournament final was held at the Rothschild Arms, Aston Clinton, on Saturday, when Miss Pat Moss, the well-known horsewoman and motor driver, presented the trophy awarded by her famous brother. Winners were the Upper Winchendon Social Club "A," captained by D. Oakley. Runners-up were the Hare and Hounds (Watlington), and the losing semi-finalists the Crown (Haddenham) and the Exhibition (Marston, Beds.).

Mr. W. Bond, Chairman of the Rothschild Arms Dart Club officiated at the presentation.

Bucks Advertiser 2.9.55

Once again, for Monza Mercedes-Benz took a confusing plethora of car configurations for the drivers to try in practice. Stirling tried long and medium wheelbase Streamliners, a medium open-wheeler and a "closed special medium". In the race Fangio and Moss drove long wheelbase Streamliners, while Kling had a long wheelbase open car and Taruffi a short chassis open-wheeler. The "closed special medium" probably refers to a car on which Mercedes experimented with various front body shapes to increase what then they called 'frontal adhesion' and today we would call 'downforce'. The first gave the desired effect but the engine overheated due to lack of airflow. There were three different frontal treatments tried but in the end they gave up and reverted to the 'normal' Streamliners. The Daimler-Benz budget for 1955 must have been astronomical by the standards of the day.

During the next day's practice, Stirling lapped in 4.48 but was baulked. "Jag. 4.49! No Fangio. Changed drivers to Fitch & not Simon."

Saturday dawned. "Had a good start in the race & was 1st till 29 laps by over 1 min. Then my rt tyre burst at 6,000rpm in 5th! Drove in at 100mph. Change to John Fitch. He did six laps & then I took over -3.25 mins. Caught up in two hours. Stopped for tyres & fuel & caught up again. Lead by 3 mins+ & on the one from last lap Mike broke. SM 1st at 88mph & 2nd J.M.F., 3rd Tripps. F. lap Mike 4.42. Three drivers were killed including Jim Mayers. To town, food & reception. J.F. was very annoyed."

Next morning Stirling went to the hospital to see Gendebien and Behra. He then flew back to London where SW cooked for him that night.

Monday morning was spent at Tring, where he joined Neubauer, the Klings and others and indulged in some horse-jumping. That evening, back in town and after a meal at the 'Wheel' with SW and Alf, he worked on his scrapbooks!

On Wednesday, he and Ken went down to Weymouth where Stirling skied behind Donald Healey's new boat, which impressed him with its speed and stability. That evening he met a Tony Barrett at the Ritz to discuss opening a club. "Food with Alf, Ken & misery on SM." Sounds as though Stirling was paying!

Next day, Stirling and Barrett viewed some property. He then saw Felix, his legal advisor, and his accountant. "Did photo for Nenettes at Lex… Later saw another club & then to Mayfair in dress for TV. To Churchill's for food with Vyvienne."

Friday saw Stirling flying up north for the first Oulton Park Gold Cup meeting. He was driving a works Maserati and achieved a lap in 1.52.6, restricting himself to 7,200rpm. He noted that Mike Hawthorn was slightly quicker on 1.52.4 in the Lancia but used 9,000rpm! That evening he had a meeting with John Webb to discuss a Vespa project.

Saturday was raceday. "Had a bad start but was 1st after one lap. Kept going well & got ftd & came in 1st by 1 min or so. Mike 2nd. Musso was 2nd till near the end when his gearbox gave up. Rushed off immediately at 4.40 & Pete & I were airborne by 5.16. Headwind all the way, but came

Stirling's only outing in a Streamliner

Final Results - Points
DRIVERS' WORLD CHAMPIONSHIP

Fangio	41	Kling	5
Moss	23½	Davies	4
Castellotti	12	Frère	3
Trintignant	10	Thompson	3
Farina	9	Faulkner	2
Taruffi	9	Gonzales	2
Sweikart	8	Menditeguy	2
Mières	7	Perdisa	2
Bettenhausen	6	Villoresi	2
Behra	6	Maglioli	1⅓
Musso	6	Hermann	1

N.B. In those days, the Indianapolis 500-Mile Race counted towards the World Championship.

Drivers

Moss on: Roberto Mières…

"Roberto Mières was a wonderful sportsman and very nice guy. He played tennis very well. Really, he was a very good amateur driver. He did race for factories but he could be described as a 'gentleman race driver'. He came from a very good family and has excellent English. I still see him around."

Bottom : TRIUMPHAL PROCESSION.—Fangio, Moss, Taruffi in formation with Castellotti just behind, during the early stages of the Italian Grand Prix. They are finishing the half-lap, approaching the pits, while in the background can be seen the end of the South Banking where it joins the finishing straight.

The Italian Grand Prix
By Peter Lewis

THE Monza Autodrome circuit outside Milan — where the twenty-sixth Italian Grand Prix takes place this afternoon—will be the scene of the fourth round in Europe of the 1955 World Championship for Drivers. In all probability it will be the final round for the October Spanish Grand Prix was cancelled after the Le Mans disaster and it is by no means certain that the postponed French Grand Prix will take place this year.

It is fitting that the rival marques of Mercédès-Benz, Ferrari, Maserati, Gordini and Vanwall are to meet for the last time on a circuit which has always been one of the fastest in Europe, and only recently has been lengthened considerably and modified to include new high-speed banked sections where speeds of well over 200 m.p.h. can be reached in safety.

In fact the race average of the winning car may well be in the region of 130 m.p.h. It is sufficient to note that last year's winning average was 111.98 m.p.h., for the new track is so different that comparisons of any value cannot be made.

New Circuit

The new circuit measures 6.2 miles, double the lap distance of the old road circuit as used last year, when Stirling Moss had such wretched luck in the Italian classic, gaining a dominating lead over the Mercédès of Fangio only to be robbed of certain victory 12 laps from the end by a split oil tank.

Fifty laps of the new circuit—some 312 miles—will, in my opinion, provide spectators with some of the finest Formula 1 racing of the 1955 season. Part of the wide, very fast straight between the pits and grandstands now has a central division, the grandstand side forming part of the old road circuit and the pits side forming part of the new high-speed section with its north and south banked curves. On each of the 50 laps cars will thus pass the pits and grandstand twice.

It is no secret, however, that drivers are not very happy about the banked sections, which, quite apart from exerting a strong upwards and outwards pull, are likely to test suspension and chassis to breaking point and wear down tyre treads at an alarming pace.

The tyre problem is certain to influence the result considerably and—in the interests of safety—the organisers have laid down that each car must make a pit stop to change all four wheels between the twentieth and thirtieth laps.

Pit Stops

Efficient pit stops (with added spectator interest) therefore become of vital importance in a race which, by the nature of its composite circuit, will test driver and mechanical endurance to the limit and is of a very open nature.

Having won the Belgian, Dutch and British Grand Prix one after the other, Mercédès-Benz will take some beating this afternoon, if only because of their ability to face up to circuit problems and to adapt themselves to new conditions.

It is worth noting that the first four positions in the 1955 World Championship table are: Fangio 33 points, Moss 22 points, Trintignant 11 1-3 points, and Farina 10 1-3 points. The winner this afternoon will gain 8 points and a further point if he is credited with the fastest lap.

The Observer 11.9.55

MOSS MAY WIN THIRD T.T. TODAY

By THOMAS WISDOM

STIRLING MOSS, 26 years old today, is tipped as the winner of today's Tourist Trophy race which is celebrating its 50th birthday.

In the final practice last night Moss, driving a Mercedes, knocked a second off the unofficial lap record set by world champion Juan Manuel Fangio, driving the same make of car, on Thursday.

Moss lapped the 7¼ miles Dundrod (Belfast) course at an average speed of 92.7 m.p.h.

But the driver of the single "works" Jaguar, Mike Hawthorn, who holds the record at 92.58 m.p.h., and Desmond Titterington, who takes on the might of Germany and Italy, were only a second slower than Moss and equalled Fangio's time.

TEAM PLANS

If Moss wins today—and I understand the German team orders plan a Moss win, if all goes well—he will be the first man to win the TT three times in its 50 years' history.

This 622 miles race—it is estimated to last for seven hours—is Britain's most important sports car race, and is the final event of the year in the world sports car championship.

Germany's Mercedes, Italy's Ferrari or Britain's Jaguar can win the championship if they win today's race.

Also to be considered is the Aston Martin team, successful in the last two long-distance sports car races including last month's "Daily Herald" international trophy. The 24-year-old Peter Collins lapped the course only three seconds slower than Moss.

Sporting Life 17.9.55

Fitch is losing to Titterington in the Jaguar which is now in the lead. Slide rules are out and an emergency pit-side conference takes place between Uhlenhaut, Lamm, von Trips, Moss and Neubauer. Moss was put back in the car after only six laps rest.

Stirling Moss in the Mercedes he drove to victory in Saturday's T.T. race.

Sporting Life 19.9.55

✎ Sally & Maglioli

PP: *"The fact you noted in your diary that Sally Weston went out with Maglioli suggests you didn't quite approve."*

SM: *"No I certainly wouldn't. He was a charming bloke and quite good-looking, and I was sure she was doing it just to piss me off."*

The Mercedes team had a fabulous coupé version of the 300 SLR at Dundrod, one of two prototypes built and known as the 'Uhlenhaut'.

to Stapleford at 7.12pm. Pete brought me to Hendon in his A30. To No. 8 and took SW to food at Chicken Inn (awful)."

He packed that night for his next trip, initially to the French Riviera for some holiday and thence to Sicily for the legendary Targa Florio. In spite of not getting to bed till 3am, he was up early and rendezvoused with David Haynes, having lunch at his house. "We came to Lydd & took off at 3.15pm. To France. David lost his lighter & found it! Left his case of clothes behind, also left his cigs at Le Touquet. Wow! X! To Paris in heavy traffic by 8pm. Went to food & a club. Bed 3am."

On Monday Stirling and David drove from Paris to Nice in 12¼ hours including a stop for lunch. "Cable from Mercs to go to Sicily!" Next day, after seeing Lance Macklin, who had an apartment in Monte Carlo, they went to Juan les Pins where the boat Stirling had hired was moored. "To boat & unloaded. Went to Moulin Rouge & then Whisky's." Next day they headed out in the boat. "Then out with the lung. A gale blew up & we only just made harbour. The boat leaks in the roof. Played chess, etc. Later … saw the marathon dance. 436 hrs!"

A postscript is added on this diary page. "I cast the anchor so we could spearfish, but Haynes (2nd mate) had knitted the rope, but not knotted it. Result - no anchor."

Next day consisted of more of the same and bed again at 5am! Stirling unfortunately had caught a cold but that did not stop them going to Maxims, the Moulin Rouge, the Casino and the Whiskey A-Go-Go that night, a good way to end the month.

Stirling Moss …

HAWTHORN IN THE 'D'

"Mike did a fantastic job with the D-type because it was certainly not comparable with the SLR."

Around 14 Worlds..

A NEW award has just been devised to be presented to the most all-round travel personality of the year. The first winner is TV dog man **Macdonald Daly**, who has flown 205,000 miles and travelled another 150,000 by train and car. The award is called the Louis Duforest Travel Trophy.

Such a rolling stone is Mr. Daly that he will have a tight schedule to-day trying to gather this latest piece of moss.

... in 365 Days

He is judging dogs at Abergavenny, and will have to fly from Cardiff to London Airport and then hurtle up to Park Lane to be at the Dorchester Hotel penthouse suite in time to receive the trophy at 7 p.m. prompt.

Wing Commander Garrett Petts, who was a Battle-of-Britain fighter pilot, will present the trophy to Daly. The day-trip Atlantic crossers—**Wing-Commander Hackett** and **Mr. Peter Moneypenny**—are guests of honour.

Various runners-up for the trophy will be at the party, including **Stirling Moss, Tommy Lawton** and four air hostesses. Miss Televisual (model **Jean Clarke**) has announced that she will arrive on horse-back, riding side-saddle in her best cocktail dress.

Evening News 1.9.55

STIRLING IS A SECOND FASTER

From Tom Wisdom

BELFAST, Friday.—Stirling Moss, who is 26 tomorrow, is tipped to make himself a birthday present of the R A C Tourist Trophy.

In final practice tonight in the open Mercedes Moss knocked a second off the unofficial lap record set by world champion Juan Fangio.

Fangio pushed his Mercedes round Dundrod yesterday at an average 92.7 m.p.h.

But the driver of the single works Jaguar, Mike Hawthorn, who holds the record at 92.38 m.p.h. and Desmond Titterington, also in a Jaguar, were only one second slower than Moss and just as fast as Fangio.

Hat trick?

If Moss wins tomorrow he will be the first man in 50 years of the T T to win the race three times.

This 622 miles and seven hours of speed is Britain's most important sports car race and by winning it, Germany's Mercedes, Italy's Ferraris and Britain's Jaguars can each win the world sports car championship.

The Tourist Trophy

Stirling took the lead during the first lap, while Hawthorn and Fangio enjoined in another of their famous battles behind the flying Moss. Stirling had built up a comfortable cushion when a sudden drama changed the whole picture. He had the exciting experience of a tyre suddenly throwing a tread while he was doing 100mph (160km/h). The flailing tread ripped into the right rear wing. Stirling nursed the car back to the pits where the mechanics cut away the damaged wing, changed the wheel and John Fitch took over.

Fitch was steady rather than rapid and was losing ground to local man Desmond Titterington who had taken over from Hawthorn. After six laps, Fitch was called in by an anxious Neubauer to be replaced by Stirling. He was now more than three minutes behind the leaders and had some work to do.

However, there was some consternation among the other teams, and in particular in the Jaguar pit, as to how the Moss 300 SLR with an exposed rear wheel, which rendered it more like a Formula car, was allowed to continue. In fact, though the International Sporting Code required cars to finish intact, the TT regulations had not included this stipulation.

Meanwhile, Peter Collins's works Aston-Martin had failed to fire up at the start and he was 48th on the first lap. He was quoted as saying he "knew the biggest hate of my life". By the end of the first lap he was up to 14th, by lap four he was ninth, sixth by lap eight and third by lap 31. It was an impressive drive which Stirling and others noted.

After his setback, Stirling was again driving superbly and the long race gave him the scope to once more take the lead as he passed the Hawthorn D-type. Then, when the battle had been decided, poor Mike Hawthorn, who had driven a valiant race, had the misfortune to experience a broken crank on the penultimate lap.

In its reporting of the Golden Jubilee T.T., Autosport described Stirling's performance as "one of the most brilliant drives ever seen on a road circuit". When it started raining and Moss hauled in the D-type, they commented, "Truly Moss is a genius in the wet, a fact which was supported by Rudy Carraciola, who, pre-war, was second to none on soaking roads".

Stirling made one of his lightning Le Mans starts to easily lead the field.

Stirling built up a healthy lead in the early laps.

THIRD T.T. WIN FOR MOSS

Jaguar's Great Struggle With Mercedes

By J. N. BENNETT

FOREIGN cars almost swept the board in the 22nd R.A.C. Tourist Trophy Golden Jubilee race, held on the Dundrod circuit, near Belfast, on Saturday. Mercedes secured the first three places in the Tourist Trophy, Porsches and D.B.'s did the same in the 1,500 c.c. and 750 c.c. classes respectively, a Maserati was the winner of the 2-litre category, while British cars, headed by a Cooper-Climax, were the first three in the 1,100 c.c. class.

To round it off, the foreign successes, Armagnac and Laureau, last year's outright winners, took the Index of Performance trophy, and the manufacturer's team prize went to D.B.

SEPTEMBER 1955

Sun rises 5.36 **Saturday 17** Sun sets 6.13
(260-105)

Up early food & off at 8.15am. Had a good start in the race & was 1st till 29 laps by over 1m. Then my rt tyre burst at 6000 rpm in 5th! Drove in at 100 mph Change to John Fitch. He did 6 laps & then I took over. — 3.25 — Caught up in 2 hrs. Stopped for tyres & fuel & Caught up again. Lead by 3m & & on the 1 from last lap Mike broke. 8pm 1st at 88mph + 2nd JMF 3rd Tripps. F.lap Mike 4:42 3 drivers were killed including Jim Mayers. To town, food, & reception. J.F. was very annoyed.
Bed 1 am

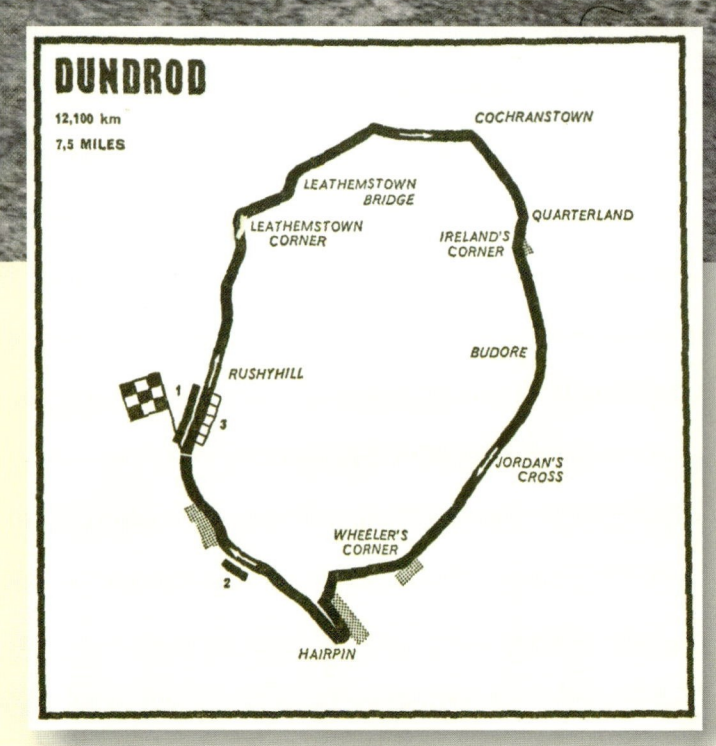

The road surface at Dundrod was particularly abrasive and caused heavy tyre wear.

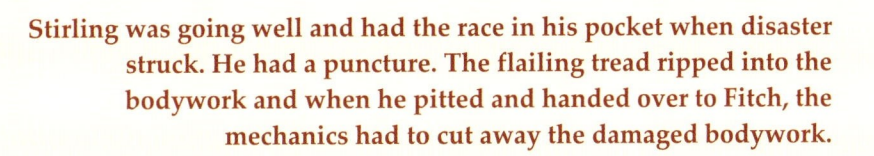

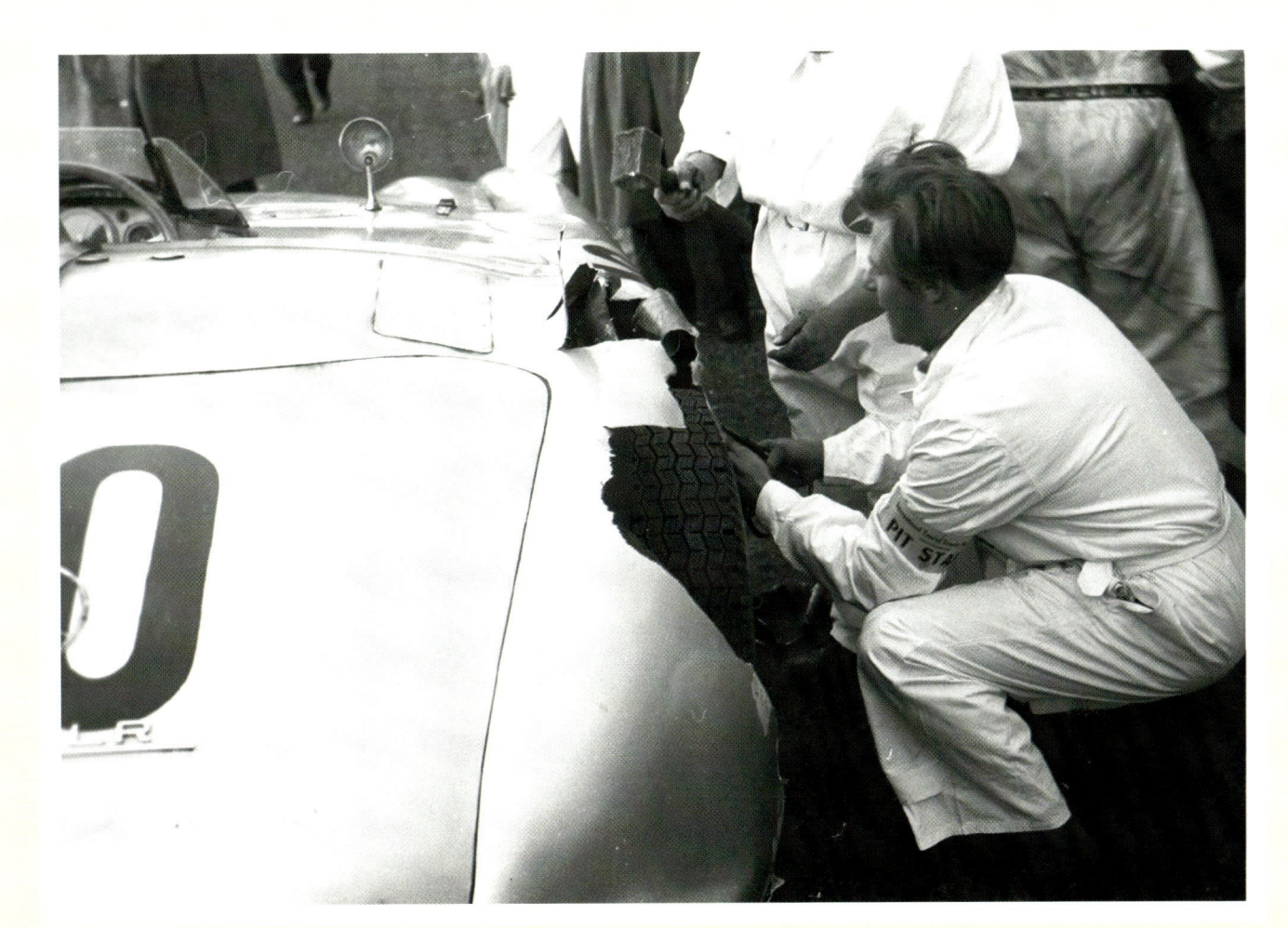

Stirling was going well and had the race in his pocket when disaster struck. He had a puncture. The flailing tread ripped into the bodywork and when he pitted and handed over to Fitch, the mechanics had to cut away the damaged bodywork.

Jenks was on hand to report for Motor Sport and give moral support.

The 'modified' 300 SLR was not a pretty sight but at least there was no major damage. Note one of the spare wheels now visible in the rear.

Stirling noted in his diary that Fangio was angry after the race and he does not look exactly happy during it!

125

EAGLE CLUB NEWS

Happy Birthday, Stirling!

16/9/55.

IT is with great pleasure that we send Stirling Moss the warmest good wishes of EAGLE Club for his 26th birthday this coming Saturday, September 17th. The year that is just over for Stirling has been a highly victorious one, and we have followed all his exciting achievements, on this page, with great enthusiasm. We wish our Vice-President the best of everything; may the coming year be even better and still more successful.

The extremely genial American John Fitch shared the spoils with Stirling.

Mike Hawthorn is no doubt telling Stirling about the Jaguar driver's incident on the penultimate lap which cruelly sidelined him after a very gutsy drive.

The errant tyre lies in shreds in the pits.

September — Stirling Moss Scrapbook

Sidelights On The T.T.

The race had once again been beset with tragedy. Jim Mayers and the very promising young Bill Smith died in a multiple accident early on and Dick Manwaring succumbed when his Elva rolled and caught fire.

The Dundrod track was far from suitable for top class motor racing, being very narrow. This was compounded by the wide disparity in performance between the competing cars. With just 12 feet (4 metres) between the car to be passed and a wall or bank, Motor Racing magazine commented that, "Such a gap is small enough at normal speeds, but at 150mph it must be like the eye of a needle".

Moss and Hawthorn both commented after the race that the course was highly dangerous. Stirling opined that it might be suitable for Formula One with only about 20 cars and drivers of suitable calibre. In reality, there were novices entered among the 100 drivers accepted by the organisers. Those same organisers were, though, excessively zealous in their conducting of the medical examinations. Dick Protheroe, who would become a very successful driver in the early sixties, was at that time a Valiant jet bomber test pilot. He was turned down for bad eyesight! Ken Wharton, though he had raced several times since suffering burns in May, was refused permission to race and had to organise an independent examination at his own expense to prove his point.

The engines of the three highest-placed cars were required by the regulations to be stripped and examined to confirm they complied with the rules. Mercedes requested that the engines be sealed and these examinations be carried out in Stuttgart where they considered the facilities were rather better. They offered to pay the scrutineer's expenses.

BIRTHDAY CAKE FOR WINNER

Stirling Moss, after his victory in the Tourist Trophy race, cuts the birthday cake, placed on the bonnet of his Mercedes by his mother.

Belfast Telegraph 19.9.55

That could be Earl Howe in the flat cap, but it looks rather like Tommy Wisdom who gave Stirling his great break in his XK 120 at Dundrod in 1950.

STIRLING MOSS TESTS BRIDPORT MAN'S SPEED CRAFT

Says "Perfectly Satisfactory"

BID TO CAPTURE DOLLAR MARKET

A DRIVE is to be made to capture American and Canadian markets with a water speed boat being built at Bridport.

To begin this drive Stirling Moss, famous racing motorist, fresh from his success in the Ulster T.T races came to Weymouth on Wednesday and demonstrated the craft both by driving her and

PERFECT LANDING

While the boat tore across the bay at maximum speed he carried out ski jumping over the waves, using only one hand and using only one ski. In a final sweeping curve the boat ran shoreward, Moss dropped the ski-rope and made a perfect landing.

For the next couple of hours Moss himself was at the helm of the boat and gave a thorough testing in a slightly rough sea.

Speaking after the trials he said that everything was perfectly satisfactory.

"HIGHLY SUCCESSFUL"

Mr. Geoffrey Lord said: "The trials were highly successful in every way. I, and others, were following in an American Chris craft but we could not keep up with the Healey boat; she had the edge on us for speed and rate of turn all the time."

The demonstration was watched by some hundreds of people gathered on the Weymouth front.

Among the Healey team for the tests was Mr. Donald Healey.

Pictured in the craft are Mr. Donald Healey (left) and Mr. Stirling Moss.

STIRLING MOSS TOWED—ON WATER SKIS. The British racing driver, who was 26 last Saturday, enjoying the unaccustomed sensation of travelling at...

Daily Telegraph 22.9.55

Bridport News 23.9.55

The Healey Ski-Master 14-ft. outboard runabout off Weymouth.

FASHION HOUSES SHOW MODELS
300 WATCH AT HOTEL
Daily Telegraph Reporter

London fashion houses displayed their latest creations when a gala night at the May Fair Hotel was presented on independent television last night. More than 300 people saw the programme at the hotel. As they waited for it to begin they watched other programmes on eight television sets.

After talking to Anna Neagle and Stirling Moss, Leslie Mitchell introduced Lady Pamela Berry, president of the Incorporated Society of London Fashion Designers. Lady Pamela showed a number of model dresses...

Daily Telegraph 23.9.55

A woman sums it up in one word—SUPERB
By MARION SLATER

As a woman I would say ITV fitted itself adroitly into English history. It took us on a travelogue of London—very "Ealing Studio."

It spoke movingly of the British fondness for "free speech, fair play, decency and tolerance."

This was all very elevating. But it was, alas, rather dull as a beginning.

But at 8 o'clock came the sparkle—in Channel Nine's variety show. It had everything — pretty girls, jolly comedians. It was as reviving as a glass of champagne.

And the drama that followed was superb. Into the intimacy of our homes came the top actors and actresses in play extracts that were irreproachably done.

I have only one criticism to make. It is possible to have too much of a good thing.

But it would be ungracious to quarrel with ITV for giving too much too well.

Over to the news, read pleasantly by Chris Chataway, who looked like every mother's thoroughly nice son. ITV are trying to marry public and personal news, the important and the entertaining.

RIGHT IDEA

This was not altogether successful. But they have the right idea. This is the way to make the news human and interesting.

Gala Night at the May Fair had points that every woman will have noticed. Anna Neagle's glamour, her surprisingly low-cut dress; Stirling Moss's almost schoolboy diffidence; Lady Pamela Berry's mellow voice, her "perfect hostess manner" and her ladylike plug for British fashions.

THE FASHIONS

And about the fashions . . . the predominance of long evening dresses, surely more elegant than short ones can ever be; the long, tight skirts; the continuing emphasis on bosoms and shoulders. This was a woman's programme.

What of the advertisements? Did they irritate? Did they interfere? My woman's-view is that they slipped easily into the show.

They certainly impress with their names.

Feminine summing-up... ITV offered real entertainment.

Daily Sketch 23.9.55

Scooters

Stirling has long been famous for his scooters. "The Vespa was the first scooter I owned. The problem with the Vespa was that the gear change was on the handlebars."

Why scooters? "I felt they were easier to ride than a motorbike because you step through them and you can carry a lot of stuff where your feet are, good to get through traffic, easy to park and you have a windscreen. I went to my sister's wedding on a scooter in a morning coat! It's just much easier to get around."

Danger In The Fifties

David Haynes: "The huge difference, the one thing I couldn't emphasise enough, is the difference in the danger between then and now. It wouldn't surprise us at all if somebody was killed in a race and in the course of a year there would be a half-a-dozen or so."

SM: "Then death seemed to be part of the deal.

"Speaking personally, and I can only speak personally, to me motor racing without danger would be like cooking without salt. For my era, anyway, the danger was an important ingredient that made it so great. You are gambling and you are gambling to try and beat somebody. There is nobody there holding your foot down, so its entirely down to you - that is where the buck stops. To me, I must say, if it had not been dangerous, I would not have enjoyed it so much."

DE RIJSCHOOL VAN NEUBAUER!

Striking Gold

With Jean Behra, Maserati's lead driver, injured, the works offered Stirling a drive in the Daily Dispatch Gold Cup race at Oulton Park. Scuderia Ferrari provided Lancias for Hawthorn and Castellotti, and Musso in another works Maserati completed the strong front row of the grid.

Stirling was not first off the line but took the lead between Esso Bend and Lodge Corner on the opening lap. Hawthorn occupied second spot and was attempting, and failing, to keep up with his compatriot. Meanwhile Collins, who was driving the new B.R.M. P25, had made a bad start from a lowly 13th on the grid. Driving like a fiend in a car that clearly had potential, he was up to third place within four laps before the inevitable happened and he had to retire with no oil pressure.

Stirling won by over a minute from Hawthorn and Titterington (Vanwall). He had to miss his interview with John Bolster for B.B.C. viewers because the plane in which he and Collins were flying back down south had no landing lights!

Fangio, Moss may end partnership

ROME, Thursday.

STIRLING MOSS and Juan Fangio, teammates in the Mercedes-Benz racing stable, are expected to break up their partnership next year.

Rivalry between them is the cause, say reports.

Fangio is slightly ahead of Moss in points for the world championship.

Fangio met officials of the Maserati stables at Modena, Northern Italy, to-day.

He said he has made no plans for next season.

He refused to discuss reports that he may join Maserati.

Both Fangio and Moss drove Maseratis before joining the Mercedes team.—A.P.

Moss is on holiday in the Mediterranean.

His mother, Mrs. A. Moss, of Tring, Herts, said last night: "My son has learnt a lot riding behind Fangio.

"But you cannot win championships that way.

"When you have to ride to orders—and that is behind — championships are out of the question.

"That's why Stirling may do something different next year.

"He will probably want to go out on his own for the championship."

Daily Sketch 30.9.55

Moss, Fangio "may split"

Stirling Moss and Juan Fangio, who have dominated the 1955 racing season as Mercedes teammates, will probably split the partnership next year.

An informed source said yesterday that rivalry between the two is the cause. Fangio is ranked first and Moss second in points for this season's World Championship.

The Belfast driver, Desmond Titterington, has been signed to drive for Mercedes in the Targa Florio sports car race in Sicily on October 16.

Northern Whig 30.9.55

Moss v. Fangio In Sports Cars

PP: "Why were you so much faster than Fangio in sports cars?

SM: "I don't know. I think sports cars were easier to drive in reality. I happen to like them; Fangio didn't. I think he preferred to see the wheels - didn't make any difference to me whether I could see them or not because I didn't look at the wheels anyway. To illustrate my point, if you have a broad pen your writing looks better than if you have a fine pen. That's how I would compare the difference in driving between Formula One and sports cars. With a Formula One car the precision you require is considerably greater than a sports car. With a sports car, if you have the precision, it pays off more because less people have it.

"A sports car is much more forgiving. You can put a moderately good driver, or take a driver who is really good in sports, people like Gendebien, Phil Hill, Taruffi, Maglioli - these guys were fairly moderate when it gets to Formula One, but they were brilliant in sports cars. I think it's easier to get close to the limit in a sports car. If you are going to drive at ten-tenths, then they are both the same, but if you are going to run at nine-and-a-half-tenths, which was normally how sports cars were run, then they were easier.

"In sports cars, I could beat him, as I showed in the Targa and Mille Miglia and so on, but in Formula One, where the highest amount of skill is required, in my mind he was the greatest. I couldn't compare Fangio with Senna, but I could compare him with every driver I ever drove with or against and there is no other driver who ever compared. I reckon I was nearly as fast as Fangio but he had amazing stamina, and I mean mental stamina as well. It's true he got the best cars but the best driver gets the best cars. He was amazingly quick and extraordinarily precise."

FANGIO & MOSS MAY JOIN MASERATI

MERCEDES-BENZ STEP

From Our Special Correspondent

MODENA, Sunday.

Fangio, the world champion driver, and Stirling Moss, British racing driver, are expected in Modena within the next 10 days, it was learned here to-night. It is understood that they will probably sign with Maserati, the Italian car firm for next season's racing.

The change is apparently due to the decision of Mercedes-Benz, to whom the two drivers have been under contract, to withdraw from Formula One racing. If they join Maserati they will have as companion drivers Bira and Musso.

Daily Telegraph 26.9.55

For the second year running, Stirling won the coveted Gold Cup race at Oulton Park, a track in Cheshire that was a more 'natural' road circuit than those flat, rather featureless courses based on disused airfields. His one-off 1955 drive for the Maserati works team renewed a relationship that had begun the previous year and would be one of his options for 1956.

The Shrimp

David Haynes tells the story about a certain boat of that name: "Stirling said, 'My God, I've forgotten this bloody boat I've hired. Hadn't we better go there and use it for a little bit of crumpet chasing?'

"We arrived at Juan les Pins harbour and we were both looking for a fairly meaningful boat but no sign of anything called 'The Shrimp'. Eventually, we got the pier number and we see a magnificent-looking craft and we say to the skipper, 'Excuse me, we are looking for the Shrimp'. 'Oh!' he said, 'Just walk forward.' So we walk forward to the sharp end and look over and there, nuzzling under this magnificent boat, was our piddling little Shrimp.

"The significance of the name hadn't occurred to us. Anyway, we were pretty staggered at this and there wasn't a hell of a lot of room. On the second day, Stirling decided that he wanted to go scuba diving. Bear in mind, I know absolutely nothing about boats!"

SM: "Less than nothing I would say!"

DH: "Anyway, so we go out in the boat, Stirling puts on all the gear and off he jumps into the water. It's a lovely sunny day - until about 15-20 minutes later when a breeze started. Then the breeze turned into a mistral.

"There I was on this boat. I had no idea where Stirling was. I had no idea how to start the boat or anything. I thought, 'I hope to God he comes up nearby' because the visibility was now down to about 20 yards."

SM: "I am underwater blissfully unaware of all that was going on."

DH: "One of the happiest moments of my life, I can tell you, was when suddenly, just on the edge of the visibility, Stirling appears with a cheery wave - he didn't realise what the conditions were! Came on board and, I am glad to say, got us back to port. It was the nearest Britain has ever been to losing a rather good driver."

"On the third day Stirling gets a message to phone Neubauer. So Stirling says the immortal words to me, 'Dave, I'm afraid I'm going to have to go. You can either go back to England or you can come with me!' So I said, 'Well, I think I would rather come with you, Stirling - it sounds quite interesting.' I little knew how interesting. If what I have just described on the water was one of the more alarming incidents in my life, one of the more amazing experiences was what happened when we got to Sicily."

OCTOBER

1955 Calendar

16   Targa Florio, Sicily - 1st Moss/Collins in 300 SLR

Stirling and David Haynes picked up the plane tickets for the next stage of their adventure and found they were "All cocked up". From Nice they flew in an Air France Armagnac. "The stewardess was the pinnacle of incivility! The undercarriage stuck up & we circled for over an hour. All OK & to Rome. Stayed at the Massimo d'Azegho & food at Alfredo's."

Unfortunately the hotel woke them an hour earlier than they were supposed to and they then caught a plane to Palermo, via Naples. "No-one met us as the cable hadn't arrived. Took a robbing taxi for 2500 lire! [£1.50]." They stayed the night at the Albergo Igua and next morning booked into the Hotel Palma. "Then to circuit (1 hr) & a lap with Karl. Lunch & Dave & I did three laps in Hans's car. 1 hr 4 mins." That night they met up with Pete Collins, Des Titterington, Hans Hermann, John Fitch and Carroll Shelby.

"Up at 9am & to circuit with Karl & David in an SL [must have been a little cramped!]. I did one lap in the SLR (51 mins) & then lunch & two more laps (50 ½ & 50) & then two laps with Pete in a 220. I now know the circuit fairly well."

Next day, Wednesday 5th, was also spent practising. Stirling commenced with one lap driving Kling in the latter's 220. After lunch he did two laps in an SL with Haynes, recording times of 53 and 52 minutes, and then had a swim. Meanwhile Peter Collins took the SLR round the tortuous circuit and also managed a time of 50 minutes. Next day Stirling had "a touch of flu" and did just a couple of laps in the rain with Collins in a 190 SL.

The following day, still feeling the effects of flu, SM did a lap in the SLR with Collins (50 ½) and later a lap in an SL (53) and 220 (59). "J.F. did 47 ½ in SLR! Back to town. Met Deli."

Nicholas Watt's superb painting sums up the atmosphere of the uniquely-challenging Targa Florio course around the mountains, towns and villages of Sicily.

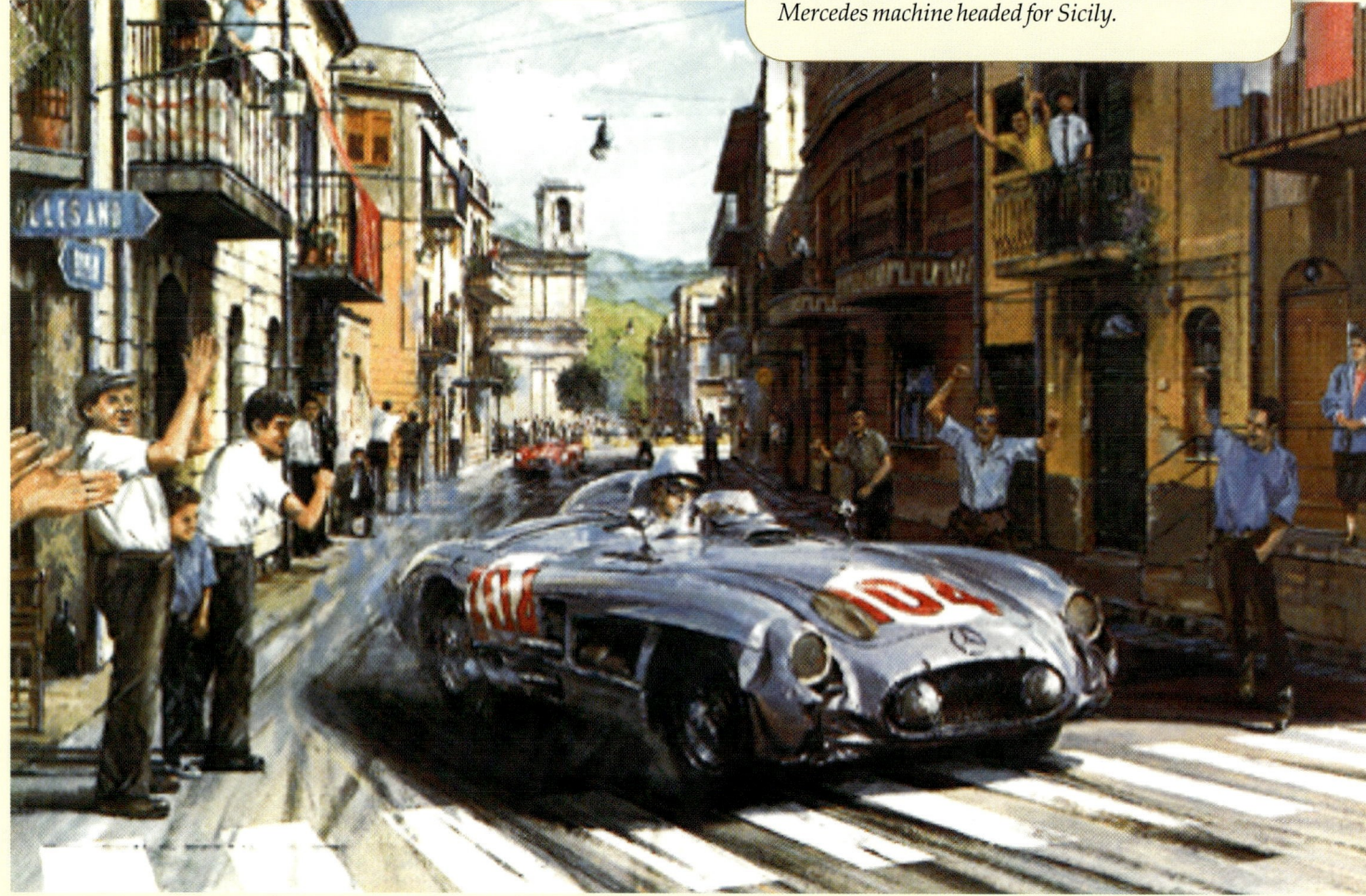

The Targa Or Not

Originally, Mercedes-Benz were not going to contest the uniquely-challenging ancient Targa Florio in Sicily. There was a relatively minor sports car race, the Grand Prix at Caracas in Venezuela that very same weekend and, with South America being an extremely important market for M-B, the senior management at Stuttgart had decided that that was the better option in commercial terms.

Furthermore, Ferrari were leading the World Sports Car Championship (with M-B having withdrawn from Le Mans and Jaguar having won there and at Sebring) and the chances of Mercedes being able to clinch the Championship were not looking good until they managed to take the first three places in the T.T. Even so, winning the Championship remained a remote possibility. There was not a strong case for the Targa.

However, the redoubtable Neubauer had other thoughts. He was absolutely determined Mercedes would give it their best shot and argued and lobbied at the highest levels until he got his own way. To take the overall honours, M-B were going to have finish in first and second places. Thus the mighty Mercedes machine headed for Sicily.

Driver Choice

With so much at stake for Mercedes, they needed a strong line-up of drivers. Rather curiously, Neubauer asked Stirling to decide with whom he would like to share a 300 SLR and also for him and Ken Gregory to suggest another driver.

Stirling had no hesitation about choosing Peter Collins, provided he could be released by Aston Martin to whom he was contracted but who were not entering this event. Collins, though something of a playboy off the track, was a deadly serious competitor once behind the wheel. He had shined in the little 500s and sports cars but had not yet made his mark in Formula One so it was quite a bold suggestion.

As to the other driver, Stirling and Ken came up with a driver who had impressed them at Dundrod where he had been sharing a D-type with Mike Hawthorn. Desmond Titterington, a native of Belfast, had shown great skill and determination, and was to prove another sound choice.

Together with Fangio from the Argentine, genial American John Fitch and just one German, Karl Kling, it was certainly a very international line-up.

This delightful drawing was sent to Stirling as a Christmas card that year.

The Armagnac

Retired Australian Air Traffic Controller, Jack Russell, described the French Sud-Est SE2010 Armagnac as, "...an 80-ton aircraft which resembled two shipping containers welded together lengthways with a wing and two under-powered engines protruding on each side. The aircraft's performance matched its appearance. It carried up to 107 passengers and had an amazing internal cabin height of 3.6 metres." A TAA pilot, when asked to report sighting and passing an Armagnac replied, "If it's that block of flats below us, we're passing it now!"

The Targa Florio

The Targa Florio was the inspiration of one Vincenzo Florio, a sportsman and industrialist. With the exception of the war years (1915-1918 & 1941-47), it had run every year since 1906 over roughly the same course in the Madonie Hills near Palermo in Sicily. There were said to be over a 1,000 corners to the approximately 40-mile (70km) lap, with the course rising from sea-level to 3,500ft (1,200m). The dangerous nature of the event is illustrated by the story of Tazio Nuvolari once rebuking Enzo Ferrari for buying him a return ticket. "You're supposed to be a businessman. You should know better than to buy a driver a return ticket." Nuvolari's 1932 record lasted until 1952.

Saturday consisted of more of the same though on this occasion he practised in Uhlenhart's fabulous 300 SLR Coupé. In this, he managed 46½ minutes but "damp & shunted wall. Not too bad. Des & Pete had a shunt as well." He later did some laps in the dark before eating in the Jolly Hotel and returning to Palermo. "Had a grog." Sunday was a day off and Stirling and Pete saw a couple of films in Italian.

It was raining on Monday and a pretty indifferent day. Stirling did one lap in a 220 and one on the 190. "J.F. hit a sheep in the SL." Tuesday included a lap in the race SLR (46 mins) "It skates about a lot. After dark did two laps with Pete in the SL (53 mins)."

The weather was so bad next day that there was no practice. The following day was better and Stirling travelled to the circuit "with Titt & Pete. I did one lap in our SLR which felt better with the softer front dampers. It was ½ wet. 48 mins, J.F. 49." French journalist Bernard Cahier took him round the circuit for some lunch and managed to spin his Fiat 600 on the way back! Stirling hung around to do some laps in the dark but heavy rain ruined his plans.

With the race on the Sunday, Friday was not too arduous. Stirling did a couple of laps in an SL with Jenks and then scrutineering took place before lunch. "The circuit is covered in mud after all the rain. It was decided to start the race at 7am to not have any darkness. Sally arrived with Brookie!"

Next morning Moss, Collins and Hermann ran out of petrol in a 220 on the way to the circuit. He then did a lap with Collins in a 190 (53 mins) and later two in the SL also with Peter Collins. "Maglioli had a shunt on the new road surface in a 3.5 practice car. He was OK. We moved to the Jolly Hotel in Cefalu for tonight. Cast. [Castellotti] is supposed to have lapped in 45 mins (maybe).

"Up at 5am after the worst night ever 1½ hours sleep. To circuit. Off at 7.25½am. Took lead on 1st lap by 1.08 from Cast. J.F. 3rd on 3rd lap. +5 mins, then crunch! Much fear. After 12 mins & with 40 odd bods got the car up two metres on to the road again! Peter took over at 4th lap & went like a bomb. He shunted a wall I'm glad to say. I took over on 8th to end. We won at 96kph by 5 mins. Took lead on 8th lap. Pete 43.22. J.F. 44 plus. SM 43.07. Was about to do a sensational 41+ but ….!"

Stirling went to bed at 4am and "Up at 6.45am! (Night worker yet)." He flew to Rome

Practice

David Haynes: *"To start with, we went round in a cooking Mercedes with me feebly taking notes like Denis Jenkinson. I didn't have a lavatory roll, but Stirling was telling me the things that I should note down. It was 40 miles a lap, so it took quite a long while. At the end of this, I thought that he and I were quite in harmony. Then Neubauer said, 'Right you are out in the SLR'. So I get into the SLR, Stirling in the seat with the proper headrest behind him, me in the seat with no headrest, because it's virtually a one-seater. No windscreen either!*

"Anyway, after having been out in this cooking Mercedes, I suddenly find myself in an SLR, going up a mountainside at about 150/160mph. I could only vaguely remember what happened at the corner at the top, but fortunately Stirling did remember and went round it.

"I completed the first lap in a total daze because, to start with, I was terrified. Suddenly, I relaxed. It was rather like being with the pilot of Concorde and you see all these switches. You assumed he knew what he was doing and, by Christ, he did! Not many people have had the privilege of actually driving with Stirling in an SLR, round a place like

Preparations

Once the decision had been made, the whole force of the Mercedes over-organisation swung into operation. They invaded Sicily three weeks in advance with eight cars for practice, eight trucks, 45 mechanics and a positive fleet of touring cars. In contrast, Ferrari turned up with three cars and eight mechanics.

To enable the Targa Florio to qualify for the World Sports Car Championship, the distance had been extended from the usual eight laps to 13 circuits, over 500 gruelling miles (over 800 kilometres) and some 10,000 bends.

The first driver was not allowed to do more than five consecutive laps and the second driver had to do a minimum of three laps. Ferrari planned to make four pit stops to change drivers, due to the extreme physical challenge of the course to the drivers. Neubauer decided they had to manage with two. Fangio thought four laps was the most any driver could manage but Neubauer was adamant they must try and do more.

Pete Collins drove the car he shared with Stirling exceptionally well.

Palermo

David Haynes: "One thing that was quite amazing, other than going up these hills and down at vast speed, was when you actually came to Palermo and you had to go through it. In rallies in those days you used to head towards a wall of people [spectators filling the streets] and you hoped that they would move out of the way. Anyway, we were going through the main street of Palermo and first time we went round - no problems! The second time we came round, we were hurtling through - I think he slowed down a bit - but we were doing a good 130mph and suddenly, an old dear, with a shopping basket, suddenly stepped out, oblivious of everything, right in front of the car. Stirling had two options, either to go behind her or ahead of her. Thank God, he decided to go behind, so she moved that much further away. He missed her by the grace of God. I looked round to see what had happened and there was this dear old lady spinning like a top ... because he had just clipped her basket!

"I said to Stirling, 'I pray God she hasn't been hurt' and Stirling, typical Stirling, said, 'We will find out when we get round next time!'

"So, we go around again, approach at slightly less than 130, waiting to see if there are police cars, flashing lights, ambulances or what. Instead of that, whereas the first time round everybody had just moved out of the way, this time as Stirling went through they are all going 'Yea, yea, yea'. They had seen this and thought it was a great bit of driving that he had actually missed this lady, who obviously hadn't suffered too much."

Stirling Moss ...

LEARNING THE COURSE

"Well, the Targa Florio took me several days to learn. You see it took you getting on for an hour to do a lap and that was going quickly. But, the thing with the Targa was that as well as the corners, you needed to know the surfaces too, because the surfaces on the Targa Florio were very moderate in places. The trouble was you had to go round the night before the race, literally, because they would go out and they would see a place where it was breaking up. They would throw a bit of tar onto it and they would sprinkle on a bit of gravel, which of course is the worst thing in the world. You would come round the corner and you were suddenly on this bloody loose gravel."

Stirling Moss ...

POTHOLES

"I remember Dave and I going out the night before to see if they had filled in any of the potholes."

What a scene. What a backdrop. What a challenge. What a motor race!

Moss wins, smashes records

STIRLING MOSS won the perilous Targa Floria race at Palermo, Italy, yesterday, and so secured for Mercedes the world car championship for 1955.

He was closely followed by Juan Manuel Fangio, world individual racing driver, and captain of the Mercedes team.

Moss, and his British co-driver Peter Collins, covered the 13 laps, totalling 580 miles of mountainous roads, with 898 bends in every lap, in 9hr. 43min. 14sec., to average just under 60 m.p.h.

Moss, the pace setter of the Mercedes team, sent the crowd of more than 100,000 into a pandemonium of excitement as he set up one lap record after another.

He lost time and dropped back to fourth place during the fourth circuit after he had skidded wildly when entering the only straight kilometre of the course. The tail of his car hit the sandbags and he stopped at the pits while mechanics checked that no serious damage had been done.

Fangio, whose co-driver was the German, Karl Kling, finished nearly 4½ minutes behind with a time of 9hr. 47min. 41sec.

Only opposition

The race gave Mercedes the world championship for the first time since the war with 24 points, one ahead of Ferrari, holders of the title. Ferrari were leading with 18 points to the 16 of Mercedes before yesterday's race.

Moss and Collins added more than 3.73 m.p.h. to the record for the race set last year by the Italian Taruffi.

The only opposition to the two Mercedes came from the Ferrari driven by Eugenio Castellotti (Italy) and Robert Manzon (France). They finished third in 9hr. 53min. 20.8sec.

Race of tactics

Next was another Mercedes, driven by the Britons Desmond Titterington and John Fitch.

It was a great race of tactics between Moss and Fangio. When Moss had his mishap Fangio surged ahead after Castellotti had shown in front and afterwards, with Moss back in the lead, Fangio hung on to Castellotti's tail, ready to take up the challenge if anything happened to his pacemaking team-mate. Then in the end he took over second place to give Mercedes their complete triumph.

M'chester Eve. Disp. 17.10.55

and then on to London Airport where he was met and taken to a Mercedes reception. Next morning he and Collins did a recording with Peter Garnier and had lunch with the Autocar Editor. "To Motor Show and rehearsals for T.V. show. Later to John & Mary Morgan's for cocktails."

Next morning was spent at the Motor Show. In the evening, "Met David Haynes & June R at the Savoy. We saw *Spider's Web* and then Lena Horne. VG. The following day was a long one at the office. David Yorke phoned to talk about the Vanwall and in the evening Stirling took Jean to see a film. Friday 21st was another day in the office before Stirling, Pete, Jean and Mary Rose went in an Aston Martin to London Airport to fly, presumably, to Stuttgart.

At the ensuing Mercedes reception, "Received my pins, etc., also Targa medals & cups. Heard Mercs are completely withdrawing from racing! Had press phoning all day. Later food & made deal to meet Neubauer in 1962 in the restaurant of today. I do hope we make it. Felt awful."

Stirling rose late and caught a plane to Nice, via Geneva and Zurich. "Arrived at 7pm. We went to the Cagnard. I feel awful and can't eat." He was still feeling bad next day but went to Cannes. He collected his stuff from the boat and went to Monte Carlo. There he paid 32,000F for two pairs of black overalls, two blue pairs, four pairs of trousers, etc. From Nice he flew back to London. "Bed & doc."

Next day the patient stayed in bed and was visited by Jean and SW. Tuesday he was filmed in bed for the BBC Sportsview programme and had six visitors, including the girls and David Haynes. The doctor called again on Wednesday and Stirling got up at midday. Tony Parravano's offer was conveyed to him and then he went to see Roy Banaman Q.C., though it is not clear whether that was to discuss Parravano or his offer, or other matters. After a spell at the office, he took Rudi Uhlenhaut to see the Folies.

That Friday he had lunch with Tony Vandervell and David Yorke, no doubt to discuss the following season and a Vanwall drive. That evening he met June R. and they saw *How To Be Very Very Popular* (VG). Saturday's diary entry is rather cryptic. "Met David de Yong, snack, to Claridges. Later met Lionel & cleaned flat. To Embassy & I.T.V. gag spot. Remained plus J.C. £6-14-6." [£6.72]

Sunday was spent at Tring and visiting Syd Logan at Stoke Mandeville hospital. "He sure

Ristorante Neubauer

David Haynes: "Another highlight of the Targa Floria was the 'Ristorante Neubauer'. Neubauer used to prepare lunch for all the drivers, the co-drivers and everybody else. And he stopped the practice [runs] and served this [meal], a lot of it cooked by himself."

"Off the track I spoiled them," wrote Neubauer in his book which was published in 1958. "Friends of mine had lent me their villa, and every morning at seven I drove into the market myself to buy pounds of coffee, whole cases of cheese, salami and sardines, and baskets of eggs and tomatoes. When Moss showed signs of catching a cold I saw to it that he took his medicine regularly."

Stirling Moss ...

BROOKIE

"Brookie was an American Press girl."

Over The Edge

"On the morning of the race," wrote Stirling in his book 'In The Track of Speed', "I felt very little like racing. I had had practically no sleep and was up at 5am, tired and jaded. I felt much better once I was in the cockpit and waiting for the start, and better still when I discovered that I was leading the big field of competitors. Round that tortuous course I sped with the pack howling along behind, the fastest of my pursuers being Castellotti on a Ferrari, with Juan Fangio on his tail. I had built up a lead of just over a minute on the first lap, and increased this to five at the end of three laps. Then, wham!

"I had just come round a right curve and was negotiating a fast left, when I lost control; the car swung its tail out, hit a bank and then bounced off and made straight for a precipice. I was really afraid by now, and tried to bail out, but couldn't. Luckily it turned out to be only a 10 to 12 foot drop and the car landed with a heavy thump."

Contemporary reports varied about the distance he travelled from the road, one putting it at 800 feet (278m). Autosport stated that it was some time before the spectators stopped taking photographs and began to help. The magazine also said it took about a dozen attempts to clear the bank and get back on to the track.

The Race

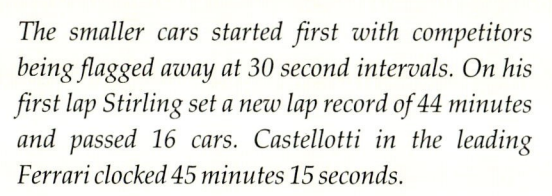

The smaller cars started first with competitors being flagged away at 30 second intervals. On his first lap Stirling set a new lap record of 44 minutes and passed 16 cars. Castellotti in the leading Ferrari clocked 45 minutes 15 seconds.

"Moss's driving is fantastic," reported Autosport. "Nothing like it has ever been seen in Sicily." His next lap is done in 43 minutes seven seconds, the first ever 100 km/h lap. Half way round the circuit, mud from the recent rainstorms was making the circuit very difficult. Stirling was now two minutes ahead of Castellotti and three minutes ahead of Fangio.

Then - disaster. Stirling lost control on the mud, smote a bank and went over the edge. Thankfully, it was not quite the precipice he first feared it was. However, he landed in a field, strewn with boulders, nine feet (3 metres) below the road. The car was relatively unscathed but he could not get any grip. Photographers and others miraculously appeared from nowhere to help and, after several attempts, he managed to regain the track and retrieved his crash hat which blew off as he accelerated away. Most of the water had boiled away and he had lost eight minutes and was now down in fourth place.

He made it back to the pits where Collins took over the battered machine. Pete then proved his worth. He completed his first flying lap in 43 minutes 28 seconds! After five laps they were back up to third, with Castellotti leading Fangio. Collins then smote a wall but got away with it.

After seven laps, Fangio's co-driver Kling led Castellotti's co-driver Manzon by eight seconds with Collins now just 36 seconds in arrears. Stirling took over again and even including the pit stop did an amazing 43 minute 41 second lap to regain the lead, just over a minute ahead of Fangio. Stirling just went quicker and quicker to win an amazing race by more than four minutes. Fangio finished second as a result of Castellotti making an extra pit-stop and Mercedes-Benz triumphed in the Championship.

Then & Now

David Haynes: *"One of the big differences between then and now was that there was always a big prize-giving dinner after a major race and all the drivers would go and they all got on well and there was a great camaraderie. Today, they all just jump in their helicopters and disappear."*

Stirling Moss ...

SYD LOGAN

"Syd Logan was a Jersey hillclimber. Very, very nice guy. I met him at Bouley Bay in my early years and we became close friends."

"Actually, poppet, I've a perfect right to be here—I'm his sort of mascot thing...."

looks much better but his sight isn't back yet." On Monday he went to Vandervell's for a car fitting and then to the R.A.C. for lunch. After a meeting with Dusty Mahon and Bob Rolophson at the Green Park Hotel, he ate at L'Epicure and ended the month at the Angel Club.

WORLD CHAMPIONSHIP FOR SPORTS CARS

Final Results - Points

Mercedes-Benz	24
Ferrari	23
Jaguar	16
Maserati	15
Aston-Martin	9
Porsche	6
Gordini	2
Austin-Healey	1

Driving Styles

Autosport commented on the contrasting styles of the drivers. First, they stated of Stirling's car, "The Mercedes come up the tricky turn under the B.P. Energol bridge to the 'tribuna' far faster than anything else. His time? 43 mins 7 secs, the first time 100 k.p.h. has been exceeded on any Targa Florio circuit!!

"Castellotti is wild in comparison; Titterington relaxed and fast; Shelby clean as a whistle; Fangio indecisive; Musso very rapid; Maglioli strangely subdued.

"The sun is very hot now, even at this early hour, and tar is forming on the approach road to the pits."

Drivers

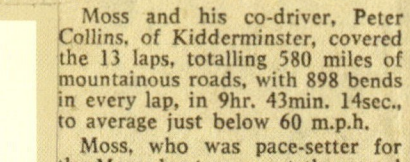

Moss on: Umberto Maglioli ...

"Very good sports car driver. Never really quite made it in Formula One. As good as most in sports cars. Quite talented."

MOSS WINS THE WORLD TITLE FOR MERCEDES

He and Collins add nearly 4 m.p.h. to mountain course record

PALERMO (Italy), Sunday.

STIRLING MOSS today won the perilous Targa Florio race here and so secured for Mercedes the world car championship for 1955.

Juan Manuel Fangio, world individual racing driver and captain of the Mercedes team, partnered by Karl Kling (Germany), followed 4min. 41sec. behind.

B'ham Gazette 17.10.55

Moss and his co-driver, Peter Collins, of Kidderminster, covered the 13 laps, totalling 580 miles of mountainous roads, with 898 bends in every lap, in 9hr. 43min. 14sec., to average just below 60 m.p.h.

Moss, who was pace-setter for the Mercedes team, sent the crowd of more than 100,000 into a fever of excitement as he set up one lap record after another.

He lost eight minutes and dropped back to fourth place during the fourth circuit after skidding wildly when entering the only straight kilometre of the course.

Hit sandbags

The tail of his car hit sandbags, and he stopped for a while mechanics checked serious damage had...

Moss and Collins... than 3.73 m.p.h. to... the race set last... Italian Taruffi...

The only opposition... Mercedes came from... driven by Euge... (Italy) and Ro... (France). They fi... 9hr. 53min. 20.8sec...

STIRLING MOSS

Local 'Colour'

Spectators' cars were parked on the edge of the circuit! The confusion in the pits brought scenes reminiscent of the Marx Brothers, according to Gregor Grant in Autosport. Two Lancias pitted and competed to be first out ... and collided! A Gordini over-shot the pits, so calmly reversed back!

17.10.55

ALLA MERCEDES IL TITOLO MONDIALE CATEGORIA SPORT
Moss precede Fangio nella "Florio"

NOSTRO SERVIZIO

CERDA, 16

Una folla straboccevole si è riversata alle tribune di Cerda, 50 chilometri da Palermo, migliaia e migliaia erano le macchine che su cui partenti; dodici non avevano ai bordi della strada, prime di arrivare al traguardo.

Quarantasette sono stati i partenti, dodici non avevano nemmeno punzonato, ed uno aveva rinunziato.

Moss realizza nel primo giro la media di Km. 98.182, al secondo forza ancora e al terzo Km. 100.186, riesce in tre giri a portare il suo vantaggio a 3' e 21". Un incidente a Moss ridà spettacolo e fasi alterne e combattive alla gara che se no poteva divenire un monologo della casa tedesca. Al quarto giro, sul rettilineo di Buonfornello Moss esce di strada, danneggiandosi nella fiancata destra. Otto minuti perduti, per l'inglese e il ritorno spettacoloso di Castellotti che riesce, per pochi primi, a prendere il comando della gara, tallonato e poi superato da Fangio.

Molti speravano che il percorso fiaccasse la potenza dei mezzi e l'organizzazione spettacolare della Mercedes, man mano che i giri passavano, si delineava sempre più evidente il risultato finale.

Così anche a Palermo una massiccia vittoria che le è valso il titolo mondiale per macchine della categoria Sport.

E' stata una affermazione derivata dallo strapotere col quale la casa di Stoccarda si era presentata fra le colline delle Madonie, dovuta a una meticolosa preparazione dei motori, alla perfetta conoscenza che gli uomini di Neubauer hanno voluto avere del percorso da affrontare, alla grande disponibilità di uomini e mezzi di rincalzo.

Prodigiosa, senza dubbio, la corsa di Stirling Moss, intelligente quella di Fangio, e prudente quella di Titterington che ha dovuto rispettare e subire la legge della graduatoria dei valori.

Contro i campioni e le macchine di Stoccarda si sono levati prima: Gigi Villoresi, con la sua «Maserati» estromessa poi da una rottura del ponte, quindi Maglioli con la «Ferrari» e infine, più tenace fra tutti il meraviglioso Castellotti, che da solo doveva lottare contro mezzi meccanici perfetti e contro Fangio, Stirling Moss, Kling e Collins.

Ha tentato anche Maria Teresa De Filippis di inserirsi con Giardini, pure su Maserati, e Cabianca con la sua Osca, ma tutto si è ridotto a una dimostrazione di spirito sportivo e perseveranza, senza eccessive mire. Lo stesso può esser detto per Scarlatti e Giuseppe Musso, pure su due Maserati 2000, e per la Fiat 8 V di Zagato, la Mercedes di Zampiero e l'altra Fiat 8 V di De Sarzana.

La «Ferrari», però, non ha perduto a Cerda e sul circuito delle Madonie, il primato per il campionato del mondo, ma a Belfast, quando al «Tourist Trophy» si dovè accontentare di un sesto posto e di un sol punto. A Cerda malgrado quello che si possa dire, le «Mercedes» sono state signore incontrastate. E' stata la dimostrazione che contro la potenza e l'organizzazione, il cuore non basta, anche se altro è stato il valore sportivo e la condotta di gara di Stirling Moss e di Fangio.

Federico Bossoli

Ecco la classifica:
1) Moss - Collins (Mercedes) in 9.43'48" media 96,290;
2) Fangio - Kling (Mercedes) in 9.47'55"
3) Castellotti (Ferrari) in 10'6";
4) Titterington (Mercedes) in
5) Giardini (Maserati) in primo della 2000;
6) Musso (Maserati 2000) in a un'ora
7) Cabianca (4-1500) in ad un'ora mo della 1500).
8) Scarlatti (2000) 1.20'14";
9) Bellucci (Maserati 2000) a 1.39'39"
10) Starrabba (Maserati 2000) in (fermato al 12. giro)

Moss e Collins subito dopo l'arrivo (Tel. a IL MATTINO)

Stirling Moss has the Italian fans cheering

PALERMO, Sunday.

STIRLING MOSS, the British motor-racing driver, today won the perilous Targa Floria race here and so secured for Mercedes the world car championship for 1955. He was closely followed by Juan Manuel Fangio, world individual racing driver, and captain of the Mercedes team.

Moss and his British co-driver Peter Collins covered the 13 laps, totalling 936 kilometres (about 580 miles) of mountainous roads, with 898 bends in every lap, in 9hr 43min 14sec, to average 96,290 kph (just under 60 mph).

Moss was the pace setter of the Mercedes team, and he sent the crowd of over 100,000 into a pandemonium of excitement as he set one lap record after another.

HIT SANDBAGS

Once he lost time and dropped back to fourth place during the fourth circuit after skidding wildly when entering the only straight kilometre of the course.

The tail of his car hit the sandbags and he stopped at the pits while mechanics checked that no serious damage had been done to the car.

Fangio, whose co-driver was the German Karl Kling, finished nearly 4½ minutes behind the British team, with a time of 9hr 47min 41sec.

SET NEW RECORDS

Moss and Collins added more than 6 kph (3.73 mph) to the record for the race set out last year by the Italian P. Taruffi.

Both Moss and Fangio started and ended the race, thereby taking full advantage to drive the maximum quota of ten of the thirteen laps.—Reuter.

Morning Advertiser 17.10.55

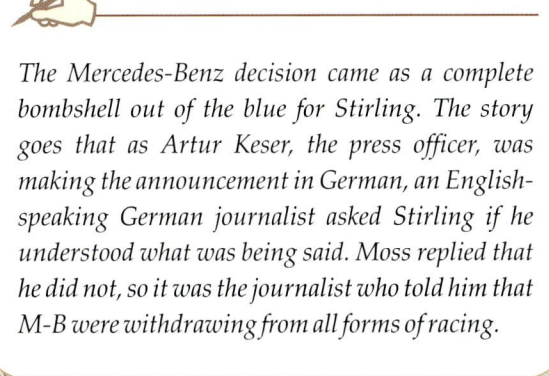

Mercedes Decision

The Mercedes-Benz decision came as a complete bombshell out of the blue for Stirling. The story goes that as Artur Keser, the press officer, was making the announcement in German, an English-speaking German journalist asked Stirling if he understood what was being said. Moss replied that he did not, so it was the journalist who told him that M-B were withdrawing from all forms of racing.

Vincenzo Florio si congratula con la coppia MOSS-COLLINS vincitori su «Mercedes» della XL TARGA

La classifica

1. — MOSS - COLLINS, su «Mercedes». Hanno percorso 13 giri del piccolo Circuito delle Madonie, Km. 936, in ore 9. 43' 14", pari alla media di Km. 96.290.
2. — FANGIO - KLING su «Mercedes» in ore 9, 47' 55" 2/5 a 4' 41" 2/5.
3. — CASTELLOTTI - MANZON su «Ferrari» in ore 9, 53' 20" 4/5 a 10' 6".
4. — TITTERINGTON - FITCHE su «Mercedes» in ore 9, 54' 53" 2/5.
5. — GIARDINI - MANZINI su «Maserati» in ore 10, 41' 15" a 58' 01" (primo della Categ. Sport 2000).
6. — MUSSO - ROSSI su «Maserati 2000» in ore 10, 48' 53" 1/5 a un'ora 05' 39" 1/5.

Mercedes Cars Withdrawing From Racing
Firm's Staff Had "Grossly Overworked"

Moss and Fangio 'not told' of directors' 10 day-old decision
MERCEDES TO QUIT RACING— SHOCK ACES

Stirling Moss ...

THE BOMBSHELL

"It was a hell of a shock. They used the excuse of Le Mans but, truthfully, I think the reason that they withdrew was that they were using too many top personnel running the racing fleet. There were Uhlenhaut and Neubauer plus God knows how many others and I think that was probably the reason. Once you'd won like they did, and they had been winning throughout '54/55, the only way they could go was down. I remember Rudi Uhlenhaut telling me that it took him six months to design and build a racing car to win, but two years to design and build a production car - very much more complex."

OUT OF WORK

STIRLING MOSS, who, with world champion Juan Fangio, is out of a job as a result of the decision by Mercedes cars to retire from racing (see Page 7). Moss who looked crestfallen at the news, said: "It is a terrible decision—the worst news I have ever had. I am out of work. It came as a complete shock." He said he had no idea for whom he would now drive.

MERCEDES QUIT OVER NEW SAFETY RESTRICTIONS

By **LEN SMITH**, Daily Sketch Motoring Correspondent

A SECRET tip off about new safety regulations is believed to be behind the withdrawal of the triumphant German Mercedes organisation from all motor racing.

But Britain's premier sports car manufacturers—Jaguars of Coventry—have no intention of quitting.

Mr. W. Heynes, Jaguar's chief engineer, told me last night: "We have not seen the new regulations but we have made no decision to abandon racing."

The Mercedes announcement has parted the world's two best drivers, champions Juan Fangio, of Argentina, and Britain's Stirling Moss, as members of the same team.

A FIGHT

Moss is expected to drive for the Italian Maserati firm, and Fangio will fight him for future championships at the wheel of a Ferrari.

The new regulations, outcome of the Le Mans and Dundrod tragedies, are framed to ban disguised racing cars from sports car events.

The regulations will be announced almost any day by the international federation governing motor sport.

They are expected to ban the use of such unorthodox equipment as air brakes—introduced by Mercedes.

Such normal road car features as two doors, adequate seating, weatherproof hoods, and even luggage space will be insisted on.

A limit on engine size—2½ litres or less—is also being considered to keep speeds down.

But this limitation is unlikely to worry Jaguar's since the introduction of their new 2.4 litre engine.

The Mercedes withdrawal came as a great surprise. Their engineers had planned new model sports cars for 1956.

Mercedes had planned an all-out attempt to sweep the board in next year's sports car events.

Daily Dispatch 24.10.55

Moss goes to Ferrari

BRM prepare car for Stirling Moss

DISPATCH REPORTER

THE BRM organisation is getting a car ready with a view to Stirling Moss driving it.

This was stated last night by Mr. Raymond Mays, BRM racing director.

Moss, who said on Saturday that he was out of work through the withdrawal of Mercedes from all racing next year, was asked before the *Daily Dispatch* Oulton Park meeting whether he would drive the BRM.

'We hope'

He won the Gold Cup in a Maserati. The BRM made a sensational debut before withdrawing.

Mr. Mays said: "We hope Moss will drive for us, but he is in a position to choose. We are hoping the car will be good enough for us to negotiate terms with him."

M'chester D'ly Disp 24.10.55

MOSS—'BACK TO THE PIGS'

STIRLING MOSS, Britain's crack racing driver, found himself without a job yesterday.

The German Mercedes company, for whom Moss has driven brilliantly this year, announced: "Our cars will not race next year—we are concentrating on passenger car production."

So what will Stirling do?

"I think I'll go and help my father and sister run their pig farm at Tring," he said last night.

But Moss is unlikely to be out of work for long. Italian firms Ferrari and Maserati are both eager to sign him up for Grand Prix racing. And Jaguar would jump at the chance of having him for sports car events.

Mercedes Sensation

THE Mercedes people have caused quite a sensation by their decision to drop out of motor racing altogether. Next year we shall not see them even in the sports car series.

I wonder why? Possibly they consider that it is a good time to retire when at the top of the ladder—and they have carried all before them this year.

But could it also be that as their successes have been achieved with foreign drivers this is considered poor propaganda for Germany?

Their decision leaves several race drivers, including Stirling Moss and world champion Fangio, stranded, but not for long.

Stirling will probably do what he always has wanted to do and that is to drive only British cars in the classic events.

STIRLING MOSS—"It is a terrible decision, the worst news I have ever had."

STIRLING MOSS: 'I AM OUT OF WORK'

Commercial Telly

Ending the BBC's 18-year monopoly, commercial television came to Britain in September, 1955. The Independent Television Authority (ITA) began broadcasting from the Guildhall. The Postmaster General assured viewers that Hamlet would not interrupt his soliloquy to tell the world of his favourite brand of toothpaste or a violinist stop in the middle of a solo to advise what brand of cigarettes he favoured. Some 24 adverts were broadcast that first night and ranged from Gibbs SR toothpaste to Cadbury's chocolate and Esso petrol. A separate organisation, the Independent Television News Company (ITN), was set up to provide all news broadcasts.

MOSS GETS OFFER

ROME, Friday.—Ferrari Motors have made an offer to Stirling Moss to drive in next year's Formula One events.—D.M. Cable.

Moss would like a British car

Stirling Moss arrived at London Airport from Rome last night with his co-driver, Peter Collins, after winning the Italian Targa Florio.

Moss said that Mercedes were not entering Grand Prix races, and added: "I have had offers from Ferrari and Maserati, but I would much prefer to drive a British car."

B'ham Gazette 18.10.55

Mercedes Quit Racing—A Terrible Shock Says Moss

STUTTGART, Saturday.

THE world champion Mercedes cars which came back last year to beat the rest of the world are being withdrawn from racing.

The surprise announcement came to-day as the makers, Daimler-Benz, were celebrating their brilliant success this year in winning the triple world championship.

The Mercedes were withdrawn from Grand Prix racing after the Le Mans disaster in June. Sports car racing will be abandoned "for some time."

Drivers had not been told of the decision. World champion Juan Manuel Fangio, of Argentina, and Britain's Stirling Moss don't speak German and did not understand the decision when it was announced.

They were told a little later. Moss looked crestfallen. "It is a terrible decision—the worst news I have ever had. I am out of work. It came as a complete shock." Moss said he had no idea who he would drive for now.—Reuter.

*** An official of the Jaguar Company said this afternoon: "Our plans are not affected. We shall definitely be at Le Mans next year."

Evening News 22.10.55

New Models On TV Tonight

By J. N. BENNETT

FIRST live television broadcast of the Motor Show will be seen at 7.30 tonight, when Associated-Rediffusion cameras will visit Earls Court for a preview.

The programme will last for half-an-hour, and expert opinions on some of the new cars will be given by Stirling Moss, whose sister Pat, together with Miss Sheila van Damm, will provide the feminine point of view.

Although the technical difficulties of cabling and lighting do not permit a complete tour of the Show, it is hoped to include as many of the leading manufacturers as possible.

Sporting Life 18.10.55

Independent television at the show

THE first live television broadcast of the Motor Show from Earls Court was seen at 7.30 in the evening on Wednesday.

In the 30-minute programme expert opinions on some of the new cars were given by Stirling Moss. His sister, Pat Moss, was present with Sheila Van Damm, the famous rally driver, to provide the feminine point of view.

The technical difficulties of cabling and lighting did not allow a complete tour of the show. Two cameras toured the exhibition floor and a third was mounted on a balcony overlooking the main hall for a bird's eye view.

Swindon Advertiser 19.10.55

Stirling Moss off on world tour

Off for a six-month motor racing tour of the world is Britain's champion driver Stirling Moss. Over dinner recently, before setting off to drive a Mercedes in the famous Targo Florio race in Sicily, Stirling outlined a programme which would take him to Venezuela, Australia, New Zealand, South Africa, Argentina, America and the Bahamas.

Far from chatting about cars Stirling was full of the delights of speedboats and water-ski-ing. He is hoping to buy a yacht so that he can give his parents a rest from their pedigree pig farm in Hertfordshire and take them out to the Bahamas.

KING Hussein of Jordan tried out six British sports cars yesterday one after the other at Goodwood.

Occasion: The Guild of Motoring Writers' Motor Show test day.

The DUKE OF RICHMOND AND GORDON is president of the guild.

Expert

King Hussein is an expert driver. He has driven in races and has hill-climb experience.

Yesterday he told me he is thinking of starting a motor-racing "stable" in Jordan.

Perhaps we shall yet see Jordan's colours on the big tracks of the world.

The test day was staged by the guild, as in past years, to give foreign journalists visiting London for the Motor Show a chance to try out the new British models on view at Earls Court.

There were 60 of the latest British cars for them to try—of 29 different makes. They ranged from the £7,000 Bentley Continental to the £542 de luxe Ford Anglia.

Disappointed

Also among the guests were MR. AND MRS ALFRED MOSS, parents of STIRLING MOSS, Britain's motor-racing champion.

Mr. Moss told a colleague that Stirling was taken greatly by surprise by the decision of the German Mercédés-Benz firm to withdraw from sports car racing as well as from Grand Prix events next year.

"He was disappointed as well as surprised," said Mr. Moss. "He regards himself as an out-of-work racing driver, and I have invited him to help me on my pig farm in Hertfordshire. Somehow I do not think he will accept."

What is more likely is that Stirling will sign up with another Continental firm who will be racing both Formula I. and sports cars—Italy's Maserati firm, for example.

Daily Mail 24.10.55

British Driving Champion Tells Of His Life

'I Earned £12,000— Tax Left Me £1,400'

SAYS STIRLING MOSS

By W. R. PAULSON

STIRLING MOSS, who has flu, sat up in bed in his West Kensington flat to-day and told me: "It's true that Mercedes' withdrawal from all racing next year is a bad knock, but I am still confident of coming out on top."

Moss, 25-year-old British champion, and now bracketed jointly with his Mercedes team mate Juan Fangio as world's No. 1 driver, is nursing a temperature "something over a hundred."

Stirling went on: "Mercedes were a wonderful team and had a wonderful car. However, it has always been my ambition to find a British car really capable of winning a Grand Prix.

HOW MUCH?

'I Don't Know'

"I have had an invitation to try out the new B R M and also the British Vanwall. Maserati and Ferrari have both made offers. I will have to go to Italy to talk it over. If possible I will choose the British car."

Moss believes that income tax is stifling enterprise in this country.

"In my first big year of motor racing I earned £12,000. After tax, I was left with £1,400. This year I don't know, frankly, what I have earned, but as chairman and director of Stirling Moss, Inc., I draw £2,000, on which I have to pay tax."

The racing driver has to pay tax a year in arrears; so he has to earn enough next year to pay the tax on the considerable sums that he has won in the last ten months.

That may be the deciding factor against taking a chance with a British car.

He has already told me, to d Maserati.

"It is quite break even on car," was his o

Stirling recko active career of driver at 12 ye early (at 18) an level only last y I reckon with lu

Evening News 26.10.55

Stirling Moss

ALTHOUGH he is down with influenza, Stirling Moss, the 26-year-old British racing motorist, hopes to be fit enough to try out the B.R.M. next week.

From his sick bed at his Fulham, London, flat to-day, he phoned that he would be up to-morrow. He has cancelled a television appearance arranged for to-night.

Mercedes, for whom he drove this year, have withdrawn from all racing for 1956.

A spokesman for the Owen Motor Racing Association, which owns the B.R.M., told me: "We hope Stirling Moss will be able to try out the new B.R.M. There is no special significance to be drawn from that fact at the moment. Moss will no doubt try out a number of makes during the winter."

M'chester Eve. News 26.10.55

Nice to be home—even with flu

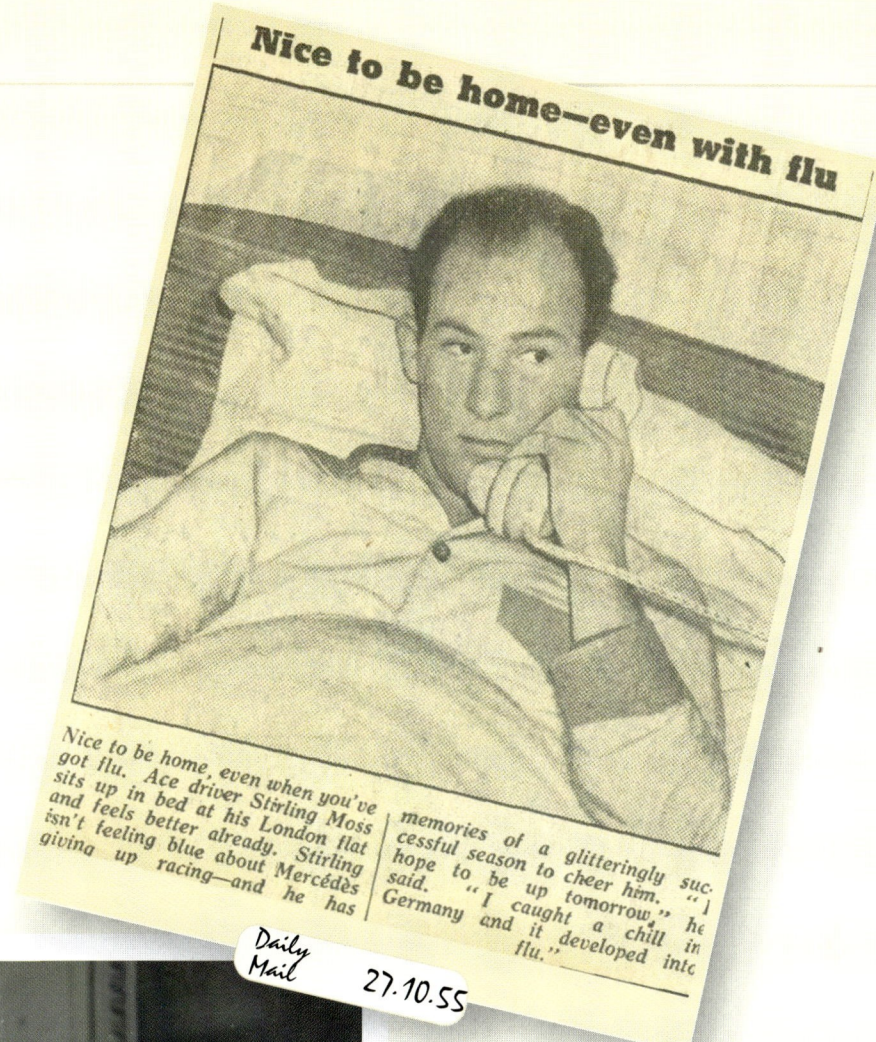

Nice to be home, even when you've got flu. Ace driver Stirling Moss sits up in bed at his London flat and feels better already. Stirling isn't feeling blue about Mercedes giving up racing—and he has memories of a glitteringly successful season to cheer him. "I hope to be up tomorrow," he said. "I caught a chill in Germany and it developed into flu."

Daily Mail 27.10.55

All After Moss

STIRLING MOSS, in bed at his Fulham flat under doctor's orders, is on a rest cure after a most strenuous season of racing.

The retirement of German Mercedes cars from all forms of racing has left him free to consider other offers.

His services are in great demand, but he will not enter into any contract until he has tried out the various Grand Prix cars he has been asked to drive. These include the new-style BRM and the Vanwall Special, the two main British hopes for next season's racing, and the British Connaught.

The two great Italian firms, Maserati and Ferrari, are also interested, but Moss would prefer to drive a British car

The Star 26.10.55

Stirling helps Rudolf Caracciola, one of the greatest pre-War racing drivers, launch his autobiography. Like Moss, Caracciola was a master in the wet and a great fighter with single-minded determination.

Stirling Moss—Motor Yachtsman

Stirling Moss has won a front-rank place in motoring circles but I wonder how many, apart from his close friends, know that he is very keen on the water. I had a most enjoyable lunch with him during the latter part of the past month at Weymouth and we talked, not very much about motor racing, but of various cruises he had made in hired craft. In point of fact he was then about to embark on a week's holiday afloat. In view of that it is not surprising to learn that he is seriously considering entering the company of boat owners and has looked over several cruisers but, at that time, had not discovered a craft which fully fulfilled his requirements. He also likes water skiing and during the morning he had given a demonstration towed by a fast runabout driven by his old friend Donald Healey, also of motoring fame. The event gave a large number of late holiday makers at Weymouth an unexpected thrill and when Moss came ashore he was besieged by autograph hunters. As it was not a particularly warm day he was shivering, but he scribbled away until everybody was satisfied. Certainly fame demands its pound of flesh!

Stirling Moss.

Motor Boat October '55

NOVEMBER

1955 Calendar

3	Testing B.R.M. at Oulton Park
12	Testing Vanwall & B.R.M. at Oulton Park
18	Testing at Modena, Italy
22	Testing Connaught, B.R.M. & Vanwall at Silverstone
24	Testing B.R.M. at Silverstone

Tuesday 1st: "Up to Pan-Am for photos. Snack lunch & work. Saw a flick and then met Turle & BP chaps & Parravano at Cabaret Club." On Wednesday, "Judy ill. Met SH [Sally Hindmarsh] for lunch. Then Parravano at 2.30. Talked until 5pm. More work. Met Haynes & to Windmill & sat in the box! Food at Angel. SW called round!"

With the shock Mercedes withdrawal Stirling was having to weigh up his options for next year. On Thursday he caught a train at Euston Station and went up to Crewe in Cheshire where he was met and taken to a "dark & damp & slippery Oulton. Tried B.R.M. - fantastic power. Difficult to drive, darty. Load of torque. Got 9,000rpm. Best lap 2.06.8. Returned to town on the 4.24. Met Sally H. & to Colony & danced."

In spite of going to bed at 3.45am, Stirling was up fairly early and went to the Grosvenor House Hotel for a TV interview with John Morgan. Another recording followed, he did some work, changed into tails, collected Jean "and to 'do' at B.A.R.C. Gave me a beautiful medal. I made a speech. Bed at 4am."

On Saturday Stirling had another seat fitting at Vandervell's for the Vanwall, Sally H. brought round a record for him and in the evening he collected JC (Jean Clarke?) and headed for Tring. He spent a relaxing day with friends at the farm and, delayed by fog, did not drop JC off until 1.30am. Then "Met Judy. Bed at 7am."

As the season had ended, Stirling was spending most of his time at the office but his days and evenings were spiced with various

Gold Medal

At the British Automobile Racing Club's annual dinner, attended by some 1,100 members and guests, the Club's President, the Duke of Richmond and Gordon, presented Stirling with a B.A.R.C. Gold Medal for his outstanding achievements during 1955. In his reply, noted Autosport, Stirling "paid compliments to Denis (The Beard) Jenkinson, the Daimler-Benz mechanics and to John Heath for giving him his first chance to go motor racing in a team".

Among the line-up of leading drivers, entrants, team managers and magazine editors was Peter Ustinov, a great enthusiast.

John Morgan

SM: "John Morgan was the owner of the Steering Wheel Club and Secretary of the BARC."

The Steering Wheel Club was very much a Mecca for motor racing enthusiasts. It was situated in Mayfair, just off Shepherd's Market and close to where Stirling has lived for many years. The premises basically consisted of a small bar area and a dining room, all decorated, not surprisingly, with notable steering wheels. Very sadly, it closed down some years ago.

A MEDAL FOR MOSS
B.A.R.C. Honour Britain's Most Successful Driver of 1955

Stirling Moss: I didn't sign

Stirling Moss last night denied he has signed to drive next season for Tony Parravano, an Italian-American business man whose car-racing headquarters are in Italy. He announced in Rome yesterday that he had signed Moss and two other racing drivers, Peter Collins and Tony Brooke.

Daily Mail 7.11.55

Out and About

SUCCESS OF THE ANNUAL DINNER

THE Annual Dinner/Dance at Grosvenor House on 4th November attracted a record crowd of 1100 members and friends who appeared to have had a thoroughly enjoyable evening. The guests were received also remarked upon the great increase in Club membership, which was now well past 9000.

Professor Low, Chairman of the Council, followed, and his task was to welcome specifically the official guests of the Club. These included many notabilities in the motoring and motor sporting world. As always, Professor Low's effort was spiced with anecdotes of the usual spicey character!

Then came the presentation of the Gold Medal to Stirling. The Duke, speaking with obvious and deep sincerity, paid tribute to the achievements during 1955 of this young driver. The Club had decided to give Stirling this medal as a result of his Mille Miglia and Grand Prix wins, but after that he claimed the laurels in both the T.T. and the Targa Florio. The presentation was made to the accompaniment of enthusiastic applause from the guests, and afterwards Stirling Moss, who is very nearly as competent a speaker as he is driver, thanked the Club for the award and paid tribute to those who had assisted his efforts during the past season. One good little touch in Stirling's speech was his acknowledgment to John Heath for having given him his first drive in a big car.

Stirling spoke warmly of the potentialities of the new B.R.M., but gave no direct indication of his own plans for the future.

Sydney Jerome's dance orchestra and Miguelita's Latin-American Combination.

Later, one of the best cabarets so far assembled by

Photo: P.A.-Reuter
Stirling Moss receives the first B.A.R.C. Gold Medal from the Duke of Richmond and Gordon.

Racing drivers present included: Stirling Moss, Mike Hawthorn, Peter Collins, Reg. Parnell, Raymond Mays, J. Duncan Hamilton, R. D. Poore, Ron Flockhart, Graham Whitehead, E. W. Holt, Ivor Bueb, John Cooper, John Heath, David Hampshire, Les Leston, P. W. C. Griffiths, P. Fotheringham Parker, A. P. O. Rogers, John Coombs, Mrs. Nancy Mitchell, John Young, P. Crabb, G. H. Grace.

* * *

SOCIAL life is in full swing in motoring circles, both

Cars

THE B.R.M.

The B.R.M. had again and again promised so much and virtually always disappointed, yet every native of Britain was willing it to succeed. For 1956, they produced a new 2½ litre car and, according to Autosport, it was almost certain that Moss would drive it the following year.

Whereas the 16 cylinder B.R.M. was a very complex machine, the new four cylinder car was relatively uncomplicated. The chassis was based on a triangular space-frame design. The new car retained the oleo-pneumatic struts previously employed but now used unequal length wishbones. Rear suspension was said to be unique amongst GP cars in that it used a de Dion set-up but with the tube mounted forward. Location was by tubular radius arms. Interestingly, with a view to saving unsprung weight, the car had just one transverse disc brake on the rear. A pair of discs were mounted outboard at the front. Wheels were Dunlop alloy, which had been introduced on the Jaguar D-type in 1954.

Details of the engine were not forthcoming initially but it seems the rumoured over-square bore/stroke ratio gave a very narrow power band which may explain why Stirling found the car quite difficult to drive.

On Stirling's left are Sally Hindmarsh, McDonald Hobley and Noel Hobley.

MOSS (B.R.M.) AT OULTON

Testing the new four-cylinder 2½-litre B.R.M. at Oulton Park last week-end, Stirling Moss returned a lap in 1 min. 52.3 secs., bettering his lap record with the G.P. Maserati of 1 min. 53.2 secs. He sampled a G.P. Vanwall as well, and though he did not drive fast, Moss commented very favourably on its handling qualities. At the same "meeting", Peter Collins drove Stirling's Maserati.

It is probable that the Formula 1 B.R.M. will be undergoing long-distance tests on a British circuit shortly, possibly at Goodwood.

Autosport 18.11.55

Model Jean Clarke admires the gold medal for outstanding achievements awarded Stirling Moss by the British Automobile Racing Club, London, last night.

L'pool Daily Post 6.11.55

MOSS AND B.R.M. BREAK LAP RECORDS
Dazzling display at 90 m.p.h.

Stirling Moss, the British racing driver today set up three new lap records in a secret trial of the B.R.M. Later he told a reporter "This car could be a world beater." With a dazzling display, Moss pushed his lap time up to over 90 m.p.h. The trial, arranged at the request of Moss himself, formed a dramatic background to the struggle between two millionaires, Mr. A. G. B. Owen, backer of the B.R.M., and Mr. Tony Vandervell, who sent the Vanwall, raced by Mike Hawthorn in several Grand Prix races last season.

On the result may depend the future of the British hopes on the Grand Prix circuits of the world next year. If Moss, after his trial today, decides to sign up for the B.R.M., it is understood that Mr. Owen is prepared to back this British venture "up to the limit," which may mean a sum of £200,000.

TEMPTING OFFERS

Before going out Moss said: "I feel the responsibility very much. I am desperately anxious to drive a British car, but in face of the tempting offers put out by the Italians it may mean gambling my whole future as a racing driver."

In a trial in the Vanwall, Moss put in a lap of 1min. 54sec. and said: "This is another good car. The handling is better but the power is not so impressive. He deferred his decision on which car to sign for. Owing to a conflict with some local interests which sought eto ban to trial on account of noise, both cars were fitted with silencers—a fact which makes their performance today all the more impressive.

B'ham Mail 12.11.55

activities. On Monday 7th he met journalist Lawrie Cade and went to a B.R.D.C. film show. On Tuesday he saw *The Glass Slipper* (VG) and later "saw Dick Clements in a play. G. but leary". Wednesday: "Did Hercules do with 49cc cycle for C. Fothergill" and had lunch with 'Lofty' England, the Jaguar Team Manager. No doubt they discussed SM driving for Jaguar again in 1956. On Thursday he saw SH for lunch and later "Met Peter Collins, Anne & Jean for food. SW tantrum."

Friday saw Stirling at the R.A.C. for the '19thC Motorists' Lunch'. That evening SM, SH and David Haynes caught a train to Chester. On Saturday he was "Up very early & to Oulton. Tested Vanwall. Flat spot at 4,700rpm. Missing badly at 6,800. 7,000 max poss. Usual 7,500. Damp & 1.55.0. B.R.M. damp (little less) & 1.52.3, new record. Then oil pressure dropped away."

That Sunday he was at Tring and being photographed by various, including commercial television and Reuters news agency. Later he was practising for a cabaret involving the Lord's Taverners and then went to London Airport to collect Bernard Cahier. "No planes from Paris due to strike." On Monday he had lunch with John Wyer, the Aston Martin Team Manager. After work, "Dress & to Lord's Taverners. VG. I was in the cabaret."

Stirling had to go to court on Wednesday 16th. "Wasted 2½ hrs. Defendant paid £5 + 4. Endorsed. Changed, met Bernard, collected SH & Diana. Saw *To Catch A Thief* VG. Colony." This was presumably in connection with the accident when a chap in an Austin A50 struck Stirling's 300 SL Gullwing in South Kensington.

Next day: "Pete [Collins] and I went to LAP [London Airport] & caught plane to Milano via Zurich where we had a good lunch. Alberta met us & drove us to Modena. Saw Tony & food." Presumably this was Tony Parravano and Stirling and Pete were at the home of Ferrari and Maserati to do a little sampling of Italy's finest.

"Up early & to autodrome. Tried the 150S 1500cc. Time 1.05.3. 3-litre 1.02.0 ftd. I did 1.01 in the GP car whilst warming up. Pete did 1.03.0 in the 3-litre. Had lunch & then discussed with Ken, Parravano & Orsi." Signor Orsi ran Maserati.

They flew back next day and together with a crowd of chums went to see *To Hell and Back* (VG) Next day Stirling saw *At Dawn We Die* (G) with JC.

Stirling Moss tries out a new British mo-ped

The battle for sales in the mo-ped markets between Midland and Continental manufacturers. One answer to the Continental challenge is this Hercules Grey Wolf mo-ped (motorised pedal which sells at £61 15s. Here, motor racing ace Stirling Moss is trying out the Grey W

B'ham Gazette 14.11.55

First All-British "Mo-ped"

Britain's biggest cycle manufacturer has entered the motor-cycle field. First all-British "mo-ped," a little pedal-assisted motor-cycle which will do 180 miles to the gallon, is capable of 35 miles an hour, is taxed at 17/6 a year, and costs, inclusive of purchase tax, £61 15s., will be announced today, writes Tom Wisdom.

It is the Hercules "Grey Wolf," and, says Hercules chief, Mr Arthur Chamberlain, "This is a straightforward challenge to the Continent."

Stirling Moss is to try-out the "Grey Wolf" today. The machine has a 49 c.c. J.A.P. two-stroke engine, a two-speed Burman gearbox, powerful brakes and was designed by Mr G H Jones, designer of the O.K. Supreme racers of pre-war days.

At the Motor Cycle and Cycle Show, which opens at Earls Court on Saturday, the big feature will be the "mo-peds" and the new scooters.

Sporting Life 9.11.55

NEWS DIARY

Stirling goes west after dollars

RUNNING motor races for millionaires is the new job of **Stirling Moss**. The young British champion is off to New York on November 26, accompanied by his manager, **Ken Gregory**, and a couple of days later he will be at Nassau in the Bahamas preparing a programme of sports car events being promoted as a new attraction for tourists.

A number of rich Americans who race very fast motor cars on the mainland are going over for the event. Moss himself, in addition to acting as organiser, is racing an Austin Healey.

Moss, who was awarded the British Automobile Racing Club's gold medal, flies to New Zealand for the grand prix immediately on his return to London.

Evening News 5.11.55

MOSS TRIES OUT A CHUG-CHUG BIKE

Stirling Moss, British motor-racing champion, cruised through the West End to-day on a new British motorised bicycle, the Hercules Grey Wolf, and afterwards placed the first order accepted for delivery in this country. The 25-year-old ace, used to speeds of up to 200 m.p.h., said: "This is the nippiest British two-wheeler I have been on, and about the quickest means of getting through Town."

Evening News 9.11.55

Discussions With Jaguar

With the Mercedes withdrawal, Jaguar saw an opportunity to lure Stirling back to the Jaguar team for which he had driven from the beginning of 1951 until the end of 1954. The idea of a Moss/Hawthorn 'dream ticket' was irresistible to Team Manager 'Lofty' England. He arranged a meeting with Ken Gregory and Alfred Moss at White Cloud Farm.

"They said they wouldn't want Moss," recalled 'Lofty', "driving a different car from Hawthorn, so that restricted it to Moss driving 'with' Hawthorn. I agreed to that and said, 'I will pay him £1,000 a time'. We had Le Mans, Reims, Sebring and Nürburgring - four races. We only paid Hawthorn £2,000 a year so I was being rather generous, especially as I obviously expected to pay Hawthorn the same as Moss. Then I asked them to understand that Hawthorn would be the number one driver, but they couldn't accept that."

Obviously, Hawthorn was established at Jaguar, having been there during 1955, but Jaguar could hardly expect the driver who had just finished second in the World Championship, was quicker than the World Champion in sports cars and was going to lead the Maserati team in Formula One to play second fiddle.

Alexandra goes to a slap-up do

IF I had a prize to award for the most **striking** sense of humour, it would go to Princess Alexandra for her splendid performance the other day.

The Princess watched the cabaret at the Lord's Taverners' Ball at Grosvenor House, London with scarcely a smile—at first.

Not so the Duke of Edinburgh. He laughed at everything from start to finish.

The Duke appeared to find the slapstick antics of Stirling Moss, Richard Hearne, Pat Smythe and other celebrities irresistible.

Twice Princess Alexandra winced at the more obvious jokes. Once she turned to the laughing Duke with a look that seemed to say: "What's so funny?"

Then, suddenly, actor Richard Hearne slipped on his backside.

Instantly the Princess roared—and gave the man in the next seat a terrific shove on the shoulder.

That man was Commander Michael Parker, the Duke's secretary — a sturdily-built chap, I'm happy to say. Anyone less sturdy might have vanished under the table. For the Princess is an athletic type.

Afterwards I thought I noticed that Parker's chair was placed rather more apart from the Princess's than before.

FOOTNOTE: Princess Alexandra had trouble with the straps of her evening dress. They kept falling. She must be used to it by now. I first mentioned it on my page nine months ago.

Sunday Mirror 19.11.55

Stirling with American actress Louise King.

Tony Parravano

"Tony Parravano offered me incredible things, he did!"

Parravano sounds an amazing character. Described variously as a successful Manhattan Beach contractor and a Los Angeles real estate developer, he built a team in California based around Italian Ferraris and Maseratis. Bill Pollack, who drove for him, says in his book 'Red Wheels & White Sidewalls', that he "bought fast Italian machinery by the handful". He also commented that he was known as "the man with the golden screwdriver" because he could not resist fiddling with banks of Weber carbs, much to the consternation of his mechanics. Pollack stated that most of the cars Parravano bought from Enzo Ferrari had been "raced hard and put away wet". He says that Parravano was a cash buyer and always in a hurry, and implies Ferrari may have seen him coming on one or two occasions.

"He was the most enthusiastic guy," said Carroll Shelby in an interview for 'Motor Trend'. Shelby, the father of the A.C. Cobra, started driving for Parravano in early summer 1955 and spent the rest of the summer in Modena with Dino Ferrari buying, he reckoned, about 15 Ferraris and Maseratis. "He'd buy anything. I drove my first Grand Prix for him at Syracuse and finished fourth." The magazine stated that he became "a missing persons statistic a few years later". They speculated that it might have been tax problems or "too many disagreements with the wrong Italian families".

Whatever, he was a tremendous motor racing enthusiast and ran one of the three most successful sports racing teams in California in the fifties and gave some well-known names a leg up the ladder. Clearly Stirling took him seriously but a private entrant is very rarely ever able to match a works entry.

Stirling Moss is offered £23,000

In Modena, Italy, Stirling Moss, Britain's champion racing driver, has been offered £23,000 to become No. 1 driver for Tony Parravano's Maserati's team.

In The Cabaret

It seems that Stirling rose to the occasion and amused the audience with his antics in a pedal car on stage, complete with his crash hat, of course. Also involved was that old 'pro' Richard Hearne, better-known as 'Mr. Pastry'.

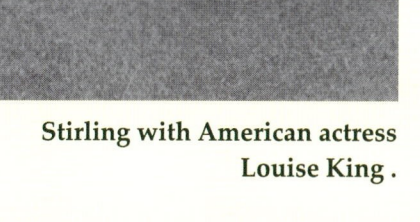

MOSS SIGNED UP
He'll Test Team's Cars

Moena, Italy, Friday. — Mr. Tony Parravano, American organiser of a new racing car team, said here that three British aces, including Stirling Moss, will start to test his cars shortly. The 37-year-old president of the Parravano Stables in Los Angeles announced earlier this month he was establishing a new racing enterprise with a fleet of 24 Aston-Martin, Ferrari and Maserati cars.—A.P.

Evening News 18.11.55

MOSS DENIAL

Modena, Saturday. — Stirling Moss denied report he had agreed to join Maserati team organised by Mr. Tony Parravano, of Italy.—Reuter.

Daily Mail 19.11.55

Moss denies offer of £23,000

Cabaret

For the cabaret, the Taverners held their own "Olympic Games."

Highlights: Racing driver **STIRLING MOSS**, wearing a crash helmet and evening dress, pedalling a toy car round the dance-floor;

Actor **RICHARD HEARNE** turning somersaults a few feet from Prince Philip's chair;

Athletes **DIANE LEATHER** and **THELMA HOPKINS**, with horsewoman **PAT SMYTHE** (dressed as a cow-girl), winning a four-legged race.

On Monday evening he went to the Grosvenor House Hotel for the Olympics Dinner. Next day he was at Silverstone for testing. "Track wet. 1.53.0 Connaught on Dunlops, 1.50.3 on Pirellis. 1.50.5 B.R.M.. Vanwall 1.46.9! & 1.47.9, full tanks. To town via Tring. Took SW out and saw *Les Clandestines* G. Food at the Mirabelle."

Wednesday 23rd: "To No. 8, saw Pete & his Pa. B.R.M.s put 60 lbs of iron on front of B.R.M. & Pete has done 1.45.5! (Dry). Talked till 6pm. Sportsview & then R.A.C. to get help of the press."

On Thursday Stirling went to Elstree from where he flew up to Silverstone. "Tested B.R.M. but wet. SM 1.58.2. P.J.C [Collins] 2.02.8. Later 1.54.3 damp. Oil filter blew up, exhaust fell off & later more oil. Returned & worked at office until 8.30. Saw Ken & Pa re. '56 contract. Decided. Had to put Jean off at the last moment. Phoned [Raymond] Mays." How could he choose the B.R.M. after all these problems?

"Up early & off to hospital for special tests. Harrods & did some shopping. To Festival Hall & luncheon for Dr. Roger Bannister to launch his new book. Office & work. Later to B.R.M.S.C. Dinner & on to Bug. Owners do & received presentation. Bed 3.30am."

On that note Stirling's diary for 1955 ends, which is most inconvenient! However, we know that he flew to New York on November 26th and the press said he was going on to Nassau in the Bahamas "a couple of days later". According to Ken Gregory, as he and Stirling flew out, Alfred Moss and Felix Nabarro arrived back from Modena with a Maserati contract for 1956.

Books

As Stirling's stature grew, his name was applied in various ways to a growing number of publications. His own 'Stirling Moss's Book of Motor Racing' was something a little different with chapters on 'How to become a racing driver', 'What is a racing car?', 'The art of driving fast', 'Team control and tactics' and suchlike.

More and more articles were appearing in journals under Stirling's name and the latest edition of 'The Observer's Book of Automobiles' had a foreword by SM. Everything was, of course, ghosted!

Right: Stirling attended Roger Bannister's book launch and met various interesting personalities. Bannister was, of course, the first 'four-minute miler'. Sheila van Damm was Britain's top woman rally driver and finished second in the 'Coupe des Dames' category of that year's European Touring Championship, as the rally championship was then known. C.B. Fry was a sporting phenomenon - unbeaten England cricket captain, played soccer for England, holder of the world long jump record, a brilliant scholar, at Oxford he won 12 'Blues' and uniquely captained the university at cricket, soccer and athletics in the same year and was offered the throne of Albania!

SPORTING TRIO

'First Four Minutes" is the title of the book. Racing driver Stirling Moss is looking at it—Mr. C. B. Fry points out an illustration. Its author, Dr. Roger Bannister, the first four-minute miler, looks on. There also is his wife. They were at Foyle's Literary Luncheon in London yesterday.

Daily Mail 26.11.55

NEWS DIARY
Stirling Moss will race for the Italians

NEXT season Stirling Moss will be driving Italian cars. That is my reading of the present situation.

To-night the 25-year-old British champion is flying off to Nassau in the Bahamas, where (as mentioned last week) he and manager Ken Gregory are organising car races for Sir Sidney Oakes, the millionaire sportsman.

Before leaving Moss will hand to his father **Mr. Alfred Moss**, a sealed envelope containing his decision and the reasons for it. The contents are to be released on Monday, when he will be in New York.

1, 2 and 3

Meanwhile he has wired **Signor Orsi**, boss of the Maserati team And Signor Orsi will tell the world that Moss will be his No. 1 driver and **Peter Collins** a probable No 3. **Jean Behra** is No. 2

And **Fangio**? The present world champion will probably join forces with Ferrari-Lancia Or retire altogether.

World Tour

BRITISH champion driver Stirling Moss will leave soon for a world tour.

First stop is Argentina, where he hopes to take part in one or two races; from there he flies to New Zealand, then to Mexico, and back to South America.

By the time he gets back to England for the next racing season he may have acquired a lead in the points competition for the World's Championship, which is about the only honour he has not won yet.

He has not made up his mind yet on the car he will drive in the Grand Prix series. He is impressed with the speed of the new BRM and will probably decide on that if the remaining "bugs" can be eliminated.

Juan Fangio, the present world title holder, like Moss, has not signed on with anybody yet, and though there have been rumours of his retirement, I expect to see him at the wheel of an Italian car next year—if he isn't invited to team up with Moss for BRM.

The Star 16.11.55

Moss not for Maserati

MOSS DENIES THAT £23,000 OFFER

Moss denies offer of £23,000

Dr. Roger Bannister (left) with Miss Sheila van Damm and Stirling Moss, the racing motorists, at a luncheon in London to celebrate the publication of Dr. Bannister's book "First Four Minutes."

B'ham Mail 26.11.55

Vanwall & Connaught

The Vanwall and Connaught single-seaters were valiant British contenders for Grand Prix honours. Young dental student Tony Brooks had taken the Connaught to victory in the non-championship Syracuse GP only a few weeks earlier to record the first GP win by a British car driven by a British driver. Even though this was against the might of the Maserati works team, Connaught could not quite maintain the momentum and suffered from relative under-funding.

Vanwall was not short of money as it was funded by millionaire Tony Vandervell of the famous bearings company. He began as a backer of B.R.M. but lost patience and set out on his own to beat what he famously called, "Those bloody red cars!" Beginning with the Thinwall Special, which was a modified Ferrari, he gradually made progress and Vanwall's time would come, and the two lead drivers would be ... Moss and Brooks.

JAGUARS TO RACE NEXT YEAR

By TOM WISDOM

THE "speed-king" auction is on. The sky is the limit for the services of the world's top five racing drivers—three of them British—for next season's Grand Prix motor races.

Five-figure contracts are being offered by Italy and Britain. But the foreigners will make the big money—£15,000 a year and more—while the British drivers must be satisfied with about £2,000—plus "expenses," after income tax.

Stirling Moss, now in New York, announced through his father last night that he still had not made up his mind which of six offers to accept.

He has previously turned down the three British "possibles"—B.R.M., Vanwall Special, and Connaught, and has a big offer from Maserati as their No. 1 driver.

In another 48 hours he would announce his decision, so his father said last night.

The other two leading British drivers, Mike Hawthorn and Peter Collins, are to try out the B.R.M. on Thursday, though Moss is dissatisfied with it.

Hawthorn told me last night: "I am not signing again with Ferrari. They wanted me to drive sports cars as well as the Grand Prix cars, but I have signed again with Jaguar for sports car events. I am going to try the B.R.M. If it's not right, then I shall go to Maserati."

TRYING B.R.M.

This is big news—it means that Jaguar, winner of many races, including Le Mans and the "T.T."—will be racing again next season, despite suggestions that, following the example of Mercedes, they were pulling out of motor racing.

Peter Collins, the 24-year-old driver from Kidderminster, is also driving the B.R.M. in further tests. He awaits Hawthorn's opinion of the car, on which millionaire owner Alfred Owen has said he would spend £200,000 if Moss would agree to drive it.

TONY BROOKS

But Collins wants many alterations made to the car; if Owen does not agree he will join Maserati probably with Moss.

What of Britain's new star, C A S (Tony) Brooks, the first man since the war to win a Grand Prix—at Syracuse—last month in a British car?

The 21-year-old driver is not turning professional—he is sticking to his career as a dental surgeon, but will still drive when he has got time.

And the best and richest of them all, Argentinian world champion Juan Manuel Fangio—he cleared more than £30,000 this year, and, despite his friend Peron's downfall, is still a "peso" multi-millionaire—though he announced his retirement, is likely to sign on with Ferrari.

Moss & Collins

Peter Collins had done such a superb job in the 300 SLR during the Targa Florio when he and Stirling had shared a car that they had clearly made plans to try and team up in 1956. Thus they tested together during this period, exchanged information and had a variety of discussions. In the end it did not work out which is a shame as they would have made a superb British team.

HOME OR AWAY? It's up to Moss

TO-DAY Britain's top race-driver, Stirling Moss, must decide. Will he race a British car or an Italian car next year?

Two days ago (writes colleague Len Smith) 26-year-old Stirling Moss spoke of his dilemma. "I'd like to win the World Championship with a British car," he said.

"I have to choose between the Italian Maserati, where I'd be No. 1 in the team, or the B.R.M. or Vanwall —both British cars.

"The Vanwall is so beautifully balanced you can throw it around anywhere you like.

"The B.R.M. has all the power you could want and can make up on the straights what you may lose on the bends."

OLD LOVE

THE Maserati is an old love of Stirling's. It behaves as near perfectly as any driver could wish.

But, says Stirling: "I'd never forgive myself if I chose a Maserati and won and a British car chased me home."

Stirling flew up to Silverstone yesterday in a last attempt to make up his mind.

For several laps he swept round the rain-soaked course averaging just on 100 m.p.h. in a brand-new B.R.M.

The B.R.M. financed by millionaire industrialist Mr. Alfred Owen, had been drastically modified following a report by Stirling after an earlier test.

He complained then that the car was "lifting at the front and snaking."

NEW LOVE?

SIXTY pounds of ballast strapped to the front axle has part-cured the trouble, but Stirling Moss said dejectedly last night:

"It was not as good as I hoped. I think the car might be able to be got right. But it is not right yet."

Which? BRM? Vanwall? Maserati?

Stirling Moss must choose before he leaves on a round-the-world race tour this weekend.

Daily Sketch 25.11.55

LAST NIGHT'S TV

SPORTSVIEW: Less momentous than usual. Stirling Moss rather disappointed Peter Dimmock by being unable to give a decision on whether he'll drive British or Italian cars next year. Stirling is in the first three in the voting for the Television Sportsman of the Year. Who's beating him? My guess is Gordon Pirie by virtue of that great televised race against Zatopek.

24.11.55

PAULINE and LARRY FORRESTER — People We Meet

WHEN Stirling Moss sets off on his next spell of foreign travel—to drive in motor races in Australia, New Zealand, and the USA—he will take with him a large, metal-bound chest. As usual, customs officials will eye it suspiciously and demand to see inside.

The chest contains Stirling's swimming togs. But these include: a complete naval frogman's outfit, with depth and pressure guages; two huge aqua-lungs; special underwater torches, and an armoury of spear-guns.

Stirling was trained in the art of undersea fishing during a visit to the Bahamas a few years ago. He has caught barracuda, huge eels, octopi and even sharks. Whenever he's in a warm country, as soon as his work's done he dons his "rubber coms" and relaxes thirty or forty feet below the sea.

A veteran TV personality, Stirling told us the other day: "I wish now and then some interviewer would ask me about undersea fishing, not just racing. In fact, one day I'd love to do a short programme on this sport. Maybe we could get the OB cameras at a public baths, then I could demonstrate the equipment."

"Maybe we could get a shark, or an octopus in the programme, too . . ."

Seriously, it's a good idea, and we've passed it on to the planners.

Stirling Moss, crack racing driver, is as much at home speeding on the water as on land. He also likes to relax forty feet under the water

TV Mirror 19.11.55

Stirling Moss is still undecided

STIRLING MOSS, Britain's leading racing driver, said as he left London Airport last night for America, that he had not yet decided whether to sign for an Italian company or drive for Britain.

"It is quite definite that I will sign a contract while I am away," he said, "but at the moment I cannot say who I shall be driving for next year."

Moss, who is to drive in Nassau, said that he would make his final decision during the week.

Sunday Despatch 27.11.55

MOSS MAY DRIVE FOR MASERATI

Moss denies he has joined Italian team

Stirling Moss driving for Maserati in 1956?

Stirling Moss Denies £23,000 Offer

PC Tells Moss How To Drive

A green Mercedes-Benz with German number-plates and a left-hand drive became caught up in traffic today outside Victoria Station.

A young policeman walked up and said to the driver: "Excuse me, sir, but when you are in England you filter to the left."

The driver?—Stirling Moss.

He had been to Victoria Airways Terminal to be inoculated before leaving tonight for New York.

Sporting Life 22.11.55

Advice From The Press

Stirling had always made it very clear that, whenever possible, he wanted to race British cars and the public loved him for this. For 1956 he had two choices - British or Italian. Faced with this dilemma, he had the brilliant idea of consulting the Press. By doing this, and heeding their advice (provided they made the right decision!), they could hardly criticise him afterwards for whatever decision was made. As they were the interface between himself and the great British public, it would be very helpful to have them on his side. It would also make the various motoring correspondents feel very involved and important, and allow them to share their importance with their readers.

Who's Who

Stirling mentioned, earlier in the year, having a meal with Mr. and Mrs Macklin. This was Sir Noel Macklin, who ran the Invicta company before the war, and their son was Lance. Sir Noel's sister was Violet Cordery who made history when she drove an Invicta around the world at an average speed of 24.6mph. She married John Hindmarsh, who won Le Mans in a Lagonda M45R in 1935 and was a test pilot who was killed in a Hawker aircraft in a test flight in 1939. Sue and Sally were their daughters - Sue is married to Roy Salvadori and Stirling went out with Sally in 1955.

Continuing: MY TWO WORLDS by Sheila Van Damm

My opinion of Stirling Moss

HIS tremendous driving brain

HIS washing... and mine!

HIS contrast with Mike Hawthorn

HIS legendary 'eye' for showgirls

CHAPTER 2

FATHER sacked me from the Windmill Theatre in 1946—but he hadn't finished with me. Oh, no.

He wanted to start a private charter airline so he said to me: "You will go and learn to fly."

And that is how I became a pilot before I became a rally driver.

I went down with mother to White Waltham, near Maidenhead, to learn privately. About six of the Windmill girls came down with me—and they learned too.

One of our loveliest girls, Anita D'Ray, learned to fly very successfully: she won a race in the Isle of Wight the next year.

And it was at White Waltham she met her husband.

★ ★ ★

THOSE were the years when father discovered Harry Secombe—and **didn't** discover Norman Wisdom.

They both turned up at the same audition in 1946. Secombe knew very little about the business, but he had a lovely voice (as opera fans are now beginning to learn).

But the most memorable sound he produced in the act he did at the Windmill was an incredible giggle. It was a miming act with shaving brush, a razor, and a lot of soapy lather. Father engaged him on the spot.

To Norman Wisdom, father said: "No." Wisdom came back at the end of the audition and pleaded for another chance. "Thank you very much," said father, "but I'm afraid not...."

That is how the Windmill lost Norman Wisdom.

I did about 100 hours private flying at White Waltham purely as a hobby; and then got myself commissioned in the W.A.A.F. V.R. as a pilot officer. Me—the ex-acting corporal.

I liked flying but just as I was never satisfied with my car driving until I could put my foot on the brake without thinking so I never felt that I could be a real pilot until I could make a forced landing 10 times out of 10. I never had to make a forced landing; but I did have one narrow escape.

I was flying a Tiger Moth—off course as usual (I could never read a map in the air)—and suddenly found myself in the middle of what appeared to be four squadrons of jets all trying to land on Odiham airfield in Hampshire. Fortunately I missed them—or they managed to miss me; but I have never been so frightened in all my life. That goes for all my rally experiences too.

★ ★ ★

I WAS still flying in September 1950 when I saw that the Daily Express was organising a 1,200-mile national motor rally. "A thing like that must be rather fun," I thought, and then forgot all about it.

But that night Zita Irwin, my father's personal pilot, announced that father was going to enter my sister Nona (then 31) and myself in the rally as promotion for the theatre.

I thought of my old Ford 8... but father said: "Don't worry, the Rootes people are going to lend you a car."

Next week I was sized up by Norman Garrad, the very tall—and very tough—competitions manager of the Rootes Group. I passed the "sizing up" and on November 8, 1950, Nona and I were in the front seats of a new Sunbeam-Talbot on the starting line of the Daily Express 48-hour non-stop national rally.

I learned a lot on that rally—two things above all: never overdo the pep pills; and never lend anything to anyone on a rally.

When we had done the eliminating tests at Torquay I had lost my voice through shouting at Nona for 48 hours. (I still shout; but my voice is stronger now.)

Nona was so relieved to be alive that she burst into tears the moment we reached our hotel room. (That was Nona's first and last rally.)

But we had not done so badly: we took the third women's prize. Next day Norman Garrad asked me if I would be interested in driving for Sunbeam in future rallies. I said "Yes"—flattered.

★ ★ ★

TWO months later, in January 1951, I joined Mrs. Elsie Bill Wisdom as third crew in the 1951 Monte Carlo rally.

This was the real thing: snow, black ice, hairpin mountain bends—and there they were the real seasoned people of the Rally Set.

Stirling Moss for instance. Stirling was only 21 then but his tremendous skill, his brain and his thoroughness impressed me immediately—and have been impressing me ever since.

I remember once standing at a control point when Stirling swept in with an exhaust pipe adrift. Before mechanics or his co-drivers could touch it Stirling was under the car like a flash tearing that exhaust off with his own hands.

★ ★ ★

THAT'S the secret of Stirling Moss: he is out of this world as a driver; yet he is supremely careful, thinks everything out beforehand, leaves nothing to chance and — unlike many another driver—is always ready to get his own hands dirty.

Another thing about Stirling that endears him to me is that he does his own washing on rallies—and offers to do my smalls too! In the off-season Stirling often comes to tea at the Windmill, not, I suspect, because he's mad about me but because he has an eye for the girls. After tea he slips in to see the show.

The Stirling speed is as legendary at the Windmill as in the Monte.

I remember once he was sitting in the stalls with that other famous driver Leslie Johnson. Leslie told me later: "One minute I was talking to Stirling and the next minute the seat beside me was empty. I looked ahead at the stage—and there was Stirling sitting in a newly vacated seat five rows nearer the footlights and motioning me to follow!"

I often get a message these days to go round backstage at the Windmill. The girls ask me: "We think we have seen Stirling out front. *Is he?*"

★

MIKE HAWTHORN is in the same top class as Stirling—but no two people could be more different. Stirling

① Jacking up the car with my own two hands when we had a puncture near Grasse — and watching the Norman Garrad and Basil Cardew team flash by as we were struggling with a puncture.

My first rally

SISTER NONA, COMEDIAN ARTHUR ENGLISH, AND ME.

STIRLING AND I DANCE AT A WINDMILL PARTY.

At Monte

NORMAN GARRAD, ME, AND (RIGHT) STIRLING MOSS AT MONTE.

£250,000 may depend on Moss

By Alan Brinton

AFTER wrestling with the 170 m.p.h. B.R.M. on the rain-swept Silverstone circuit, Stirling Moss last night tussled with the toughest decision of his career.

Before tomorrow—when he flies to America—he has to make up his mind what make of car he will drive in next season's Grand Prix races.

He stands a good chance of becoming the first British world champion, but he badly wants to do it in a British car. That is why he drove the dark green prototype B.R.M. round Silverstone for the second time in three days.

He could not approach record speeds on the wet track. An oil seal failed, then the oil tank split.

To the limit

So he has to decide without knowing the car's full potentialities, for it was wet on Tuesday, too, when he tried the B.R.M., the Vanwall and the Connaught.

He said: "The B.R.M. has oceans of power, but on Tuesday it was the very devil to handle. At times the front end was lifting quite frighteningly."

Mechanics toiled on it and yesterday he said it handled far better, though it still needed more work.

Raymond Mays, "father" of the B.R.M., was undismayed. Said he: "I think we have more than a fair chance of bringing the world championship to Britain for the first time."

I understand that Mr. Alfred Owen, the B.R.M.'s millionaire backer, is prepared to help the organisation "to the limit"—a quarter of a million pounds, it is said—IF Moss and his friend, Peter Collins, drive.

Stirling has to weigh an offer from Maserati's, a firm with years of hard Continental experience and with cars that should be difficult to beat. He would be their Number 1 driver, with Collins as Number 3.

News Chronicle 25.11.55

£20,000 for Moss?

STIRLING MOSS is now back in London after having again tried out the latest B.R.M., Vanwall and Connaught Grand Prix racing cars. At the weekend he flew to Italy for trials in the new petrol injection Maserati and some of the cars belonging to the wealthy American, Parravano, who now owns the biggest private team of racing cars in the world.

Tony Parravano has offered Moss and Fangio more than £20,000 each to drive in his team and is reported to be trying to buy a new B.R.M. if this can be negotiated.

Fangio is said to be seriously considering the offer, but Stirling Moss may drive for B.R.M. or Maserati in Formula I Grand Prix races and possibly for Parravano in sports car races.

Moss will make his decision some time this week before leaving on Saturday for the United States. While in America he will drive a British Austin-Healey in a sports car race at Nassau, before going to New Zealand to race his own Maserati for the last time.

Northern Despatch 23.11.55

Plywood Motor Boat Trial

Mr. Donald Healey at Nassau

Mr. Donald Healey, the Warwick rally driver and sports car builder, is at Nassau (Bahamas) for three weeks demonstrating a motor boat fitted with a modified car engine, and which is cheaper than many similar models.

The boat is made of light, cheap plywood and is glued together. Fitted with an Austin inboard motor, it is designed principally for towing water skiers and has a speed of 30 knots per hour. Stirling Moss, who is with Mr. Healey, will take delivery of the first boat next spring.

The Healey family and Mr. Geoffrey Lord, a marine engineer, have formed the Healey Marine Company to build a light and cheap craft at Bridport.

During this year's Motor Show Mr. Healey took 100 firm orders for his boats, which sell at £149 10s. without an engine, and £395 complete. It is planned to sell the boat extensively abroad and in Britain.

B'ham Post 29.11.55

Moss May Drive for Maserati

STIRLING Moss, British driver, who was runner-up in last year's world championship, may race for the Italian Maserati firm next season, the Rome sports daily, "Correire Dello Sport," reported to-day.

Moss said, when he left London on Saturday for the United States, that he had not yet made up his mind for whom he would drive in 1956.

"Correire Dello Sport" also said that world champion Juan Manuel Fangio, Moss's team-mate with Mercedes last season, might sign a contract with Ferrari.

Provitials 26.11.55

...oss still undecided

Stirling Moss, champion British racing driver and runner-up in the world championship, said today that he had not yet decided what make of car to drive in next season's Grand Prix races.

Moss has had trial runs in the BRM, the Vanwall and the Connaught, Britain's three Grand Prix hopes.

Moss, who drove today to the Airways Terminal at Victoria to be inoculated before leaving tonight for New York, said there would be no decision for "some days."

Evening Standard 26.11.55

Stirling Keeps His Herr On

STIRLING MOSS, off to New York to-night, got caught in traffic outside Victoria station to-day in his green Mercedes Benz.

A young policeman approached the car. He saw the German number plates and left-hand drive.

"Excuse me, sir," he said, "but when you are in England you filter to the left."

Evening Standard 26.11.55

FANGIO GIVES UP MOTOR RACING

By Tom Wisdom

THE world champion driver, Juan-Manuel Fangio, 44-year-old Argentinian, has retired from motor racing, and—Stirling Moss, aged 26, the next best, has been told that the Mercedes sports car with which Moss won the three most important races of the year is not for sale.

On top of this news yesterday came the announcement that the millionaire racing driver, Briggs Cunningham, the only American to race a team in Europe, is closing down his Florida factory.

After the Le Mans disaster in which Cunningham drove, his wife insisted that he should stop racing and building racing cars.

It is also most unlikely that the British Jaguar team, winners this year at Le Mans, will race next year, though no firm decision has been made.

Evidence that the Maserati factory is anything but idle is provided by this picture of Stirling Moss and a new 12-cylinder, 3-litre sports car that he has recently been testing at Monza. The factory is producing four 3½-litre Gran Turismo cars a week, there are four new formula I cars under construction, and the factory is still busy maintaining private owners' cars

STIRLING MOSS'S STRANGE DINNER

He invites in seventeen friends—and asks them to decide: IS MY FUTURE BRITISH or FOREIGN?

by BASIL CARDEW

STIRLING MOSS is a driver with a torn conscience. Should he take the big chance of becoming next year's world champion by driving a foreign car? Or should he jeopardise his chances and fight for Britain by signing up with a British racing stable?

In the chandeliered, portrait-hung Mall Room of the Royal Automobile Club in London's West End I went to the most astonishing dinner party of the year, ending in the early hours of yesterday.

Stirling Moss had called together 17 journalistic friends of wide experience in the niceties of international motoring—and he put those questions to them.

Sipping soda-water (he never drinks), the pale, wiry-figured driver of 26 sumptuously dined and wined his writer guests. The only outsiders with the "jury" were Papa Alfred Moss and 29-year-old Ken Gregory, Stirling's racing manager.

Quickly...

WHEN the coffee and the port had gone round the long oval table Stirling got to his feet and said:—

"Gentlemen — I have a decision to make, and quickly. In fact, I must make up my mind by Saturday, for then I leave for New York and the Bahamas for racing.

"Afterwards I go on to New Zealand and perhaps the Argentine. I cannot get back before February."

In complete silence he then put his problem:—

"I believe the Italian Maserati will have the best chance of winning the world championship next year, and I have the chance of driving No. 1 for them.

"But there are some promising British cars that have been built during the last 12 months, and you know the dearest thing to my heart is to win the world championship in a British car.

"Money does not come into this. Whatever you earn—here or abroad—the tax man takes the same."

Testing

HE had the choice of three British cars. All three he had driven in tests round the three-mile Silverstone circuit in Northants.

On a wet track, in slippery conditions, these were his best times and speeds in the 2½-litre, unsupercharged British racing cars:—

Connaught. — Lap, 1min. 50.6sec.; speed, 95 miles an hour. B.R.M.: Lap, 1min. 50.5sec.; speed, 95 miles an hour. Vanwall: Lap, 1min. 46.9sec.; speed, 98 miles an hour.

Compared with this, Moss believed the Maserati would lap the circuit in 1min. 43sec., at a speed of 102 miles an hour.

"But," he added, "this is not really a fair comparison, because the Maserati could only do that in fine dry conditions."

Then he reported that Peter Collins, his 23-year-old friend, after modifications had been made overnight to the B.R.M., clocked 1min. 46.3sec., a speed just on 99 miles an hour.

Some round the table took out their diaries and compared these performances with the official Silverstone record for 2½-litre Grand Prix cars of 98.48 miles an hour, set up this year by two Maseratis at the Daily Express International Trophy meeting.

So it was obvious that the British cars were going faster than they had ever gone before.

Problems

STIRLING MOSS summed up his British choices:—

He thought the Vanwall had one problem—and that was to make it lighter.

The B.R.M. had one problem too—to make it hold the road better.

The Connaught had two problems and therefore it fell between the two—it had to be made lighter *and* more powerful.

He explained that the wealthy sponsors of both the Vanwall—Anthony Vandervell—and the B.R.M.—Alfred Owen—wanted him to give his decision before he leaves on his travels.

The vote

IF he goes to either of their stables they will spend large sums on producing full British Grand Prix teams next year.

If he goes foreign they may cut down their plans. This was an added responsibility for him.

He summed up: "It is now really a choice of Maserati, or Vanwall, or B.R.M.

"What would you do, gentlemen?"

For hours those round the table discussed his problem.

Each of the 16 journalists—one had been called away—was allowed to speak for one minute. And then we voted. The result: Seven for Britain, nine for Italy.

FOOTNOTE *from Italy last night*: The new Ferrari is reported to have passed 190 miles an hour in a trial run at Modena. Enzo Ferrari hopes to engage Stirling Moss to drive it.

How his friends voted...

Sixteen of Stirling Moss's journalist friends voted on his dilemma. Like this:—

Moss for BRITAIN
Basil Cardew, Daily Express
Courteney Edwards, Daily Mail
Alan Brinton, News Chronicle
Len Smith, Daily Sketch
Robert Walling, Evening Standard
William Paulson, Evening News
Keith Challen, News of the World

Moss for ITALY
Harold Nockolds, Times
William McKenzie, Daily Telegraph
Patrick Mennem, Daily Mirror
Laurence Cade, Star
Peter Garnier, Autocar
Richard Bensted Smith, Motor
Denis Jenkinson, Motor Sport
Roy Pearl, Motor Racing
Peter Lewis, Sunday Observer

How would YOU vote?

Send YOUR decision on postcards to : Letters, Daily Express, Fleet-street, E.C.4.

STIRLING MOSS FOR THE B.R.M.

Moss in the B.R.M.

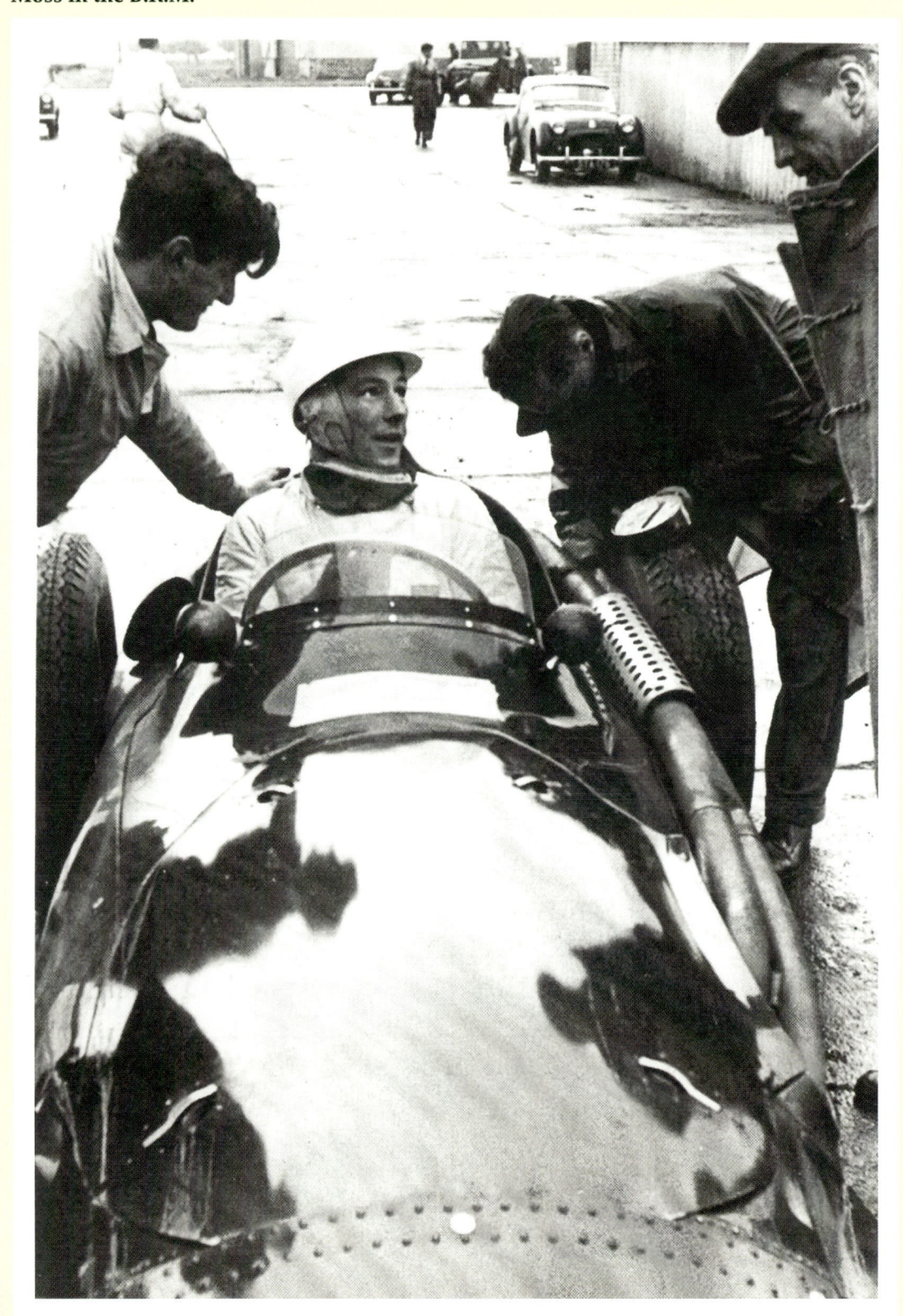

Watched by B.R.M. co-founder Raymond Mays, Stirling climbs into (or is it out of!) the 'great British hope'.

The B.R.M. mechanics strapped lead to the front of the chassis in an attempt to improve the handling.

Moss plans to try out B.R.M. next week

Moss is still undecided
News Chronicle Reporter

STIRLING MOSS, now in America, has deferred his decision on which car he will drive in next season's Grand Prix races.

His father, Mr. Alfred Moss, himself a former racing motorist, should have announced his son's decision yesterday. Instead, he said at his Tring farm: "He wants further time to think it over."

Stirling also wants to discuss plans with Mr. Anthony Vandervell, millionaire sponsor of the British Vanwall, who is in the United States.

He will also see Tony Parraveno, who is reported to have offered him £23,000 a year to drive Maserati cars in his stable.

News Chronicle 29.11.55

Colour Film of Ill-fated Le Mans Race

Many of the British drivers who were racing at Le Mans this year when the most tragic track crash of the century occurred were at the Royal Empire Society Hall on Monday night to see Jaguar's film of the race.

Mike Hawthorn and Ivor Bueb, who won the race for Jaguar after Mercedes had retired in mourning for their driver Pierre Levegh, were there to see the film have its premiere. So were Stirling Moss, Tony Rolt and Duncan Hamilton.

It is believed to be the only fully documented film in colour of this ill-fated 1955 Le Mans 24 Hours, and it includes a complete record of the crash.

Of the six camera men employed to film the sequences, one narrowly escaped with his life as Macklin's car, which had been struck by the Mercedes, hurtled out of control only inches away.

This cartoon has been inscribed by the pre-eminent motoring cartoonist and given by him to Stirling. In pencil is written across the top: "Young Moss wasn't long out of a job." At the bottom, after his signature, Russell Brockbank has written "to young Moss". Also in Stirling's scrapbooks is the printed version that appeared, with the same type-set top line, in The Motor.

December

1955 Calendar

10   Governor's Cup - 6th in Austin-Healey

11   Nassau Trophy - retired in Austin-Healey

Stirling's time in Nassau was part-work, part-holiday. While there, he took part in the Bahamas Speed Week, more for the fun of it than as a serious racing driver. It appears that he drove an Austin-Healey belonging to Lady Greta Oakes who drove her Healey competitively. She was married to Sir Sydney Oakes, son of the famous Harry Oakes, a very wealthy man who lived in Nassau and was murdered in his bed during the war years. Sir Sydney was one of the guiding lights of the Bahamas Automobile Club.

Stirling had a particular fondness for Nassau and he was there to help promote the event. He was accompanied by Ken Gregory, who combined his role as Stirling's manager with that of General Secretary of the B.R.S.C.C. (British Racing & Sports Car Club). He was there to bring some order to the chaos and had a pretty fraught time. The racing was to take place at the palm-lined 3½ mile Windsor airfield circuit.

A number of American drivers were there, including Phil Hill, Sherwood Johnson, Lou Brero, Jim Kimberley, Ed Crawford, Masten Gregory, Art Bunker and Jack MacAfee, all of whom were well-known in the USA. The 90 or so drivers were out to have a good time. One American publication referred to "some of the fiercest, most violent, dangerous cocktail parties ever to 'grace' a sporting weekend".

The event was supposedly being organised by a large, volatile American called Sherman 'Red' Crise who had no experience whatsoever of running a race meeting and with whom Gregory well and truly clashed. There were no time-keeping facilities and the course of the airfield track was indicated by 50-gallon oil

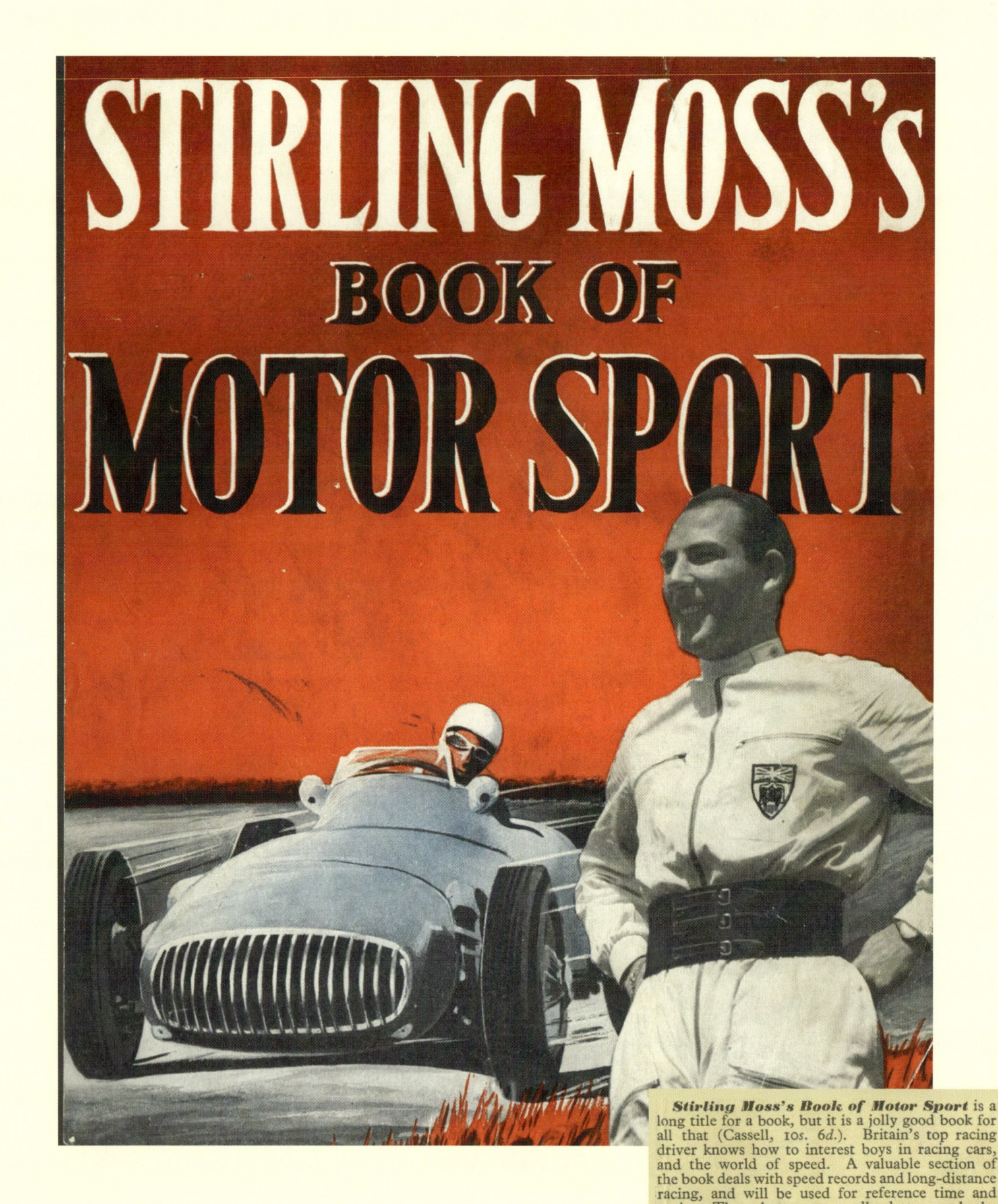

Stirling Moss's Book of Motor Sport is a long title for a book, but it is a jolly good book for all that (Cassell, 10s. 6d.). Britain's top racing driver knows how to interest boys in racing cars, and the world of speed. A valuable section of the book deals with speed records and long-distance racing, and will be used for reference time and again. The photos are well chosen and the captions above the average in a book of this type, being well written and informative.

Stirling Moss joins Maseratis as Number One driver

TWO TOP AWARDS FOR STIRLING MOSS

Stirling Moss has been awarded the Gold Star and the Seaman Trophy by the British Racing Drivers' Club, the Gold Star for being the most successful British driver, and the Seaman Trophy for being the British driver most successful abroad.

The John Cobb Memorial Trophy—for all-British successes—goes to Mike Hawthorn, and Tony Brooks is awarded the E.R.A. Club trophy for his victory with a Connaught in the Syracuse Grand Prix.

Evening News 2.12.55

Moss joining Maserati

By Daily Mail Reporter

STIRLING MOSS, Britain's top racing driver, is to be No. 1 driver in the Italian Maserati team next season.

For weeks he has been wondering whether to join a British team—his ambition is to win the world championship in a British car.

Last month he tried out Britain's three Grand Prix hopes—the B.R.M., Vanwall, and Connaught cars—at Silverstone.

He was still undecided when he flew to New York last week to see millionaire Tony Vandervell, the Vanwalls' sponsor.

But last night, from the Bahamas, where he is racing, he telephoned his decision to his father, Mr. Alfred Moss, in London.

Mr. Moss said Stirling thought the new British cars were good, but not good enough to beat the Continental challenge until well into next season.

"Stirling would very much have liked to drive solely for Britain, but as he has decided that he cannot, he has insisted that he should be free to drive British cars in six of the major sports car events. The Maserati Company have agreed."

Daily Mail 3.12.55

Stirling Moss, the racing driver, is so rarely in England—and so busy when he is here—that I thought myself lucky to be able to catch him for lunch a few days before he left for the Bahamas.

So far this year he has spent only six weeks in this country. "And that means that I have to work jolly hard when I am here," he said ruefully. "It's not all driving, there's a lot of office work: for I get 12,000 letters a year to answer."

Stirling, who is now our most famous racing driver, maintains that he has learnt more about Grand Prix Racing in one year with the German Mércèdes-Benz team than he could have done in five years here. Of the man thought to be his rival on the German team, Fangio, he said, "We were the best of friends. There was no friction between us at all—despite what some people think."

Stirling Moss

I remarked that Mr. Moss looked remarkably fit. "Racing with Mércèdes—particularly in the Mille Miglia and the Targa Florio—has made me appreciate the need for physical fitness more than ever," he said. So he still is a teetotaller and smokes only four or five cigarettes a day.

When I asked about his plans for the future, or if he had any ideas for business if and when he retired, he replied, "Well, no, not really. I'm just busy building up as much goodwill as I can."

Which proves that our fastest man on wheels still has—to use an ambiguity—his feet firmly planted on the ground.

Stirling Moss decides to race for Italians

'BRITISH CARS ARE NOT READY YET'

STIRLING MOSS, who was yesterday chosen by the British Racing Drivers' Club as the most successful British driver of 1955, is to join the Maserati company as their number one driver for next year.

B'mingham Gazette 3.12.55

Stirling is top again

By Tom Wisdom

FOR the fifth time Stirling Moss is champion British racing motorist.

The British Racing Drivers' Club last night announced the award of their Gold Star to Moss, the most successful British driver this year.

The Seaman Trophy has also been awarded to him.

The John Cobb Memorial Trophy goes to Mike Hawthorn, winner, at record speeds, of the Sebring 12-hours and Le Mans 24-hours races.

Daily Herald 2.12.55

MOSS JOINS MASERATIS

No. 1 driver next year

Stirling Moss, champion British racing motor driver, has decided to join the Italian Maserati Company as their number one driver for next year.

This was announced in London last night by his father, who added that it was felt the new British Formula One cars "will not be ready to compete on even terms with the Continental challenge until well in to the season."

Morning Advertiser 4.12.55

drums full of shale. Steel spikes were inserted into these and the spikes connected by rope.

With a complete lack of practice times, Ken decided on a Le Mans-type start, with the largest capacity cars at the front end, to at least reduce the overtaking somewhat - cars ranged in size from 500cc to 4.4-litres. The Americans did not like this idea because they preferred to use their safety belts and this would put them at a disadvantage with this type of start.

Apparently, there was near anarchy at the drivers' meeting until Stirling stepped forward and said there was nothing to stop the drivers putting on their belts after they had sprinted across the track and before departing. They would just lose a few seconds but the Le Mans-type start was the safest way to start the race and surely safety was paramount. This swayed them and a nasty crisis was averted.

There were 11 races in two days but Stirling took part in just two. In the Governor's Cup, he finished sixth in the Healey but had a top wishbone break in the Nassau Trophy and thus failed to finish.

After Christmas, Stirling's next destination was New Zealand where, on January 7th, he was to drive his old faithful Maserati 250F to victory in the non-championship New Zealand GP, before heading for Argentina and beginning his Formula One campaign for 1956 as Number One driver in the Maserati works team.

It had been an amazing year for Stirling. He had finished second in the World Championship, would have won the World Sports Car Championship had there then been such a prize, had won his first Grand Prix and would very likely, had Mercedes not withdrawn at Le Mans, have won the 'Grand Slam' of the greatest sports car races - the Mille Miglia, Le Mans, the Tourist Trophy and the Targa Florio.

He had started the year as a coming man and ended it as team leader at one of the two best Formula One teams for the following season. He began the year as a well-known racing driver and ended it as a household name. It was a vintage year for the 26-year-old but he had another six brilliant seasons ahead of him.

STIRLING MOSS WILL BE MASERATI No. 1
By Daily Mail Reporter

STIRLING MOSS, Britain's top racing driver, is to be number one driver in the Italian Maserati team next season. For weeks he has been wondering whether to join a British team—his ambition is to win the world championship in a British car.

Last month he tried out Britain's three Grand Prix hopes—the B.R.M., Vanwall, and Connaught cars—at Silverstone.

He was still undecided when he flew to New York last week to see millionaire Tony Vandervell, the Vanwall's sponsor.

'Free' events

But last night, from the Bahamas where he is racing, he telephoned his decision to his father, Mr. Alfred Moss, in London.

Mr. Moss said Stirling thought the new British cars were good, but not good enough to beat the Continental challenge until well into next season.

"Therefore, as a professional driver, he feels he must continue to drive for a foreign firm," he said.

"Stirling would very much have liked to drive solely for Britain, but as he has decided that he cannot, he has insisted that he should be free to drive British cars in six of the major sports car events. The Maserati company have agreed."

Moss, runner-up in the world championship last year, will probably have Jean Behra, of France, and an Italian driver as team-mates. His rival, Juan Manuel Fangio, last year's champion, is reported to have signed

Daily Mail 3.12.55

Gregory's Challenge

Typical of Ken Gregory's challenge was an incident with a telephone line around the circuit, connecting the marshalling posts. A car had gone off and broken the vital wire. The individual detailed to go and repair it thought he had done so satisfactorily merely by knotting the two ends together!

The Bahamas Auto Club Trophy

Ken Gregory tells the amusing story of this race which was restricted to local residents. Not surprisingly with the good weather, the Nassau car-hire companies had small sports cars among their fleets. Apparently, several enterprising but rather unprincipled locals hit on the notion of hiring these for a few days and entering the cars in this race. Not surprisingly, they took quite a hammering.

During the race, Ken needed his fellow Stewards for a swift ruling on some point. Looking around he failed to find 'Red' Crise and Oakes but then realised they were out on the circuit racing!

MOTOR RACING INVADER FROM THE STATES

A wealthy Californian building contractor, Mr Tony Parravano, is planning a full-scale invasion of international motor racing next season in a bid to scoop the top places in Grand Prix and sports car competitions.

A fleet of 22 Ferrari and Maserati racing cars is to be his striking force. He hopes it will win for him the number one racing position vacated by Mercedes-Benz, who have retired temporarily from the championship battle.

Drivers will be chosen from a team of six or eight men — two 'aces' supported by brilliant young men with growing reputations.

Skilled German mechanics from

"DROVE LIKE MASTER"

"No one outside Britain had heard of Brooks before he won the Syracuse Grand Prix (Sicily) in October, but he drove like a master," said Mr Parravano. "I have talked with him briefly, without making any offer, but he is a student dentist, and I do not think he wants to drive full-time."

Mr Parravano agreed that he had made offers to the British champion, Stirling Moss, runner-up to Argentina's Manuel Fangio in the 1955 world championship; Peter Collins, Britain, who also drove Mercedes cars; and Italy's Eugenio Castelloti, who came third in the championship.

B'mingham Gazette 10.12.55

Bright Hopes for Sports Car Events
WILL MOSS JOIN HAWTHORN IN JAGUAR CAMP?

Mike Hawthorn  — Stirling Moss

CONFIRMATION by Jaguar yesterday that they intend to compete next year in selected sports car events is one of the brighter features of what has been a disastrous year for motor sport.

Coventry Eve Tel 14.12.55

JAGUARS TO KEEP ON RACING
By COURTENAY EDWARDS

JAGUARS will be racing next season. Mr. William Lyons, head of the Coventry firm, last night dispelled fears that he might be quitting.

He said he had hesitated because of the uncertainty over the regulations for the race in which he is mainly interested, the 24-hour Le Mans classic next August.

Jaguars have won three of the last five races at Le Mans. Another victory there will be the Jaguar team's main target for 1956 with Mike Hawthorn as No. 1 driver.

There is still a chance that Stirling Moss may drive in the Jaguar team when his commitments as No. 1 driver for the Maserati Grand Prix team permit. But it seems unlikely that Moss will be willing to drive as No. 2 to his old rival, Hawthorn.

The Motor 9.2.55

AT MODENA: Tony Parravano, wealthy American sponsor of an ambitious International racing stable for 1956, seen during recent trials at the Modena aero-autodrome with Peter Collins, pulling a face as he adjusts his helmet, preparatory to trying one of the Parravano sports Maseratis.

MOSS DECIDES FOR MASERATIS
British cars not ready for Grand Prix

News Chronicle 3.12.55

By ALAN BRINTON

STIRLING MOSS, Britain's ace racing driver, has finally decided to "go foreign" for next season's Grand Prix events. He will join the Italian Maserati team as No. 1 driver.

With offers from the world's best racing teams, Moss has had a worrying time making up his mind. In the past fortnight he has tested three British cars — B.R.M., Connaught and Vanwall.

He was keen to win the world championship — now within his reach — in a British car. But promising though the British cars are, the 26-year-old racing ace feels they need further tests and modifications before competing on even terms with the Continental challenge — at least until well into the season.

Last night he phoned from America, where he is racing sports cars, to tell his father, Mr. Alfred Moss, he was going to Maserati.

Both his parents think he has made a wise decision.

Said Mr. Moss, "Stirling feels he must continue to drive for a foreign firm until the necessary developments are completed on the British designs, and an adequate number of cars are built to ensure a full season's racing."

But though driving for Maserati in Grand Prix, Moss has insisted he should be free to drive British cars in six of the major sports car events. Maserati's have agreed.

Interlopers

To the horror of Stirling and Ken, Americans were driving their cars along the circuit, during practice, in the wrong direction! The primitive roping made it difficult to police the situation and keep people off the track.

THE NASSAU MEETING

HEROES of the Bahamas three-day meeting on the palm-lined Windsor airfield circuit at Nassau were undoubtedly the young Spanish Marquis Alfonso de Portago and the American Phil Hill. De Portago carried off the Governor's Trophy race, over 30 laps, as recorded in last week's issue, and the following day beat Hill a second time

SUNNY SCENE above shows Stirling Moss in summery attire, riding on the Austin-Healey of Lady Greta Oakes, during the parade which preceded the sports car races at Nassau, in the Bahamas.

Stirling met a lot of air stewardesses on his travels.

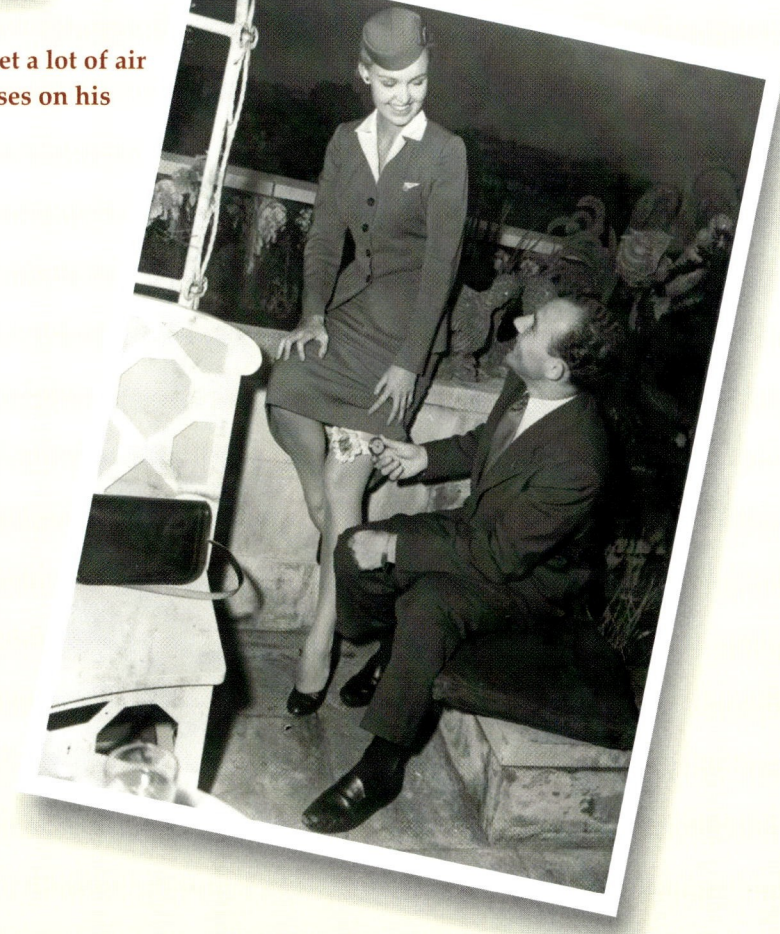

Moss
...ET GENTLEMAN FARMER

Reportage photographique Kurt Wörner

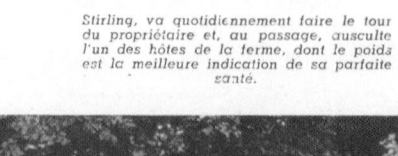

L'équitation est un excellent entraînement pour les pilotes en automobile... « Les mains basses, les coudes au corps... » que voilà d'excellents principes. Stirling sort le cheval pour une randonnée dans la campagne...

« Maman » Moss est, elle aussi, une assidue de la course en automobile. Le « Nuage Blanc » est, pour elle, une réelle détente et surtout en compagnie de la « meute » familiale !

Stirling, va quotidiennement faire le tour du propriétaire et, au passage, ausculte l'un des hôtes de la ferme, dont le poids est la meilleure indication de sa parfaite santé.

...Mais c'est Patricia, sa sœur, automobiliste distinguée elle aussi, à ses heures, qui « saute » sur la bête et lui « grille » la politesse !

SAVING HIS BACON

167, FLEET STREET,
Friday night.

PIG breeding and motor racing may seem a curious combination, but the Moss family have successfully combined them. The pig, in fact, might be regarded as Stirling Moss's badge.

But a real pig will be representing him at the Boxing Day race meeting at Brands Hatch track. Moss will not be back from America in time to race himself but, to keep the family name to the fore, his father is sending along a pedigree Large White. After the meeting it will be roasted on a spit to provide a barbecue feast for the race-goers.

Stirling Moss spends a great deal of his spare time on the family farm at Tring, Hertfordshire, and intends to take over on his father's retirement.

B'mingham Gazette 10.12.55

It was the perfect end to a near-perfect year. In December, Stirling relaxed in Nassau in good company. The lady in the middle is Louise King but Stirling is not sure who the other girl is. Louise was an American actress who would marry Peter Collins in 1957. They lived on a yacht in the harbour at Monaco but tragically he was killed that very year at the Nürburgring.

Who is this? None of us have a clue! Answers, please, to info@xkclub.com

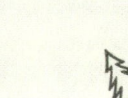

SPORTS CAR Journal
FEBRUARY
Vol. II No. II

CHRISTMAS WITH STERLING MOSS
by BILL BARRETT

CHRISTMAS WITH STERLING MOSS
by BILL BARRETT

One of the finer jewels I received for the holidays was the opportunity to spend Xmas night with the great Moss and other close friends. Mary Hefley, race secretary of the California Sports Car Club, called Stirling at his hotel. Because of a cancelled appointment, Moss was able to spend the evening with us.

Some background into the "flying Englishman's" career is necessary to acquaint a few who may not be familiar with it.

Age 26, a bachelor, second only to Fangio as the greatest driver in the world in 1955. First British driver to win the Italian Mille Miglia, a thousand mile course, with a record 98 mph over the course. Teamed with Fangio for the Mercedes factory last year, it was not possible to shoot for that pinnacle of racing, world's champion, but this year Fangio and Moss are driving for different factories, Moss with Maserati and Fangio with Ferrari. What a wild season this will be!

We discussed racing Xmas night of course but also other bits outside of racing. One interesting observation, Moss said "I prefer the Eldorado for street driving here. Quite relaxing you know." Parravano had lent him his Eldorado during his brief visit here.

Stirling is a very calm and collected young man. Though he has that twinkle in his eyes, indicating enjoyment of a prank, one he told me which backfired. He lost several front teeth in an accident at Naples in 1950, so his father, a dentist, made him partial plates. At the movies one night with a girl friend he slipped the plate out and into his hand grasping his friend's hand. This proved to be rather startling to her, so much so she refused to give the plate back to him. For this reason Stirling now owns several sets.

Again one time while water skiing, he lost the plate. Returning to the hotel desk, you can imagine his difficulty getting the keys for his room—222—without those front teeth.

Racing has been kind to Moss financially too. Something in the neighborhood of $100,000 last year. Though he tried very hard to get clearance to run at Torrey Pines with no remuneration. Unfortunately FIA flatly refused to give him clearance.

Moss does not drink, though he has a great capacity for orange juice at a party. He is quite kind and generous with his time, a great deal of humility, coupled with a burning desire to win.

And it isn't very often when he is entered that he doesn't win.

"I have a great deal of respect for your two drivers, Gregory and Shelby," he said. "They are quite good, and drive a very calculated race."

"I do like Hollywood, particularly the freeways, which enable one to get about quite fast, with a minimum of effort."

He feels that American women are not quite as warm as the Europeans. In Europe it is quite unusual to see a woman driving and during his first trip here, he found it difficult to drive and look at our beautiful women at the same time! Thinks it unsual that American racers talk about nothing but racing, while the lovely ladies are shunted to the sidelines!

Stirling told me that General Motors is going to participate at Sebring this year, and also enter Indianapolis.

That the Polaroid camera will soon have a negative for each picture and color film available in the near future.

His clothes are custom tailored for him in England, beautifully cut, but a bit austere.

We spent nearly an hour trying to get a good cover picture, in front of our tree. He was quite kind about it though, and eventually instructed me how to get the picture and this after a long day of personal appearances, studio lunch, etc.

Yes, he is quite a man, and it will be a gratifying memory to look back to the Xmas night we spent in the presence of the Champion Racing Driver of the World.

Sterling Moss surrounded by several well known sports car drivers at a recent reception given in his honor. From left to right are Jack McAfee, Internationally known Masten Gregory and Phil Hill.

LOVE TO STIRLING!

THIS could be the picture blonde Jean Clarke will send to the Bahamas.

Twenty-two-year-old Jean is the girl friend of racing driver Stirling Moss—and that is where he is practising for the next racing season.

Sketch cameraman Don Price took the picture yesterday at a London fashion show, where Jean modelled glamorous transparent nighties.

It was at a fashion show that Jean—ITV's Miss Televisual—first met Stirling three months ago.

"MEN OF THE YEAR"

ANGLO-AMAL. BRITISH. 2,319 FT. CERT. "U." REL.: NOT FIXED.

Interest. Macdonald Hobley presents ten outstanding British personalities, from among whom he invites his viewers to choose their own "Man of the Year." They include Stirling Moss, who confides his ambitions in motor sport, Sir Gordon Richards speaking on his retirement as a jockey, film star Anthony Steel on his debut as a singer, Chris Chataway, the President of the Royal Academy, Major Draper (who flies under Thames bridges), Eden and Churchill. Smoothly presented. Good.

Today's Cinema 12.12.55

Is this Stirling trawling the papers for more cuttings for his scrapbooks?

Wishing you a Happy Christmas and a Prosperous New Year

Stirling

P.S. As I am somewhere in America the good wishes are mine but the signature isn't.

"Just started to flog the sixpenny dip—and some little perisher yells 'Look, there's Stirling Moss!'"

Daily Sketch 23.12.55

ACNOWLEDGEMENTS

I would like to thank Doug Nye, Ted Walker (Ferret Fotographics), Erik Johnson, Robin Bynoe, Paul Vestey, Matt and Di Spitzley, Rob and Sue Fleetwood, Roger Bonnet, John Davenport, Val Pirie, Judy Addicott, Estanislao M. Iacona, Cristián Bertschi, Deborah Gregory, Simon Thomas, Geoff Goddard, Merlin and Karen Unwin, Jane Arnold-Forster, Dermot Bambridge, and David and Lesley Haynes. All have been extremely helpful and supportive, and Doug Nye has given exceptional assistance. I would like to also thank Nicholas Watts (www.automotiveart.com) for permission reproduce two of his superb paintings. In our office, Claire Bryan has worked tirelessly to sort out copyright issues, research obscure subjects and is always full of great ideas and very supportive. To anyone I have forgotten, please forgive me.

Andy Garman, who has designed this book and with whom it has been a privilege to work for the last seven years, has been fantastic, showing extraordinary patience and flexibility in the face of horrendous deadlines and ever-moving goalposts! Julie, my wife, has provided tremendous support and lots of positive input.

Finally, Lady Susie and Sir Stirling have been just wonderful. Susie is a very special lady and has been so charmingly helpful in every possible way. As for the great man himself, Stirling has done me the honour and privilege of agreeing to these books and then has thrown himself into them with all the energy for which he is rightly famous, to say nothing of his enthusiasm, time, patience and great humour. Above all, he has made it a lot of fun.

GLOSSARY

M-B = Mercedes-Benz
Rudolf 'Rudi' Uhlenhaut - Head of Experimental Engineering at M-B
Alfred Neubauer - M-B Team Manager
Artur Keser - M-B Head of PR

Ken Gregory - Personal Manager
Felix Nabarro - lawyer & friend
David Haynes - best friend
Sally Weston (SW) - longer term girlfriend
Jenks - Denis Jenkinson (DSJ) - pre-eminent motor racing journalist, died in 1996
Alf Francis - Stirling's Chief Mechanic - in 1955 looked after Stirling's own Maserati 250F

ftd = fastest time of day
No. 8 - Challenor Mansions - flat shared by Stirling & Ken Gregory, cost £3 10s 0d (£3.50) week
Crumpet - (Stirling's favourite word) delectable females of the species
Films & meals, etc., rated by Stirling: VG = very good, F = fair, etc.

MORE SCRAPBOOKS...

This book is intended to be the first in a series covering Stirling's remarkable career and private life. Years will be covered at random. The second in the series will be the *Stirling Moss Scrapbook 1961* another great year when he took on the might of Ferrari and famously beat the more powerful Italian machines at Monaco and the Nürburgring through sheer ability on these drivers' circuits. You can keep up to date will all information about these titles, learn the latest news about Stirling and register to receive ongoing information at **www.stirlingmossbooks.com**

We welcome relevant anecdotes and photographs.

Fifty Years On - 2005 Postscript

During the writing of this book, Lady Susie very kindly organised a supper party to spark off as many stories and anecdotes as possible. Sir Stirling invited his best friend, David Haynes, and his wife Lesley. David provided the splendid tale about the awful 'Shrimp' and his unforgettable Targa Florio experiences. Val Pirie was invited to add some background to the office side of things though she didn't, in fact, actually join Stirling until later in the fifties (but she will be very involved in the next Scrapbook - 1961). American Herb Jones, who coincidentally is a member of our *Jaguar XK Club*, happened to be staying at the 'Moss's Mayfair Mews' and chipped in with various US stories. Then there was the great man himself, my wife Julie, and me. Val did a great job of trying to keep the party in order and generally failed!

I am not sure how many printable stories came out of the evening but we had an absolute ball.

Then, to my great surprise, Stirling tracked me down on Christmas Day to pass on that he had had a card from Judy, his actual secretary in this period. Subsequently, I went down to the Cardiff area to meet up with Judy Noot, as she was, and Judy Addicott as she has been for many years, having married sometime racer and highly distinguished test pilot Dizzie Addicott. Judy was delightful and regaled me with many stories for this and future Scrapbooks.

Judy (Noot) Addicott.

Top: Sir Stirling, Val & Philip. Middle: Lady Susie & David. Bottom left: Julie & Sir Stirling. Bottom right: Lesley & Herb.

Top left - The Le Mans start was always a Moss speciality and here Stirling demonstrates his agility at the 1st Swedish GP. *Top right* - From left: Piero Taruffi, Juan Manuel Fangio, Karl Kling, Alfred Neubauer, Stirling and Andre Simon. - *Bottom left* - Victory in the classic Tourist Trophy demonstrated Stirling's 'never say die' approach to motor sport. *Bottom right* - The young British duo of Stirling Moss and Peter Collins drove brilliantly to win the gruelling Targa Florio and clinch the World Sports Car Championship for Mercedes-Benz. *Facing inside back cover*: Stirling leads the pack into the Gasometer Hairpin at fabulous Monaco, a race he so nearly won until cruel luck played its part. *Inside back cover*: The drama, the frenzy, the tension of a pit stop in the Targa Florio as Stirling hands over the battered 300 SLR to Pete Collins. (DaimlerChrysler Archive)

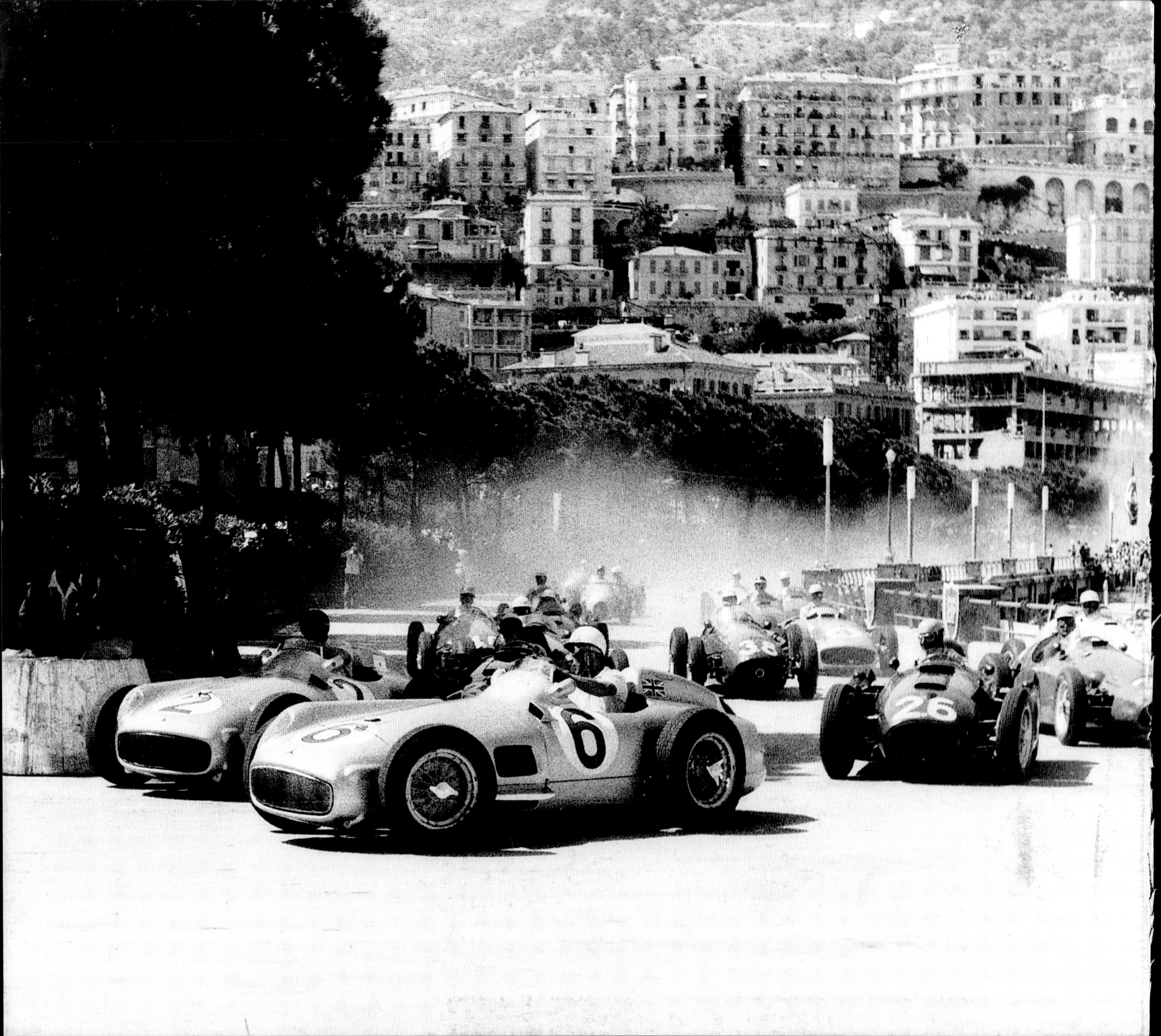
6
26